W9-BEQ-960

# TEACHING LITERACY IN FIRST GRADE

# TOOLS FOR TEACHING LITERACY

Donna Ogle and Camille Blachowicz, *Series Editors*

This highly practical series includes two kinds of books: (1) grade-specific titles for first-time teachers or those teaching a particular grade for the first time; (2) books on key literacy topics that cut across all grades, such as integrated instruction, English language learning, and comprehension. Written by outstanding educators who know what works based on extensive classroom experience, each research-based volume features hands-on activities, reproducibles, and best practices for promoting student achievement.

TEACHING LITERACY IN SIXTH GRADE
**Karen Wood and Maryann Mraz**

TEACHING LITERACY IN KINDERGARTEN
**Lea M. McGee and Lesley Mandel Morrow**

INTEGRATING INSTRUCTION: LITERACY AND SCIENCE
**Judy McKee and Donna Ogle**

TEACHING LITERACY IN SECOND GRADE
**Jeanne R. Paratore and Rachel L. McCormack**

TEACHING LITERACY IN FIRST GRADE
**Diane Lapp, James Flood, Kelly Moore, and Maria Nichols**

# TEACHING LITERACY
## in First Grade

Diane Lapp
James Flood
Kelly Moore
Maria Nichols

Series Editors' Note by Donna Ogle and Camille Blachowicz

gp

THE GUILFORD PRESS
New York     London

© 2005 The Guilford Press
A Division of Guilford Publications, Inc.
72 Spring Street, New York, NY 10012
www.guilford.com

All rights reserved

Except as indicated, no part of this book may be reproduced, translated,
stored in a retrieval system, or transmitted, in any form or by any means,
electronic, mechanical, photocopying, microfilming, recording, or otherwise,
without written permission from the Publisher.

Printed in the United States of America

This book is printed on acid-free paper.

Last digit is print number:   9   8   7   6   5   4   3   2   1

LIMITED PHOTOCOPY LICENSE

These materials are intended for use only by qualified professionals.

The Publisher grants to individual purchasers of this book nonassignable
permission to reproduce all materials for which photocopying permission
is specifically granted in a footnote. This license is limited to you, the
individual purchaser, for use with your own clients or students. It does not
extend to additional professionals in your institution, school district, or
other setting, nor does purchase by an institution constitute a site license.
This license does not grant the right to reproduce these materials for
resale, redistribution, or any other purposes (including but not limited to
books, pamphlets, articles, video- or audiotapes, and handouts or slides for
lectures or workshops). Permission to reproduce these materials for these
and any other purposes must be obtained in writing from the Permissions
Department of Guilford Publications.

**Library of Congress Cataloging-in-Publication Data**

Teaching literacy in first grade / Diane Lapp . . . [et al.].
       p.   cm. — (Tools for teaching literacy)
    Includes bibliographical references and index.
    ISBN 1-59385-182-0 (hard) — ISBN 1-59385-181-2 (pbk.)
       1. Reading (Elementary).   2. Language arts  (Elementary).
    3. Literacy.  4. First grade (Education).     I. Lapp,   Diane.  II. Series.
    LB1573.T364 2005
    372.4—dc22

                                                      2004030039

# ABOUT THE AUTHORS

**Diane Lapp, EdD**, is Distinguished Research Professor of Language and Literacy in the Department of Teacher Education at San Diego State University (SDSU), and has taught in elementary and middle schools. Her major areas of research and instruction have been issues related to urban struggling readers and their families. Dr. Lapp directs and teaches in field-based preservice and graduate programs and continues to team-teach in public school classrooms. She has coauthored and edited many articles, columns, handbooks, and children's materials on reading and language arts. These include *Teaching Reading to Every Child*, a reading methods textbook in its fourth edition, and the *Handbook of Research on Teaching the English Language Arts*, second edition, coauthored and coedited with James Flood. She has also chaired and cochaired several International Reading Association (IRA) and National Reading Conference committees. She is currently the cochair of the IRA's Early Literacy Commission. Her many educational awards include being named Outstanding Teacher Educator and Faculty Member in the Department of Teacher Education at SDSU, Distinguished Research Lecturer from SDSU's Graduate Division of Research, member of the California Reading Hall of Fame, and the IRA's 1996 Outstanding Teacher Educator of the Year. Dr. Lapp is the coeditor of the literacy journal *The California Reader.*

**James Flood, PhD**, is Distinguished Research Professor of Language and Literacy at San Diego State University (SDSU); has taught in preschool, elementary, and secondary schools; and has been a language arts supervisor and vice principal. He was a Fulbright scholar at the University of Lisbon in Portugal and the President of the National Reading Conference. Dr. Flood has chaired and cochaired many committees of the International Reading Association (IRA), National Council of Teachers of English, National Council of Researchers in English, and National Reading Conference. Currently Dr. Flood teaches graduate courses at SDSU. He has coauthored and edited many articles, columns, handbooks, and children's materials on reading and language arts. These include *Content Area Reading and Learning*, second edition (edited with Diane Lapp and Nancy Farnan), and the *Handbook of Research on Teaching Literacy through the Communicative and Visual Arts* (coedited with Shirley Brice Heath and Diane Lapp). His many educational awards include being named Outstanding Teacher Educator in the Department of Teacher Education at SDSU, Distinguished Research Lecturer from SDSU's Graduate Division of Research, and member of both California's and the IRA's Reading Hall of Fame. Dr. Flood is the coeditor of *The California Reader* and a member of the board of directors of the IRA.

**Kelly Moore, PhD,** is a literacy resource teacher in the San Diego Unified School District, where she teaches at a large urban elementary school that has formed a unique collaboration with a middle school, high school, and San Diego State University. Within this partnership, Dr. Moore collaborates with teachers from all grade levels on literacy staff development, preservice education, and beginning teacher support. Her primary interest is the assessment–instruction connection in early literacy classrooms. Her recently completed dissertation focused on teachers' effectiveness at planning diagnostic instruction. She was awarded the Constance McCullough Research Award by the California Reading Association for this study. Through her continued research, writing, and teaching, Dr. Moore hopes to promote teacher education and future research in the area of early literacy.

**Maria Nichols, MA,** is a literacy staff developer in the San Diego Unified School District. An elementary school teacher for 16 years and a National Board Certified teacher, Ms. Nichols now supports teachers at all grade levels in urban elementary schools as they strengthen their content knowledge and instructional practice. She has worked previously as a demonstration and resource teacher in an elementary professional development site and has led workshops nationwide on literacy content and instruction. Ms. Nichols received the Outstanding Achievement in Literacy Award from the Greater San Diego Reading Council of the California Reading Association in 1998 and the Distinguished Elementary Educator of 2002 Award from the San Diego Chapter of Phi Delta Kappa. Her current focus is on classroom environments and instructional design that encourage students of all ages to use talk as a tool for developing comprehension.

# SERIES EDITORS' NOTE

As teacher educators and staff developers, we have become aware of the need for a series of books for thoughtful practitioners who want a practical, research-based introduction to teaching literacy at specific grade levels. Preservice and beginning teachers want to know how to be as effective as possible; they also know there are great differences in what students need across grade levels. We have met teacher after teacher who, when starting to teach or teaching a new grade, asked for a guide targeted at their specific grade level. Until now we have not had a resource to share with them.

We also collaborate with staff developers and study group directors who want effective inservice materials that they can use with teachers at many different levels yet that still provide specific insights for individual grade levels. Thus the Tools for Teaching Literacy series was created.

This series is distinguished by two innovative characteristics designed to make it useful to individual teachers, staff developers, and study groups alike. Each Tools for Teaching Literacy volume:

➤ Is written by outstanding educators who are noted for their knowledge of research, theory, and best practices; who spend time in real classrooms working with teachers; and who are experienced staff developers who work alongside teachers applying these insights in classrooms. We think the series authors are unparalleled in these qualifications.

➤ Is organized according to a structure shared by all the grade-level books, which include chapters on:

- the nature of the learner at a particular grade level
- appropriate goals for literacy
- setting up the physical environment for literacy
- getting to know students with appropriate assessments and planning for differentiation

- a week in the grade-level classroom—what this looks like in practice with important instructional strategies and routines
- resources for learning

With this common organization in the grade-level books, a staff developer can use several different volumes in the series for teacher study groups, new teacher seminars, and other induction activities, choosing particular discussion and learning topics, such as classroom organization, that cross grade-level concerns. Teachers can also easily access information on topics of most importance to them and make comparisons across the grade levels.

First grade is a critical year in literacy development. Teachers new to this grade have numerous decisions to make to orchestrate effective, appropriate, and engaging instruction. In this volume, two university educators, Diane Lapp and James Flood, and two public school teachers, Kelly Moore and Maria Nichols, have collaborated to describe how beginning first-grade teachers can design rich literacy instruction for their classrooms. This book conveys their understanding of the oral language base of literacy learning—both reading and writing—and their expertise in differentiating instruction for English language learners.

DONNA OGLE
CAMILLE BLACHOWICZ

# PREFACE

We wrote this book for you—the first-grade teacher—to share some ideas that we believe will ensure successful literacy learning for all of your students. While doing so, we reminisced about our first years of teaching and about the excitement we feel each year as we see new school supplies being shelved in stores and children suggesting to patient adults that they must have them all. The excitement of a new beginning happens not just once a year for teachers, but every day as they enter their classrooms and greet their students.

As a first-grade teacher you'll love teaching primary-age children; love their thirst to learn, their excitement when they feel successful, and their love of school in general. Experience and a commitment to staying on the cutting edge in our profession will change the way you teach and what you teach.

This book is a compilation of what we've learned about teaching first grade from hands-on teaching and research in the classroom. It's based on our own experiences and the experiences of colleagues whom we have taught, mentored, and worked with side by side. It's the result of good days and bad days, effective lesson planning, and lessons that have failed. It comes from working to understand and implement research and, most important, from watching our children exemplify what really works.

For all of us, it's been many years since our first year of teaching, but our thoughts about teaching first grade have not changed. We have taught and/or worked with teachers in every grade at the elementary level, but there is still something magical about walking into a first-grade classroom, especially early in the year. It is both an honor and an incredible responsibility to be a first-grade teacher.

It is our hope that the ideas, lessons, strategies, assessments, and examples we've included in *Teaching Literacy in First Grade* will support you in your journey as a teacher of first graders and set you on your way toward a career filled with the same joys and successes we have had and continue to have as teachers.

## ACKNOWLEDGMENTS

We wish to thank Ms. Christine Daleo-Wong, an exceptional first-grade teacher, for all of her excellent ideas and suggestions; Dr. Julie Jacobson, an excellent teacher of second-language students, for her outstanding teaching ideas and translations; and Dr. Linda Lungren, an excellent teacher of multiple arts, for her assistance throughout the entire project. A special thanks to our colleagues throughout the country, especially those in California and Massachusetts, for sharing so many insights from their many years of teaching.

# CONTENTS

# CHAPTER 1

# WHERE DO I BEGIN?

*Getting to Know Your Students, Your Classroom, and the Curriculum*

Hurrah! You got the position. You're a first-grade teacher. You're the most important teacher in each child's life, because you will shape his or her initial attitude about learning and the importance of school attendance. As you begin to assume this awesome responsibility, you're probably trying to remember everything you were taught in your teacher prep classes and during your student teaching. As you pause to think about this, we're going to help you organize what you've learned so that you will be able to address, as a professional, the almost overwhelming number of decisions you are about to make: decisions regarding such issues as room arrangement, evaluation of students' progress, effectiveness of materials, selection of optional materials, approaches to instruction based on students' needs, and classroom management. The purpose of this chapter, as well as the rest of the book, is to facilitate the necessary decision-making processes. This chapter can help you get started and help you prioritize your long list of "to dos" before your students arrive on the first day of school.

As you'll soon realize, each decision you make affects the next. We start by identifying and prioritizing what you need to think about.

1. *Fact*: My students are 5- and 6-year-olds.
   *Questions*: ➤ What are children like at this age?
   ➤ What are appropriate expectations for them?

2. *Fact*: Most of my students have been to preschool and/or kindergarten.
   *Questions*: ➤ What will they have learned in their home and school experiences?
   ➤ Where should my instruction begin?

3. *Fact*: I've been given money to buy classroom supplies and books.
   *Questions*: ➤ What should I buy?
   ➤ What can my students read?

4. *Fact*: My classroom is a fairly good size.
   *Questions*:
   - How should it be arranged to ensure comfort and productivity?
   - Where can I get things to make the classroom homey, inviting, and still functional?
   - What about charts? Should they be made before the children arrive?
   - Do I need a management plan?

5. *Fact*: I have to teach my students content based on grade-level standards.
   *Question*:
   - How can I get to know my students quickly and start meeting all their various needs?

Briefly answering these questions should get you started.

## WHO ARE FIRST GRADERS?: A BIRD'S-EYE VIEW OF YOUR STUDENTS

You may discover many differences among the children who will soon become members of your classroom family, both physical and cultural, some of which are the results of development and some from the types of home and school experiences they've had during the early years of their lives.

Some children will seem more mature than others, more or less candid, more adventurous and secure, or more timid and shy. Some will come to first grade knowing how to read, others will know a few of the letters of the alphabet, and many will be somewhere between these extremes. One thing that most will have in common is that as they come to you, they will be very eager to learn and especially eager to learn to read. It may help you to think of your first graders as emerging, developing, or transitioning readers and writers, because the different characteristics exhibited by the children during these early stages of development will help you to more successfully plan their daily instruction.

## STAGES OF READING AND WRITING

It's a Monday morning late in September, and a class of first graders is spread out around the room in "free choice" reading.

Carlie has a Big Book version of *The Gingerbread Man*, which the class has read many times. "Run, run, run, . . . " she repeats in a singsong voice as she intersperses the phrase in a retell of the story from memory, simultaneously turning the pages and studying the pictures. Once she finishes, she starts over, and Jeremy joins her. He listens for a bit, then begins to join in on the "Run, run, run . . . " portions. Midway into the story, Carlie is interrupted by Jeremy.

CARLIE: And then, a cow sees the Gingerbread Man.

JEREMY: I thought it was a horse. He chases him because he's a cookie. Cookies are real good—Mmmmm!

CARLIE: No, the cow sees him first, then the horse. See? (*Turns page ahead.*)

JEREMY: Oh, yeah.

Carlie continues to "read," with Jeremy chiming in on "Run, run, run." At the end, there is a conversation about rereading the text.

JEREMY: Read it again.

CARLIE: It's your turn.

JEREMY: I can't read it.

CARLIE: It's easy. You just turn the pages, say the part that goes with the picture, and say the "run, run, run" part. See . . .

Carlie begins to model for Jeremy. As the Little Old Lady is popping the Gingerbread Man into the oven (according to Carlie), Michael joins them.

MICHAEL: That's not what it says on that page. That part was on the other page, see? (*Turns page and points to words.*) Oven—it's right there. It has to have a *v.*

CARLIE: A *v?* Where's a *v?*

MICHAEL: (*points.*) Here—in *oven.*

CARLIE: *o—v—n—* (*stretches out word to hear*). Yeah, and the oven's in this picture, too. Then the old woman puts the Gingerbread man into the oven . . .

JEREMY: (*looking at the alphabet cards on the wall*) Which one is the *v?*

CARLIE: Then she smelled the Gingerbread . . .

MICHAEL: No, it says it this way. (*Attends to the print to correct Carlie's structuring of the idea.*)

This collaborative interaction around reading could have happened in any first-grade classroom, because first-grade teachers begin the year with students who vary widely in their understanding of and proficiency with reading and writing. Meaning is at the heart of all we do as readers and writers (Lapp, Flood, Brock, & Fisher, 2005). Children expect their world to make sense and expect stories of their world to make sense as well. These three children are no exception, despite the variance in their levels.

Researchers have identified broad stages of reading through which children progress (Chall, 1967, 1996). These stages, which include *emergent*, *early*, *transitional*, and *fluent* reading behaviors, are not discrete; rather, they form a continuum of reading behaviors. By observing the children in the introductory vignette, it is obvious that although they are all the same age and in the same grade, each is progressing along this developmental continuum in his or her own unique way. As we note in Chapter 4, through observation of your students it becomes easy to assess each child's strengths and the next steps needed to ensure his or her literacy growth.

Emergent readers and writers are characterized as "learning about print" (Clay, 1966, 1998; Flood, 1975; Sulzby & Teale, 1991; Brown, 1999/2000). During this stage children develop an understanding that print helps them send, as well as receive, information. Through exposure they learn about and develop an appreciation for a variety of text types. They learn how to handle and navigate through books (concepts of print). They also develop an understanding of words and are able to distinguish between letter shapes and names and begin to connect the sounds of their spoken language with the letter representations (phonological awareness). They are emerging as readers as they rely on memory, letter cues, illustrations, and story context. Their attitudes about and motivation to read are being shaped by all of the wonderful read-alouds that are shared with them. A number of good read-aloud books are listed in Chapter 4.

## A CLOSER LOOK AT EACH CHILD

Jeremy is an emergent reader who is just beginning to grasp concepts about print. He knows some letter–sound correlations, and has control of a few sight words. His reading is heavily supported by picture cues and other aids such as text pattern and a detailed introduction to the text. Jeremy enjoys and remembers stories and expects consistency when hearing a known story. He is able to draw on his knowledge of the world to support meaning ("Cookies . . . Mmmmm!") He needs to develop an understanding about the role of pictures in making meaning. He needs to learn letter forms, as well as some letter–sound relationships. Most important, he needs many, many successful interactions with the printed page to begin to view himself as a reader and become more of a risk taker when reading.

Emerging writers tell many stories and share ideas through drawings and a variety of letter arrangements, which are detailed in Chapter 3. Their realization that books are written from top to bottom and left to right is reflected in their developing writing. They use invented spellings to convey much of their meaning. Toward the end of this stage they write lists and single sentences.

Developing or *early readers and writers* will also be members of your first-grade family. This stage of development has been referred to as "breaking the code" (Brown, 1999/2000), because it is during this stage that children understand the alphabetic principle that the sounds of their language are represented by the letter configurations in print. This understanding enables them to manipulate chunks of letters, thereby increasing their word recognition and word writing. Much "word-to-word matching" (Holdaway, 1980) and self correction/monitoring occurs as children read in texts at their independent levels. Successful practice with print strengthens a child's decoding, fluency, and meaning making while supporting the child's sense of self as a reader.

Carlie is an early reader who has gained independence in her ability to grasp concepts about print. Like other early readers, she reads text independently with the support of pictures and a strong introduction to the text. She has most letter–sound correlations mastered and has gained control of a growing number of sight words. As an early reader, she is developing her ability to use multiple sources of information to problem solve at the word level. Carlie "reads" a book slightly above her independent level, using a mix of memory and her understanding of the plot and interactions between the characters. She understands that a text is constant and that the words work in concert with the pictures. She is able to transfer her understanding of reading to more complex texts with the support of a known story line and pictures. She sees herself as a reader and does not distinguish the familiar picture book that she reread, from her leveled, just-right reading. She needs to strengthen her understanding that pictures can be a source of information for problem solving the print on the page, and she needs to begin using these strategies independently.

Michael is well into the *early stage* of reading. He is using a mix of sources of information (meaning and graphophonic cues) to inform his reading. He is attending more to the print than the pictures, and he has well-developed understandings about the encoding of words. Like the others, he enjoys rereading favorite stories. With support and ample time to read, Michael will soon be a *transitional reader.* You will see a wide range of reading behaviors being exhibited as children move from being early to transitional readers. In fact, we like to think about them as beginning, middle, and late early readers.

These developing or *early writers* move beyond composing lists to writing simple stories and informational accounts based on classroom and personal experiences. They begin to write more, with greater ease and confidence, and to take bigger risks.

*Transitional readers* are "going for fluency" (Brown, 1999/2000) as they attempt more and more silent reading. They are able to read new text with increased independence. Text introductions by the teacher can be brief. These readers are busy broadening their knowledge of text by reading many different forms and genres.

Teachers can support this stage of development by providing lots of time for independent reading in texts that are motivating to the children and introduce a wide variety of topics. It is through this sustained wide reading that children's critical literacies are developed. A number of highly motivating first-grade books across the genres are listed throughout this text. As children's ease with chunking longer words increases, so does their fluency, speed, comprehension, knowledge of text styles, and sense of self as a reader. Most children will not complete this stage of development until third or fourth grade. Writers at this stage produce well-organized stories, poetry, and informational pieces.

Fluent or *independent readers* are not common members of first-grade classrooms. Still, we need to have a sense of this stage so that we have an end goal for the type of reader we want every child to become. These self-extending readers learn more about reading every time they read. They read a variety of texts for a variety of purposes.

As teachers, it is our responsibility to understand the reading process, the developmental levels of reading and writing, and the instructional approaches that will support children in their reading and writing development. We must use this knowledge to assess where each of our students is in his or her development so that we can design curriculum and instructional experiences to engage, support, and propel them in their learning. We need to plan for large amounts of time in the day for reading, allowing children to explore texts, practice what they know, and build toward literacy proficiency. Writers at this stage write for a variety of purposes and with a variety of structures.

Differentiated instruction that offers children support as they develop as readers and writers should be the goal of every first-grade teacher. First grade is a time of new beginnings and new experiences that should invite each of the children to actively engage in learning experiences where they make connections, compare information, and contrast ideas as they construct their personal understandings as foundations for critical literacy (Ferreiro, 1991; Heffernan, 2004). As they interact with you and their peers, they will be able to share points of view, negotiate with and question each other, and reflectively think about lots of the new information. As students engage in such experiences, you will notice developmental changes in each child's listening, speaking, reading, writing, and thinking behaviors (Piaget & Inhelder, 1969).

The more children read and are read to, the more words, concepts, and language patterns become part of their listening vocabulary. Soon the children are using these words in their everyday oral language and including them in their writing. The more sophisticated their oral language becomes, the more understandings and vocabulary they have to bring to the tasks of reading and writing (Depree & Iversen, 1994).

# LANGUAGE PROVIDES THE FOUNDATION FOR LITERACY DEVELOPMENT

By the time most children enter first grade they will be on their way to proficiency with oral language, making themselves understood and understanding most interactions. Children's language at this age is often called "egocentric." Their oral language manifests their attempts to make sense of the world around them. Frequently, when asked questions like "Will you answer the phone for Mommy?" or when sentences are phrased in the passive form, as in "Father was given a tie by Susie," they are often confused because of the unfamiliar sentence syntax.

According to Piaget (1973), children learn oral language by constructing their own rules and relationships and by being allowed to direct their own process of learning (Chomsky, 1988). Your role as their first-grade teacher is to provide an environment with experiences that expand their knowledge of all aspects of language, including their vocabulary and their knowledge of unfamiliar and complex grammatical structures. As noted by Lapp, Fisher, and Flood (2000), classroom activities designed to encourage language observation, experimentation, and discussion are those in which:

1. The underlying structure of each activity is based on the continuous assessment of each student's performance.
2. Literacy engagement is interwoven among the expressive (talking and writing) and receptive (listening and reading) language arts.
3. Oral language tasks include spontaneous activities such as conversation as well as prepared activities like singing a song.
4. Peers provide support for each other's efforts.
5. Performance expectations are realistic and obvious to all.
6. All learners are valued, and instruction occurs for all children by building on what they already know.
7. The teacher models and scaffolds literacy strategies.
8. The teacher also provides explicit instruction as needed.
9. A wide array of leveled books are available as language models.
10. Multiple genres are read and discussed; written assignments included an array of genres and formats.

We now consider the specifics of actualizing these beliefs in our classrooms. Vygotsky (1978) cogently noted that children need to develop their literacies (listening, speaking, reading, writing, viewing) while engaged in purposeful, meaning-centered literacy activities.

# WHAT ARE THE FUNCTIONS OF LANGUAGE?

It seems fair to ask about the array of oral language skills that all first graders should possess. The following list adapted from the work of Brown and Allen (1976) denotes the functions of language that first graders should have mastered:

*Controlling Function*

1. Wanting: "I want some more milk."
2. Offering: "I'll help you fix it."
3. Commanding: "Get my bike now!"
4. Suggesting: "Let's read books."
5. Formulating: "You're s'posed to pick up your toys before you go."
6. Permitting: "You can play with my boat."
7. Intending: "I'm going to the store."
8. Querying want: "You wanna play cards?"
9. Querying permission: "May I use your scissors?"
10. Querying intention: "Are you playing or not?"
11. Promising: "I'll always defend you."
12. Threatening: "I'm gonna tell your mom."
13. Warning: "You're gonna fall."
14. Prohibiting: "Don't touch my doll."
15. Using condition: "If you help me, [I'll play ball too]."
16. Contracting: "I'll give you some candy if you let me have that car."
17. Commanding verbalization: "Tell her about it" or "Stop talking right now."
18. Assenting: "Sure, okay."
19. Refusing: "No, I won't."
20. Rejecting: "I don't want to go."
21. Evading: "We'll see" or "I don't know."

22. Querying justification: "Why did you do it?"

23. Justifying: "Because my mom told me to" or "It's naughty to do" or "Children aren't allowed to do that."

*Feeling Function*

1. Exclaiming: "Wow!" or "Nuts!"

2. Expressing state/attitude: "I feel just terrible today" or "I really don't like that program."

3. Querying state/attitude: "How do you feel now?" or "What do you think about 'Popeye'?"

4. Taunting: "You're a real baby."

5. Challenging: "I bet I can stay up later than you."

6. Approving: "You had a nice idea."

7. Disapproving: "You did a silly thing."

8. Cajoling: "You know how—come on."

9. Congratulating: "Good for you!"

10. Commiserating: "I'm sorry you were hurt."

11. Endearing: "I'm your best friend."

12. Tale- telling: "And then he hit me with the truck and . . . "

13. Blaming: "John broke the glass, not me."

14. Querying blame: "Who wrote on the wall?"

15. Commanding apology: "Say you're sorry."

16. Apologizing: "I'm sorry I broke your picture."

17. Agreeing: "I love him, too."

18. Disagreeing: "I think you're wrong—he's nice."

19. Rejecting: (same as in controlling function)

20. Evading: (same as in controlling function)

21. Using condition: "I'd like her if she were nice to me."

22. Querying justification: (same as in controlling function)

23. Justifying: (same as in controlling function)

*Informing Function*

1. Using ostension: "That's [pointing] the car I like."

2. Stating: "I never hit other people."

3. Questioning—positive/negative: "Is that your car?"

4. Questioning content: "Who runs fastest in your neighborhood?"

5. Questioning why: "Why does he always win?"

6. Querying name: "What's that thing called?"

7. Responding: "Bill runs the fastest."

8. Affirming: "You're right."

9. Denying: "No, you're mistaken."

10. Rejecting: "No, it's not terrible."

11. Evading: (same as in controlling function)

12. Using condition: (same as in controlling function)

13. Justifying: (same as in controlling function, but wider in scope—includes all supporting material)

*Ritualizing Function*

1. Greeting: "Hi, how ya doing?"

2. Saying farewells: "See you tomorrow."

3. Turn taking: "And what do you think?" or nonverbal cues signaling the back and forth flow in conversation.

4. Calling: "Nancy . . . "

5. Availability responding: "Yeah? You called me?"

6. Requesting to repeat: "Say that again."

7. Repeating: "I said, 'Give it to me.' "

Other rituals include introducing someone, welcoming a person, acknowledging another's new status, and so on.

*Imagining Function*

1. Giving commentary: "And then the old man put his can down . . . "

2. Being expressive: "Wow, you sure are a pretty doll!"

3. Using heuristic: "When the sun goes down, then it gets dark and then the moon appears."

Chapter 7 provides examples of instruction that support continued language development.

# HOW IS LANGUAGE DEVELOPMENT RELATED TO LEARNING TO READ AND WRITE?

As you will realize when you initially assess your students, many children begin school with an understanding of the functions of language, both oral and in print form (Morrow, 2005; Smith, 1971), but their understanding and control over forms (letter names and sounds) and conventions (left to right, top to bottom, role of spaces, punctuation) will vary.

## Developing Phases of Word Awareness

As you observe your students, consider that on their journey to becoming fluent readers they typically progress through five stages or phases of awareness of words and word parts and the way they work in print (Ehri, 1995; Ehri & McCormick, 1998; Lapp & Flood, 2005). These phases, which include prealphabetic, partial-alphabetic, full-alphabetic, consolidated-alphabetic, and automatic-alphabetic, may not be acquired by children in a linear lockstep fashion and may overlap as they develop an understanding of how phonemes (sounds) and graphemes (letters) work together in print.

Although typical of preschoolers and kindergarteners, a few children in your first grade will be progressing from the *prealphabetic phase*, using nonphonemic visual cues for reading words (pictures, logos), because they have very limited knowledge of letters and equally limited knowledge of how spoken sounds correspond to or represent letters in written words. Some children will be at the *consolidated-alphabetic stage*, where their sight vocabularies continue to grow because they have learned how many word chunks work in words (affixes, root words, onsets and rhymes, and syllables). Most, however, will be *partially using alphabetic cues* to match some letters and sounds.

Much of the work you do with your students in word study will be concentrated on helping them to use alphabetic cues for word recognition. With this instruction the children will progress from matching individual sounds (phonemic awareness) with individual letters to reading larger chunks of letters in words (e.g., from reading words with single letter sounds like *b-a-t*, to reading chunks of letters as in *sn-ack, sn-ake, oc-to-pus, pre-view, end-ing.*)

## Spelling and Word Learning

Word study time will have to be spent with game-like activities designed to enforce these alphabetic understandings. Word-sort and word-building activities help children learn about letter forms, sounds within words (phonemic awareness), phonograms (word chunks: onset [initial letters before the first vowel] and rhymes [the vowel and letters that follow]), and nonphonemic sight words (*the, went, there*).

Children enjoy scrambling and unscrambling words with easy-to-handle magnetic letters, wooden letters, felt letters, and letter tiles. White boards and markers are also easy for children to use for copying and writing words. Many districts have mandated programs to guide teachers in their design of this block of time. However, you still need to know where your children are in their understanding of words to use these programs wisely. Assessing your children's writing samples for their developmental spelling levels will support your efforts to teach this block effectively.

Researchers have also identified five stages of spelling that are closely tied to these stages of word learning (Bear, Invernizzi, Templeton, & Johnston, 1996).

**1.** *Preliterate.* At this stage, children pretend to write. They use random letters and letter-like forms that have no relationship to sound or spelling patterns.

FHUFJKF = bug

This stage of spelling is very similar to the prealphabetic stage of word knowledge.

**2.** *Letter name.* This stage generally corresponds to the beginning of reading. Letter name spellers work in a linear, sound-by-sound progression through a word, spelling only the sounds they hear.

LIK = like

During this stage of spelling, children exhibit patterns of spelling similar to those they are becoming able to read in the partial-alphabetic phase of word learning.

**3.** *Within-word pattern.* Spellers at this stage begin to spell by patterns, using vowels.

MAIK = make

This stage of spelling parallels the word knowledge being exhibited by young readers as they become more fully aware of the alphabetic relationships between sounds and letters.

**4.** *Syllable juncture.* The more advanced spellers at this stage use meaningful units, such as prefixes and suffixes, in their spelling.

BLAZZING

This stage of spelling parallels children's consolidated knowledge of the alphabetic principal that words are composed of bigger units/chunks.

**5.** *Derivational constancy.* Spellers in this phase use their knowledge of parts of words that remain constant across words.

*translate, transport, transfer*

At this stage spellers perform similarly to readers as they automatically recognize words in print.

### Phonemic and Phonological Awareness and Phonics Instruction

Knowing your children's developmental stages will help you to determine the instruction they need. Children at the preliterate level need phonemic awareness and phonological awareness instruction that will move them into phonics. Children at the letter name stage may need to continue with phonics instruction and should be learning sight words. Children at the within-word pattern stage are ready for spelling instruction. Phonemic awareness, phonological awareness, and phonics instruction should offer a variety of meaningful experiences. The word work should be playful and social (Morrow, 2005). Using games, sorts, chants, and rhymes will allow children to play with sounds and develop understandings of sounds and words. There are many books of resources for these activities (see, e.g., Cunningham, 2000; Cunningham & Cunningham, 1992; Cunningham & Hall, 1997; Bear, Invernizzi, Templeton, & Johnston, 1996).

The following chapters provide examples of instructional experiences that acknowledge that children are different and that their learning develops through different paths and at different times. Instruction that accommodates these differences must be flexible and adaptable for each individual, must include multisensory learning opportunities that rely on all of the student's senses, must be scaffolded for each student's learning level, and must encourage and expand the student's language, which is the cornerstone of every child's listening, speaking, reading, and writing development.

# HOW IMPORTANT ARE FAMILY CONNECTIONS?

Every child in your classroom has been entrusted to you with his or her family's belief that you will continue the child's path to literacy. Parents hope their children have teachers who are kind, supportive, professional, and very approachable. The significance of home-based literacy experiences to children's school-based literacy performance continues to be supported by research, which can be summarized as advising "the more at-home literacy experiences, the better" (Darling & Westberg, 2004; International Reading Association, 2002; Lapp, Fisher, Flood, & Moore, 2003; Lapp & Flood, 2004; Neuman & Celano, 2001; Purcell-Gates, 1993, 1995, 2000; Shaver & Walls, 1998; Taylor & Dorsey-Gaines, 1988; Teale, 1978; Yaden, Rowe, & MacGillvray, 2000). Children who have learned the functional uses of literacy through their daily family life experiences are generally those who experience greater success in school literacy (Flood, 1975; Goodman, 1986; Heath, 1983; Morrow, 2005; Taylor, 1997). More specifically, Hess and Holloway (1984) have identified the following ways in which children's literacy can be developed and supported by the family: (1) parents reading to their children, (2) parents communicating their expectations about literacy to their children, (3) availability of reading and writing materials in the home, and (4) parents conversing with their children.

We offer detailed suggestions and examples in Chapter 10 that will help you to connect with families by providing them with insights about how they can better perform in these four areas. To initiate and foster a partnership with the families of your first graders that promotes literacy for each of them must be one of your primary goals.

## SETTING UP THE PHYSICAL ENVIRONMENT OF YOUR CLASSROOM

At last—a classroom of your own! Now, finally, your vision of a "palace for learning" can be realized. Yet there are so many variables to consider. Decisions about space, accessibility of materials, and general organization can impact your instruction in surprising ways.

It is important for you to create a classroom with space to learn. This will include space for meeting with your whole class, places for small groups and partners to engage in learning activities, and places for students to work individually. Think of your new classroom for a minute. You may have a barren room with nothing more than a trash can. You may be lucky enough to have a well-equipped room handed down to you from a retired teacher of 30 years. Whatever your situation, there are certain arrangement issues you must think about in order to teach your new first graders. There are a number of questions to think about as you set up your classroom. What will you place on the wall? Where will student work be displayed? How will you set up the room for literacy centers? How will you make space for students to work in small groups? Will these centers be located permanently in various parts of the room, or will they be portable because your space is so limited? You can get many great ideas for classroom arrangement by visiting other teachers. Some teachers may not have time for touring other first-grade classrooms before the first day of school. However, if you have time, take a trip around the school. You may even get some good ideas from your kindergarten and second-grade colleagues. The classroom setup you choose now will most likely not be the same setup in December or June. Revisit your classroom space often and think about how it is conducive to differentiated instruction. You have endless possibilities, and you will constantly have to be taking your students' behavior characteristics, language proficiencies, learning styles, ethnicity, and gender into consideration.

## WHOLE-CLASS MEETING AREA

First, decide where there is space for the whole class to gather. This space has to be large enough for all to fit, yet intimate enough for serious conversation. A circle is often the formation of choice, so that all can see the person talking and better focus on their thoughts to respond. Carpeting is nice, as most children will be on the floor. Some teachers fringe the space with furniture so that children have a choice based on comfort, but that decision is up to you and the furniture you have available. Many teachers put a rocking chair in this space for themselves. Our preference is always a small first-grade-size chair so we are on a level close to the children who are sitting on the rug (indicating that we are part of the group), yet slightly elevated so that we can hold a book for all to see. Access to and viewability of a Big Book stand, an easel to hold chart paper, and an overhead projector screen should be considered as well.

## PLACES FOR PARTNERS, PLACES TO WORK ALONE

Once you've selected a space for a whole class gathering, you need to decide how you will arrange desks or table space for every child to be seated at the same time. Round tables or clusters of desks allow for group interaction and are always our preference. Placing student desks in clusters can provide a cooperative learning environment. When first assigning students to the desks in your classroom, you will not know much more than each child's gender and name. Your first seat assignments will most likely be random. As the weeks go by, you will probably be changing seat assignments, creating heterogeneous groups according to literacy strengths and needs, student behavior, ethnic makeup, and gender.

## WHAT GOES IN AND ON TOP OF THE DESKS?

Limit the number of items stored inside the students' desks. Giving them several books, folders, and papers will only clutter their desks. Keeping pencils, glue, scissors, and crayons on top of each desk in a basket or box will keep students organized and ensure that work is started in a timely fashion. There's nothing worse than a student rummaging through his or her desk looking for a pencil for 20 minutes. Keep a basket of books on top of each cluster of desks. Be sure to include a range of levels and genres in these baskets. Students can read books from these baskets when they complete their work. This will prevent off-task behavior. Be sure to change the books inside each basket periodically to keep students motivated and interested in reading.

Unfortunately, with class-size reduction came classroom-size reduction, and many teachers find themselves dealing with tight quarters. In this case, a few round tables still offer a place for groups, partners, and individuals to work. Lapboards (rectangles of stiff cardboard) give children a sturdy surface on which to write when not seated at a table. When children are free to use the library or carpet space or to arrange themselves at tables in the room according to the work they are doing and their social learning preferences, the classroom space can work for all learners even if there is not an assigned seat for every student at the same time. Your comfort with this plan will depend on your pedagogical belief system and instructional style.

Many teachers use furniture such as bookshelves to create spaces that give a feeling of separateness for children who need some quiet to focus or for partners who want to be able to chat without disturbing others. If you choose to use furniture to create nooks or small-group spaces, consider whether you will be able to visually check on and make eye contact with children in these spaces while you are working with another small group or individuals. If difficulties should arise, the ability to make eye contact with the culprit(s) may save you from having to interrupt instruction.

## HOW SHOULD YOU ARRANGE THE CLASSROOM LIBRARY? HOW SHOULD BOOKS BE DISPLAYED?

Tied for first consideration in planning space is the location of the classroom library. Your classroom library communicates to all who enter the room. An invisible shelf of books banished to the far corner of the room suggests that time to read, explore, and learn independently is not a priority. A library that stands out as the center or hub of the classroom speaks of a room of learners who take reading seriously. The library must have space not only for books, but for children too. Frank Serafini (Serafini & Georgis, 2003) suggests outlining the library space with

shelves, chairs, couches, or other furniture to help define the area for the children. This arrangement can reinforce desired behaviors (how learners should behave in the class library).

Imagine yourself approaching your favorite bookstore. Most likely, the books displayed in the windows call to you before you actually cross the threshold. Attractive arrangements—books standing, covers facing out—entice you to start browsing immediately even if you are on a mission to find a specific title. Bestsellers are front and center, making you feel as if you just might be missing out if you walk on by. Often, bookstore employees have their thoughts on the books posted next to them, and professional book reviews are cut out and displayed. Books are arranged by genre and/or topic for easy location. All of one author's titles are together. The store is brightly lit and has spaces (and maybe even furniture) where you can settle in, read a bit, and make decisions about your selections. All of this, and all the store is trying to do is sell you a few books. We're selling something far more important—the desire to become passionately literate. A classroom library that says, "Come in, all of this is for you, get comfortable, settle in, and enjoy!" is crucial if your children are to become engaged readers.

To emulate the bookstore feel, the tops of bookshelves should be filled with books standing face-forward and arranged to entice. Other books will be grouped in tubs of some sort by author, series, topic, theme, or level for easy location. Signs on the tubs (and pictures for support if necessary) help the reader to locate the correct tub easily. (Office supply stores and 99-cents stores sell inexpensive plastic tubs such as those in the photograph above.) Whenever possible, books should be arranged/stored with covers showing.

If furniture won't fit or isn't available, some carpeting to sit on while browsing is a nice touch. Children who have read certain titles can post "book reviews" or recommendations on sticky notes, or a bulletin board which can also be dedicated to reviews and recommendations. Remember, the idea is to sell, and what we are selling counts for a lifetime!

## WHAT BOOKS SHOULD BE IN THE LIBRARY ON THE FIRST DAY?

When deciding what to have on the library shelves before the children come in, we generally talked to the kindergarten teachers. We wanted to know what authors and characters had been favorites of the children we would be greeting on the first

day. Having a few of those books on the shelves already will create a sense of familiarity for the children as they arrive. Favorite titles can entice the children right
into the library, build confidence, and get learning started while you are still meeting and greeting. Rather than putting out all your books on the first day, it may be a
good idea to wait until later. By doing so, you can allow your students to take part
in arranging the books with your help. This lets them feel that they are part of their
growing learning community. The suggestions shared by the kindergarten teachers
include:

*Don't Let the Pigeon Drive the Bus!* by Mo Willems
*No, David!* by David Shannon
*Brown Bear, Brown Bear, What Do You See?* by Bill Martin Jr.
*Is Your Mama a Llama?* by Deborah Guarino
*The Napping House* by Audrey Wood
*Rosie's Walk* by Pat Hutchins
*Chick Chicka Boom Boom* by Bill Martin Jr. and John Archambault

## HOW CAN YOU GRADUALLY ADD BOOKS?

Over the first few weeks (exact time depends on the number of books you have at
this point), boxes of books can be opened and explored. While exploring books,
model for children the way to begin grouping texts (books by Eric Carle, books
about bears, comic books, magazines). Show them how these books will go into a
tub and be placed in the library so they know how to locate books and why certain

---

### $$ Money-Saving Tip $$

Get to know your school librarian and local public librarian *very* well. They will assist
you in choosing titles and may even be lenient with checkout rules. Some districts
have instructional materials centers where teachers are able to check out large quanti-
ties of trade books for extended periods of time. Commercial book clubs such as Scholastic and Troll offer children monthly opportunities to buy books at a savings and earn
bonus points for the classroom purchases. (Don't worry—these companies will find
you!) Depending on your population, parents' awareness of a classroom wish list of
titles may help. Many children will lend or donate books to the classroom from home.
Parent Teacher Associations (PTAs) and other parent organizations often support library
building. Watch for grant opportunities, haunt garage sales on Saturday mornings (a
teacher we work with just bought three boxes of books for $10.00!), and watch for
hand-me-downs from retiring teachers, those changing grades, and parents you know
who have older children. Reggie Routman (2003) asserts that a collection of 200 classroom books is adequate; 1,000 titles or more is excellent. Over time you can acquire
what you need if you keep your eyes open for book-gathering opportunities.

titles are together in the tubs. In first grade, you may need to heavily support the children in grouping the books. Plastic tubs are ideal for grouping the books by author, character, topic, genre, or theme. At the beginning of the year, just distinguishing between a fiction and nonfiction section of the library may be enough.

# HOW CAN YOU PLAN FOR VARIETY AND DEPTH?

The library needs to contain not only texts the children like, but those they don't yet know they like. As a first-grade teacher, you will constantly need to broaden your students' awareness of the incredible range of genres and structures of texts. Your library should have a balance of fiction and nonfiction, as well as a wide variety of subgenres and structures in each.

You may want to begin the year by sorting and arranging texts familiar to the children, then add range and depth as you study new genres and structures.

| Fiction | Nonfiction |
|---|---|
| Narrative | Narrative |
| List (ABC) | Expository |
| Comics | Poetry |
| Magazines | Biography |
| | Brochures |
| | Advertisements |
| | Articles |
| | Magazines |

Remember, books are not the only texts we want to have available in the library. Magazines such as *Your Big Back Yard*, *Ranger Rick*, *Ladybug*, and possibly *Cricket*, are part of developing literate lives. Parents with subscriptions may be willing to send in old copies as their new ones arrive. Catalogs are fun to browse through and offer their own reading challenges, as do field guides, brochures, newspapers, and other forms of texts. There are two ways to organize your classroom library. First, organize your books so they are accessible to students. It is a good idea to level approximately 20% of your library so students can choose books that are at their independent reading levels. You can use Fountas and Pinnell (1996) as a resource when leveling your books. The goal should be to teach your students how to choose books that are right for them.

For this reason, it is best to avoid leveling each book in your library. Asking yourself the following questions will help you as you level your books:

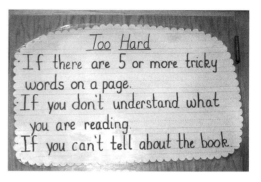

1. How many total words are in the book?

2. How many different words are in the book (e.g., count the word *come* only once)? What is the ratio of different words to total words?

3. How many high-frequency words are in the book? What is the ratio of high-frequency words to total words?

4. How many low-frequency words are in the book? What is the ratio of low-frequency words to total words?

5. How long are the sentences?

6. How complex are the sentences?

7. How predictable is the text?

8. Do the illustrations give text support?

9. How familiar are my students with the topic/concept of the book?

10. How big is the font size?

11. How much space is there between the words? The sentences?

12. How many words are there on a page?

13. What is the pattern of language? Does the text repeat?

As you review your books while answering these questions, remember that the less difficult books should be in the entry-level basket of books, labeled with a 1 or an *A*, progressing to higher-level baskets as the books increase in difficulty. Whenever possible, use books that are already leveled by a publisher as your guide. These will give you benchmarks as you level other books. Most publishers include book levels on their websites. It is important to remember, however, that publishers vary slightly in their criteria for leveling. Keep this in mind when you level your books. For example, you may place a particular book in your level K book basket, whereas another teacher may place it in his level L book basket. Don't worry—the purpose of leveling is to allow you to teach your students to pick "just right" books independently. Leveling becomes much easier after you have a few books in each level.

Another way to organize your library books is by genre or topic. With this arrangement, students can choose books that interest them and motivate them to read more. Regardless of how you organize your books, it is a good idea to store them in baskets or tubs. Students can take a basket of books to any place in the classroom, and you can easily see where you may have gaps in your library in terms of a particular level or genre. Label each book with a colored sticker so you and your students will know where to return a book when they are finished.

## WHERE SHOULD YOU PLACE CENTERS FOR SMALL-GROUP LEARNING?

When you are working with an individual or a small homogeneous group of children, the other children can be heterogeneously grouped in learning activities.

➤ *Literacy Corner.* This could be your classroom library. This area would contain leveled books for students, your reading assessment log, children's reading logs, and beanbag chairs or other comfortable places to read.

➤ *Writing Center.* This is where students can practice writing independently or in cooperative groups. Be sure to include a variety of kinds of paper (lined, blank, construction, stationery), pencils, pens, markers, erasers, envelopes, books about writing, charts (What do good writers do? Topics for writing, etc.).

➤ *Poetry Center.* Students can enjoy reading and writing poetry at this center. Be sure to include different types of poetry books to accommodate the range of learners in your classroom. Have a big chart showing the "poem of the week" and a pointer so students can point to the words as they read along. Also having the poem written on sentence strips will give students practice in sequencing the poem.

➤ *Social Studies/Science Center.* This center offers an ideal way to integrate literacy and these content areas. In this section of the room, include posters, leveled books, basal readers, maps, and hands-on materials to increase student motivation in social studies and science.

➤ *Math Center.* Get your hands on some math literature. There are many resources to choose from, and these books will make a nice math–reading connection for your students. Some great titles to include in this center are:

*1, 2, 3 to the Zoo: A Counting Book* by Eric Carle
*Anno's Counting Book* by Mitsumasa Anno
*Five Little Monkeys Jumping on the Bed* by Eileen Christelow
*The M&M's Brand Counting Book* by Barbara Barieri McGrath
*One Guinea Pig Is Not Enough* by Kate Duke
*Give Me Half!* by Stuart J. Murphy

*A Chair for My Mother* by Vera B. Williams
*Alexander, Who Used to Be Rich Last Sunday* by Judith Viorst
*Monster Math School Time* by Grace Maccarone
*The Grouchy Ladybug* by Eric Carle
*Inch by Inch* by Leo Lionni

Having manipulatives in storage bins at this center will also help your students make the connection from abstract to concrete concepts.

➢ *Listening Center.* Having a listening post in your classroom is a must! Try to borrow as many headphones as possible from other teachers. Remember to place a red sticker on the STOP button, a green sticker on the PLAY button, and a blue sticker on the REWIND button. The sooner you get your students to become independent at literacy centers, the sooner you can start your guided reading groups.

➢ *Word Study Center.* This is a great place to store white boards, markers, magnetic letters, letter cards, dictionaries, chalkboards, and chart paper. Students can manipulate the letters while learning word families, blends, digraphs, and sight words. Set up this center close to the word wall for easy reference. The children should be able to easily see the word walls from this area.

➢ *Technology Center.* Students will love this section of the room as they work through literacy-based computer games, practice keyboarding skills, and practice word processing spelling words. Be sure to hang a chart above the center that explains the procedures for using a computer.

Depending on the amount of space you have, you may want to combine some of these centers in one area. Storing everything related to a particular subject area in one place will keep you and the students organized. You will never wonder where your writing assessments are if you put them at your writing center. Additional items at each center may include:

➢ Assessment measures and forms

➢ Pencils

➢ Erasers

➢ Crayons

➢ Leveled books

➢ Teacher resources

➢ Folders

➢ Paper

Designate a bulletin board above or near each center for student work. Leave these areas blank at first. As the first weeks of school pass, place student work on the bulletin boards. You want to create a student-centered room—an environment that is print rich and represents what the students are learning.

# PLANNING WALL SPACE FOR LEARNING

## Word Wall

One large wall space should be dedicated to word walls that are visible from any place in the room where children might be writing (which is typically the whole room). Lower is better, so that the words are also in the children's sight line. In our first grade we use two word walls. One contains high-frequency sight words that cannot be phonetically decoded and should be learned by sight (e.g., *the*, *that*, *you*). Across the top of this word wall, alphabetically arranged, are all of the letters of the alphabet (*Aa*–*Zz*). As each high-frequency word is introduced, it is posted under the letter corresponding to its first letter (e.g., the word

*went* is placed under *Ww*). The words must be large enough for the children to read them easily. These words can be secured with Velcro or masking tape so that children can take them to a work area to work individually or practice them with a partner. A second word wall should contain words that can be decoded. So that children can find these words easily, we placed the vowels (*Aa*, *Ee*, *Ii*, *Oo*, *Uu*, *Yy*) across the top, and as words are introduced we list them according to their first vowel sound (e.g., *at*, *bat*, *ham* are placed under *Aa*; *bet*, *hen*, *meet* are placed under *Ee*). All of the words on both word walls are also written on index cards so that children can use them for easy word sort practice. Before any word is added to either word wall, children and teacher study its configuration, letter–sound pattern, pronunciation, and spelling. Both word walls are used often throughout the day to aid rhyming, reading, and writing activities.

## Alphabet/Phonics Cards

Children will also need an alphabet and/or sound card and a number line. If your district has an adopted literacy curriculum, it may come with sound cards. These are used for instruction and for reference. Again, the cards should be located so that children can see them from many areas in the room. Many teachers like the number line to be placed low enough that the children can actually touch and use it without having to track it with their eyes only.

Some publishers include sound/spelling cards in their programs. These are helpful for students as they begin to understand that many different letters and letter combinations make certain sounds. For example, sound/spelling cards show students that the /c/ sound can be spelled with a *c*, *k*, or *ck*. This is helpful, because students tend to overgeneralize the spelling of the /c/ sound with the letter *c*.

## Calendar

A calendar is a large part of literacy and mathematics instruction in first grade. Many teachers dedicate an entire bulletin board area to a working calendar, which can be used for counting the days of school, thinking about seasons and weather, writing the days of the week, and many other connected learning opportunities. Location is crucial. The calendar must be located for whole-class instruction and easy reference.

## Charts

As children engage in units of study in reading, you will be charting examples of the work that children can refer to as models. As the children engage in independent experiences, they will need to refer to these charts to support their efforts. The charts should be prominently displayed for easy access. Children will also need access to charts from past studies. If wall space is plentiful, keep the charts up around the room.

> ### $$ Money-Saving Tip $$
>
> There is no reason why you should buy charts for your classroom. With all the computer software, Ellison cutters, and creative students, you can have a print-rich classroom without spending much money at all.

There are many charts that you can make with your students. This will not only save money but will help build a sense of community in your classroom. You can also have the children make signs for the different centers or sections of the room.

Another good idea is to create classroom rules with your students so they can feel that their opinions matter. This will also, it is hoped, reduce behavior problems, inasmuch as the students will not want to disobey the rules they created. You can turn this rule-making activity into a social studies lesson and have each student sign this "constitution" or contract.

Other charts you may want to create with your students include:

➢ "What Do Good Readers Do?"

➢ "During Independent Reading, I . . . "

➢ "Writers' Workshop Topics"

Sharing the pen as you create these charts will also ensure that the students feel as if they are making an authentic contribution to teaching and learning.

When wall space is tight for some teachers, they hang charts on a laundry rack using pants hangers. The children go to the rack, find the needed chart, pull it out for reference, then rehang it when they are finished.

## A PLACE FOR EVERYTHING, AND EVERYTHING IN ITS PLACE

Writers' workshop, discussed further in Chapter 3, creates the need for paper of various types, pencils (keep a can with sharpened pencils available so students with dull pencils can just swap rather than disturbing learning with the pencil sharpener), erasers, staplers, and so forth. A designated shelf for these items is helpful. Expectations for neatness and thriftiness should be set so supplies don't become messy and are not wasted. Places for writing folders, tubs of independent reading books, individual collections of known texts for fluency work, and a place to turn in homework are a few of the many other considerations.

Once you think you have the room arranged, put yourself in your students' place. Sit on the carpet. Sit in the library. Try every seat at every table. Can you see the word wall? the alphabet? the charting that will be driving independent reading or writing? Remember to look through 5- and 6-year-old eyes—what's slightly too high for you is very high for the children. Will the location of all these items allow your students to access the information they need? If so, you have planned well. Will everything go perfectly on the first day now? Perhaps not, but your thoughtfulness and preplanning will set you up for more successes than not and create a first day that feels like a great beginning for all.

## WHAT MATERIALS SHOULD YOU BUY?

The title of this section should more appropriately be called "What Materials Should I Buy, Borrow, or Steal?"! We know that a first-year teacher's funds are limited, so we suggest materials to enhance literacy learning that are inexpensive at worst and free at best.

## Books! Books! And More Books!

There is no better way to let your students know that reading is important than by having a collection of books in your classroom. It is important to remember to stock your library with books at various levels, ranging from wordless books to texts that are three to four levels above first grade. Even though you may not know the exact reading levels of your students, you have to make sure there is something that appeals to them on that first day of school. It is also important to include a variety of genres in your library. You will undoubtedly have students who will rush to expository texts such as *Spinning Spiders* by Melvin Berger or *Dinosaur Babies* by Lucille Rech Penner. There will also be students who will gravitate toward known fairy tales like *The Three Little Pigs* or *Hansel and Gretel*. Talking with the kindergarten teachers at your school site before the first day will help give you an idea of your students' reading levels and interests.

## Book Baskets and Tubs

Another must-have are tubs or baskets to store your books. These can be found at 99-cents stores and come in a variety of sizes and colors. Remember to arrange your books so students are likely to peruse the baskets' contents and feel successful as readers. These baskets or tubs of books, clearly labeled by level and/or genre, will help you and your students stay organized.

## Index Cards and Sentence Strips

No first-grade classroom is complete without a print-rich environment. You will want to label items in your classroom (e.g., clock, door, overhead projector) as well as display words on a word wall. There is no better way to create this environment than with index cards, cut up sentence strips, or, better yet, paper you cut into strips or cards.

## Alphabet Strips

It is a good idea to post a large alphabet strip in your room where all students can see it. The alphabet can be made by you, printed out on a computer, or bought from a teachers supply store. Be sure that the alphabet includes upper- and lowercase letters and pictures to go with the sounds of the letters. In addition to the large alphabet strip, which will undoubtedly be located at the front of the room, have individual alphabet strips on students' desks for easy reference. The individual strips, too, should have upper- and lowercase letters. Again, these can be made or bought for very little.

## Pencils, Crayons, Markers, Erasers

You should have *many* writing tools available in your classroom. Some teachers prefer the thicker primary-grade pencils for first grade. Some teachers use regular size pencils because they are more readily available. Again, the 99-cents store is a great place to get pencils if your school does not provide many. You should also give each student a box of crayons. Labeling each child's box of crayons with a student number will help to remind students that they are in charge of their own supplies and will minimize fighting over the last green crayon. Markers will be a necessity for the students and for you as you write on charts, overhead projectors, and lined dry-erase boards. There is no need to buy white board erasers—an old cloth sheet cut into squares works fine and provides enough for everyone. Erasers are necessary tools for first graders as well. Some teachers prefer pencil erasers. However, many students press too hard and those eraser tops go flying all over the desks. We prefer the small rectangular erasers. You can label these with the students' numbers.

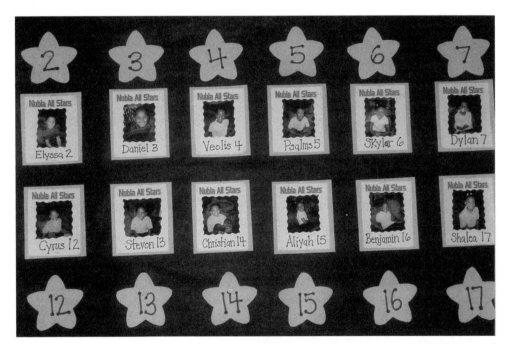

## Paper (Chart, Lined, Blank, Construction, Newsprint, Journals)

In addition to writing tools, you should also have many different types of paper on which the children can write. Chart paper is great for interactive and shared writing, and individual-sized paper is good when your students are writing independently and in guided settings. Newsprint paper is inexpensive and fine for illustrating work and for scratch paper. Multicolored construction paper will be helpful as you integrate the fine arts with literacy throughout the seasons of the year. Check the supply room at your school, an office supply store, or craft store in your community for this kind of paper.

### Sticky (Post-It) Notes

You will undoubtedly find that you are using a lot of sticky notes to write messages home to parents, label your teacher resources, and remind yourself of important dates. However, we hope that you will also give your students a chance to use sticky notes as they interact with texts. Because the sticky notes come in all sizes and colors, students can use the notes to mark interesting parts of books as they read. More ideas for using sticky notes include the following:

1. When reading independently, children can note connections they make between the text and self, other texts, and world experiences. These can be shared during whole-group discussion.

2. New words found while reading can be written on sticky notes and added to an existing word wall.

3. Sticky notes can be used to add information to message boards, Venn diagrams, KWL charts, and concept maps.

### Cassette Player with Headphones

We know that not every first-grade teacher will be fortunate enough to have a cassette player with headphones in the classroom when he or she arrives. We believe that this is the one item you *must* purchase if it isn't provided. A "listening post" can be used for so many literacy-building activities (e.g., oral language, fluency) that we know you will have gotten your money's worth after just a few weeks in school. We recommend having at least three headphones attached to the cassette recorder. Use permanent markers or stickers to label the buttons as well. Students can press, say, the green button for *play*, red for *stop*, and the blue button for *rewind*.

### Visit Your Supply Room and Get to Know Your Building Supervisor

Making a trip to the supply room at your school site and befriending the building supervisor early in the year will be to your benefit. This person will be able to help you when your desks need to be lowered or raised, when your overhead projector light bulb burns out, when your paper towel or tissue supply gets low, or when you are out of pencils. We have

**$$ Money-Saving Tip $$**

Have students make the borders for your bulletin boards. Use blank sentence strips, and have students color, paint, or glue construction paper on the sentence strips to form a pattern. Students will feel valued, their work will have contributed to creating a student-centered classroom, and you will have taught students the math concept of patterns.

listed some of the essential supplies in this section; however, we
know that you will need many
more.

## START TEACHING WHILE ASSESSING

It is most important to assess your
students quickly and thoroughly
in the first few days of school.
However, instruction should not
stop while you assess the stu-

> **$$ Money-Saving Tip $$**
>
> A good way to build a listening library in a hurry is to record your voice on a number of cassettes. Pick one of your favorite books, and record yourself reading the text. You may want to ask one of your more fluent readers to do the same. This is an excellent way to save money on purchases of prerecorded cassettes, and in this way you can personalize each recording (for example, "Hello students in Room 8. How are you enjoying the story so far? Stop the cassette here, and discuss the characters and the plot of the story as we have been practicing in class.")

dents. You may be mandated by your school, district, or state to assess your students with the use of specific measures, or you may be encouraged to use teacher-made or commercially purchased assessment instruments. The sooner you get to know your students, the better. Chapter 5 provides specific ideas about how to assess your students and the different measures to use, which can also inform your teaching. We believe assessment should begin the minute your students walk through the door, because by assessing your students in a nonthreatening way you are creating a comfortable environment where teaching and assessment go hand in hand.

# CHAPTER 2

# UNDERSTANDING HOW CHILDREN LEARN TO READ WRITTEN LANGUAGE

Our grandest hope for every child is that he or she leaves first grade with the beginning knowledge, interest, skills, and strategies necessary to become an independent, literate member of a community, able to use literacy to further his or her own life and the causes of a greater society. More specifically, we hope that by the end of first grade every child, as a reader, will be reading at grade level and, as a writer, will be able to fill a page. Although these are specific goals that can be accomplished by implementing appropriate instruction, they do not get at the spirit we hope you will instill in your first graders, to be lovers of learning.

Such a spirit would include viewing a piece of text as an opportunity to learn and dream side-by-side with an author. It would include an understanding that writing is a tool for communicating a person's needs, hopes, and persuasions. Spelling would be seen as a tool for making sure others can read these thoughts. To this end, though, there are some definite capabilities we hope children have fully in command when they leave first grade:

➢ Valuing the important role they play in their own literacy development

➢ Realizing the importance of being independent, as well as members of a community of learners

➢ Orally communicating their ideas with security and specificity

➢ Reading at (at least) an early stage

➢ Enjoying the wonder of the literature they read and have read to them

➢ Composing full sentences, linked to form bigger ideas, which they realize communicate their messages to a reader

➢ Spelling well enough to communicate their written ideas

Your modeling and instruction will support your students' literacy development as well as their love of learning. As you read this chapter, we'll help you to answer the following three important questions, which we believe support each child's engagement and development as a reader and writer:

1. How does continuous assessment promote differentiated instruction and learning for students?

2. How can I effectively design the day to support differentiated learning and engagement?

3. How can I ensure that my children are reading, enjoying, and writing a wide range of texts?

## HOW DOES CONTINUOUS ASSESSMENT PROMOTE DIFFERENTIATED INSTRUCTION AND LEARNING FOR STUDENTS?

What you learn about your children will guide your decisions about their reading instruction, which will range from their learning the forms and conventions of print to reading comprehension. Although comprehension is the primary goal of all reading instruction, learning about the forms and conventions of print is equally important. You will be designing whole-group, small-group and independent reading instruction using the release of responsibility model (Pearson & Gallagher, 1983) and its associated instructional approaches, which can be addressed through a readers' workshop model (Fountas & Pinnell, 1996). This information is detailed in Chapters 3, 4, and 5.

## HOW CAN YOU EFFECTIVELY DESIGN THE DAY TO SUPPORT DIFFERENTIATED LEARNING AND ENGAGEMENT?

The key to ensuring effective learning is to provide differentiated instructional experiences that are based on continuous student assessment. If possible, given your time constraints, a 3-hour and 15-minute literacy block will allow you an hour each for readers' and writers' workshop, an hour for small-group instruction with a rotation of centers, and a 15-minute word study block. This is an ideal plan, but we realize that many time demands may keep it from being a reality. If so, adjust your literacy study time to include all of these components. In this chapter, we discuss briefly each of the means of differentiation, as well as how to fit them into smaller blocks of time.

One instructional plan that easily accommodates differentiated instruction is referred to as a readers' workshop model (Daniels & Bizar, 1998). Before discussing the components of this model, we consider how a teacher's instructional planning relates to district and national standards.

As teachers, most of our instructional planning falls into two categories: what to teach and how to teach it. What we teach as literacy is guided first by our knowledge of the reading and writing process and our assessments of our students. Once we know where our students are in their development and have a sense of what can be accomplished based on a rigorous years' work, we look to district and state standards to help shape these goals for both individuals and the class as a whole.

Learning how to teach starts in our preservice programs and continues throughout our professional lives as we participate in professional development and work to stay in step with advances in understandings about how people learn.

Both of these issues—what to teach and how to teach it—are addressed in this chapter.

## What We Teach

In *The Art of Teaching Writing* (1986), Lucy Calkins discusses designing curriculum as decision making that is guided by a number of factors, including our students, our colleagues, the communities we teach in, and of course, the educational thought collectives of which we are a part. Many of these thought collectives we belong to by choice, others we belong to as members of a school district, which is part of a larger educational system at the state and national levels.

States have invested in the development of standards documents that spell out state educational goals. Standards for your state should be available to you at your school site, if you do not already have your own copy. For the sake of a cohesive conversation, we will be referring to the New Standards (New Standards Primary Literacy Committee, 1999) here and in Chapter 9, which are intended for a national audience.

### How Can Standards Be Used Effectively to Guide Instruction?

The authors of the New Standards worked to emphasize and define what it means to be both a reader and a writer. The volume for kindergarten through third grade, titled *Reading and Writing Grade by Grade: Primary Literacy Standards for Kindergarten through Third Grade*, describes for teachers "the full range of skills, knowledge and literacy habits that primary children need to learn if they are to succeed in later schooling and in life" (p. 8). This is not stated as specifically as the standards of many states. For example, California standards offer bulleted sections highlighting the skills and strategies readers and writers need to learn. These bulleted lists are often misused as lists of proficiencies to be taught, rather than seen as the pieces that, when fit together in meaningful ways, become the components of a rich, rigorous curriculum.

The New Standards organize the content of reading and writing instruction into three broad categories for each. These categories are used to organize end-of-year benchmarks for skills, knowledge, and daily practice.

The first-grade standards are organized in the following way:

*Reading Standard 1: Print–Sound Code*

➤ Phonemic awareness

➤ Reading words

*Reading Standard 2: Getting the Meaning*

➤ Accuracy

➤ Fluency

➤ Self-monitoring and self-correcting strategies

➤ Comprehension

*Reading Standard 3: Reading Habits*

➤ Independent and assisted reading

➤ Being read to

➤ Discussing books

➤ Vocabulary

*Writing Standard 1: Habits and Process*

➤ Writing daily

➤ Generating topics and contents

➤ Rereading

➤ Revising, editing

➤ Polishing

*Writing Standard 2: Writing Purposes and Resulting Genres*

➤ Sharing events, telling stories: Narrative writing

➤ Informing others: Report or informational writing

➤ Producing and responding to literature

*Writing Standard 3: Language Use and Conventions*

➢ Style and syntax

➢ Vocabulary and word choice

➢ Spelling

➢ Punctuation, capitalization, and other conventions

Through discussions about each of these broad categories of reading instruction and samples of children's work, the New Standards begin to define for us our goals for end-of-the-year first graders. Regardless of whether you are using the New Standards or your own state standards, your work is to assess your students, and design a journey that will enable each child to meet or exceed these goals.

This curricular design is not easy, but support is available. Many districts purchase reading programs that are required to have curriculum that matches standards. These programs, when used wisely, will support your efforts. When using such a program, your role, again, is to assess your students and choose the instruction in the program that meets your students' needs.

Many districts across the United States are now writing units of study based on standards to guide curricular decisions. Designing these units is discussed in depth in Chapter 9.

Having considered what to teach, we return to the workshop model that helps teachers understand how to teach.

## How to Teach

### What Are the Components of a Readers' Workshop Model?

The workshop model is built on the understanding that children learn best by doing (Daniels & Bizar, 1998). A workshop is a daily, ongoing learning opportunity that allows children time to practice and implement what they are learning in the real world outside of school with the support of an expert (that's you!). Workshops can be designed for any subject matter.

The workshop model has several set components that organize the time block. A mini-lesson is the first component. A *mini-lesson* is a brief (hence the name) lesson designed around an aspect of the work you have identified through assessment. It generally lasts 5–15 minutes.

After the mini-lesson, Daniels and Bizar suggest a "status of the class" *check-in* as the second component.

This is a quick, 5-minute check to see how everyone is set-up for the work. This step may not always be necessary, depending on how well organized and smooth flowing the work has been.

The largest amount of workshop time is devoted to the third component, *independent practice*. You can increase this up to 30 minutes over time. But don't necessarily expect 30 minutes the first day. Start with the amount of time your children are able to sustain their efforts, then gradually lengthen it. It's better to have the time shorter at first than to have everything fall apart because the children aren't used to that much independent time.

During the independent practice, you will be *conferring* with individual readers. This is an important assessment time for you. Be focused on the individual reader, but scan the room for trouble spots as well.

The last component is *the share*. This share is also an instructional component. During your conferring, you should identify a student whose work will benefit all and further the learning from the mini-lesson. As the child shares, allow him or her enough of a voice to have ownership of the work, but also step in and make what this particular child has done explicit, along with an explicit message about how the work this reader has done can support other readers as well.

Chapter 3 discusses using the workshop model to teach writing, and more on planning for a year of workshops can be found in Chapter 9.

## Guided Reading

In addition to implementing a readers' workshop, you will be using your assessments to form small, flexible groups for guided reading. As discussed in Chapters 4 and 5, you will be forming groups based on both needs and instructional levels. It is important to note that not all readers at a particular level have the same skills. For example, you may have several Level E readers who exhibit an overreliance on phonics for problem solving at the word level, thus needing work that focuses them on using meaning as a strategy. However, you may have another Level E reader who substitutes meaningful but incorrect words as he or she reads. This reader needs phonics as a focus. Knowing this, you look to your Levels D and F readers to see if you can form a group that will focus on matching meaningful ideas to text.

Using your assessments in this way, you can form and work with as many as five to seven groups of children at almost the same instructional levels and with similar needs at any given time during the year. You will need a block of time in your schedule to meet with your groups. If you are able to plan an hour for guided reading, you can generally meet with three to four groups on any given day. The section on small-group instruction in this chapter discusses scheduling these groups. If you do not have the luxury of an hour for guided reading, you can call students to work with you during the reading workshop. However, if you choose to use workshop time, it is important to balance time to meet with groups with time to confer with your readers during independent reading.

## Word Study

The word study block allows you time to meet the needs of children with different levels of phonemic and phonological awareness, and those children developing a readiness for spelling instruction. As mentioned earlier, a separate block of time for this is ideal. If it is not possible, you may try using the first 10 minutes of writers' workshop for word study, or perhaps 20 minutes a few days a week.

For the majority of first graders, the initial focus of their word study instruction will be learning the forms and conventions of sound and letter associations. In addition, early vocabulary instruction activities should include building fluency when reading a repertoire of known sight words. We next consider the specifics of these areas of instruction.

Word study should occur during a block of time that is specifically devoted to developing the children's understanding of words. This is separate from the readers' workshop, as readers' workshop focuses on comprehension work.

Possible instructional activities for the developmental stages likely to be found in first grade include:

### Phonemic and phonological awareness

➢ Learning songs that play with sounds
➢ Language experience opportunities, in which the teacher encodes a child's language while he or she speaks
➢ Letter sorts
➢ Learning rhymes orally
➢ Playing rhyming games
➢ Picture sorts by sound
➢ Alphabet scrapbook
➢ Picture dominoes

*Phonics*

➤ Short-vowel word family games

➤ Word sorts with short-vowel words, diagraphs, and blends

➤ Letter cubes

➤ Board games that use blends, diagraphs, or words to navigate to the finish line

*Within word*

➤ Word sorts

➤ Word hunts in texts

➤ Short vowel/long vowel sorts

Phonemic and phonological awareness and phonics instruction may also be a follow-up to shared reading with a focus on comprehension, or added to the end of small-group shared reading or guided reading groups. After the lesson, practice playing with the sounds in some of the words. Have the children locate a word such as *hop*. "How many sounds do you hear?" Play with the words orally for children in early stages of phonemic or phonological awareness, enjoying a shared read. After guided reading, for children who have a better sense of the alphabetic principal that sounds of language are represented by letters in words they speak and read, distribute white boards and pens and/or magnetic letters. Study the selected word using the look, spell, cover, write, and check method. Then begin to play: "What if we take away the *h* and add *m*?" "Take away the *m* and add *p*?" "Take away the *p* and add *dr*?"

As phonological awareness develops, children will be ready to benefit from spelling instruction. Like the previous instruction, spelling instruction should be active, social, and meaningful to create excitement about spelling in the children (Marten, 2003). Memorization of spelling words isn't bad. Some words, like sight words, have to be memorized. But memorization isn't enough by itself. To be good spellers, children need to:

➤ Learn spelling strategies (visualize, use parts of words you know to spell unknown words, use what you know about vowel patterns, etc.)

➤ Memorize sight words

➤ Use linguistic patterns to generalize

Spelling instruction should include a mix of varieties of word sorts and inquiry. As children sort words, they begin to generalize patterns, hypothesize about rules, and look for other words to support their hypotheses. This creates what Marten (2003) describes as a word crafting classroom.

We assess children's writing to better understand their development. We see what they are doing well in their spelling, and where they are wobbling. A "wobble," or what a child is trying to use but still confuses, is that child's point of instruction. Most children in a first-grade classroom are in the early phases of the letter name stage. But there are always ranges of ability, with children like Jeremy, our *Gingerbread Man* reader in Chapter 1, still using random letters initially. Because of this range, you may need some guided group spelling instruction. This, too, can be a quick 5 minutes of practice at the end of a guided reading lesson.

Children need to learn sight words to develop automaticity in reading and writing. The word wall is a tool used in most classrooms for this purpose (Cunningham, 2000). The word wall, made of chart or butcher paper, is a large space with letters in alphabetical order and a space for sight words under each letter. The word wall is a dynamic structure, changing as children master various words. When a word is mastered, it comes off the wall and new words are added. Sight words for the word wall may come from shared reading, assessed needs in children's writing, or lists of words children should master, such as the list in Chapter 10.

Once words are displayed on the wall, it is important to make sure they don't become wallpaper. Cunningham (2000) suggests many games that might be played with the word wall to make sure that children get in the habit of referring to it as a resource. Our favorite variations of these games are:

> *Three cheers.* The children clap and spell a word, then raise their fists in the air and say the word three times in a row.

> *"I'm thinking of a word."* In this guessing game, the teacher gives progressively more supportive hints:

  - "I'm thinking of a word—it's on the word wall."
  - "I'm thinking of a word—it's on the word wall and it starts with a *c*."
  - "I'm thinking of a word—it's on the word wall and it starts with a *c*, and it has 6 letters."
  - "I'm thinking of a word—it's on the word wall and it starts with a *c*, and it has 6 letters, and it means 'you can't.' "

> With each clue, the children have to write the word they think it is on a piece of paper, thus practicing many words to play the game.

For children like Jeremy who just need more practice, small-group shared reading can be used for sight word practice, and that 5 minutes after a guided reading lesson can be used for spelling sight words with magnetic letters on the white board. Again, use the look, say, cover, write, and check method.

## Vocabulary Instruction

Vocabulary instruction may also be a part of your word study time. It should also be an embedded part of your ongoing instruction throughout the day. We work to elevate and expand our children's vocabulary at every opportunity, which can vary from informal events like greeting them at the door in the morning to explicitly designed instruction. As noted in Chapter 7, children encounter new vocabulary in a variety of oral language and reading situations throughout the day. Preteaching vocabulary does not enable the children to become independent when encountering new words, and we can't possibly teach all the words children need to know. Our job is to broaden their vocabulary with smart choices for instructional words. Which words will best broaden vocabularies has been an issue for educators at many levels (Lapp & Flood, 2005; Graves & Slater, 2004). Not only do we need to choose the words that will best serve our children, but we also need to teach them skills for solving new words in context (Brassell & Flood, 2004).

Isabel Beck (2002) uses the word "robust" to describe vocabulary instruction that:

➢ Teaches about words and their uses

➢ Provides time for children to think about and use complex words

➢ Enhances language production and output

Beck further suggests using oral language to "lift" young children's vocabulary, as their speaking and listening skills are more advanced than their reading. She also discusses teaching words that are used frequently by mature language users, which she refers to as Tier Two words. Such words might include *ridiculous, ordinary, considerate,* or *argumentative.* Beck suggests that we lift vocabulary by offering a more complex form of meaning or articulating a more complex idea than the children are able to articulate on their own.

For example, if a child is discussing his or her weekend and says, "It was fun!", you might respond, "That's great—another way to describe something fun is to say it was exhilarating!" The children should be allowed time to play with this word, using it orally in conjunction with descriptions of other activities that they think fit into the category of exhilarating.

Laufer and Nation (1999) similarly classify words according to high or low frequency, domain-specific technical, and high utility. A contention of these researchers is that in choosing words for vocabulary instruction, we must consider the words' ability to support our students in thinking and articulating their thinking to others.

As children begin to read more complex texts, they have to learn to use context to make meaning of new words. They need to learn strategies such as pausing to reread and/or reading on through the text (sentence, paragraph, page) to get a sufficient sense of a word to keep meaning intact, using the tone or mood of the passage, and using an understanding of the setting. Much of the instruction for understanding new words in context can be done during shared reading.

### Read-Aloud

A read-aloud is generally a whole-class instructional activity. As noted throughout this text, we read aloud to children for many reasons. For instance, read-alouds allow the children to hear models of fluent reading, expand their vocabulary, learn more about the world, and develop a love of reading. Read-alouds are also used to model comprehension strategies and engage children in trying these strategies themselves. Comprehension is the ultimate goal of all reading instruction and the focus of the read-aloud work we discuss here. This comprehension work will be closely tied to the units of study in the readers' workshop (Chapter 9).

Your focus for read-aloud should be a step ahead of what your children are currently working on in independent reading. Through think-alouds, you model the tasks in a mini-lesson that you want children to eventually take responsibility for (release of responsibility model). The release of responsibility model refers to the differing amounts of support children need to be successful with differing complexities of text (Pearson & Gallagher, 1983; Fountas & Pinnell, 1996; see Figure 2.1).

Notice, in Figure 2.1, that the line distinguishing the amount of teacher support and the amount of student responsibility does not rise to the level of no responsibility on the part of the students, or fall to the level of no support on the part of the teacher. Even in read-alouds, the most supportive of the approaches, we want children to be mentally active and participating. Our reading frees them from the challenges of decoding, so their effort can be directed toward comprehension. Likewise, we never stop supporting. Even during independent reading, the least

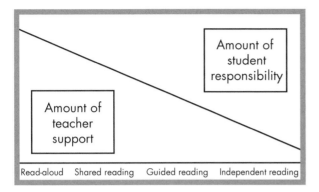

**FIGURE 2.1.** Release of responsibility model.

supportive approach, we teach through mini-lessons, conferring, and the workshop share.

Using read-alouds, you plan the first lesson or two (such as how a character changes throughout the text) knowing that the thinking work will have to be heavily modeled for the children. Eventually, the children will begin to understand your thought processes and join in, taking on more and more of the thinking themselves.

How, exactly, does this modeling work? Chapter 9 includes a possible progression of instruction aimed at the students' understanding characters in text as a means of building stronger comprehension. Although this instruction will most likely be given a little later in the school year, the progression described will work with any set of foci in any unit of study. The suggested progression of focus points for this work on understanding characters (remember, the focus points always depend on your students' needs) is:

➢ Determining the main character

➢ Thinking about what a character is like

➢ Noticing a change or surprise

➢ Thinking about the cause of a change or surprise

In Chapter 9, we share a snippet of a read-aloud in which a teacher is using a think-aloud to model her thoughts about what a certain character, Wemberly, is like. Within a week of that read-aloud, this work will have moved into shared reading. The teacher knows the work is ready to move into shared reading because the children are taking over the thinking and talking during read-aloud.

The next step for these children is to notice when a character changes, and this becomes the next focus for read-aloud. A book in which a character has an obvious change, such as *Harriet, You'll Drive Me Wild!* by Mem Fox, is a good place to start.

Figure 2.2. illustrates a read-aloud lesson plan that considers where to stop, what to ask, and how to model if the talk does not develop. In this lesson plan, we first offer the children an opportunity to think for themselves by asking a very open-ended question. Next, one or two more supportive questions are considered, then ideas for the think-aloud are included if necessary. The stopping places suggested are not the only possible stopping places in the text. They simply offer some points at which to stop and build meaning and talk.

Title: *Harriet, You'll Drive Me Wild!* by Mem Fox
Focus: Character change

| Stopping place in text | Questions to get talk started | What the talk should sound like | Modeling if talk is weak |
|---|---|---|---|
| Cover and title | Look at the mom . . . what are you thinking? How about the way her hands are on her hips? Why do you think she says Harriet will drive her wild? Why do you think she says this? | She stands like David's Mom in *No, David!* . . . Mom's mad . . . Wild is like crazy, bugging you . . . | I know that sometimes I see moms with hands on their hips . . . it means . . . Using what we know about our world can help. (*Note*: English language learners may need support with *"drive me wild."*) |
| *. . . and she was* (page after juice is spilled) | Hmm . . . what's Harriet like? What about the juice all over the floor? What about Mom? Does Mom's face look like she's worried about the juice? | Naughty! I think she knows it was an accident . . . Nice—doesn't yell. | Harriet is being very naughty, but Mom doesn't seem too upset. Some moms would give a consequence . . . I know I would have to use patience to keep from getting mad. When we think about how we would behave, it helps us . . . |
| *. . . and she was* (after she slid off the chair) | Hmm . . . what's going on with Mom now? Why is Mom grabbing things like that? What about the dish breaking? | Still nice, but her face looks a little madder. My Mom would have . . . I don't think Mom will be patient much longer. Mom said her whole name. Getting mad now . . . | When someone does things over and over, it gets harder to keep from being mad. When we think about how we would behave, it helps us . . . I'm thinking again about how I would behave . . . |
| *. . . there was a terrible silence.* | What are you thinking? Why would Mom not say anything right now? | This is it . . . She was too naughty . . . Mom won't be nice now . . . She's quiet because she doesn't want to yell . . . | I know that when I'm really mad, I won't say anything, because the wrong thing might come out . . . |
| *. . . picked up the feathers together.* | What happened with Mom? Did Mom actually change? | She had it . . . Lost her temper . . . Even nice moms get angry sometimes . . . Still nice . . . Got over it right away . . . said sorry . . . They laughed and made up . . . Still a nice mom . . . | Sometimes my mom yelled at me like that when I was really naughty. But, she didn't change . . . I'm thinking about a time in my life when the same thing happened . . . |

**FIGURE 2.2.** Sample read-aloud lesson plan.

As the children begin to take more responsibility for the talk about character change in the read-aloud, we plan some shared readings to begin to transfer this way of thinking to the children's independent reading, and then we can start modeling the next focus in our read-aloud.

But how do we know when the children are ready for the focus to be moved to shared reading? Consider the read-aloud that happened 2 days later in this class. The teacher was reading *At the Edge of the Forest* by Jonathan London. In this story, a boy lives with his family on a farm at the edge of a forest. One day, a coyote sneaks onto the farm and kills a sheep. The father grabs his gun and goes after the coyote, with the boy reluctantly in tow. The two come upon the coyote, the father aims and is ready to shoot, when the coyote's pups come running out to join her. At this point, the teacher is about to begin modeling her thinking about the dad, when the children begin to talk.

"Oh, he's not going to shoot!"
     "He's not mad any more! See, he really is a nice man—the gun was just 'cause he was mad!"

This group of children was noticing that the intent to kill the coyote was a surprise in behavior by an otherwise kind man in reaction to anger. They came to this realization without modeling. The teacher now knows she can move this focus into shared reading and begin with a new, more complex focus in read-aloud. This may happen after two or three read-alouds, or it may take longer, depending on the complexity of the work.

Think back to the three *Gingerbread Man* readers in Chapter 1: Carlie, Jeremy, and Michael. Again, this work may come later in the year, so all will have grown as readers since we listened to their reading of *The Gingerbread Man*. Undoubtedly, all three readers would delight in this text. First graders can relate to a child like Harriet. So, we would expect to hear rich conversations from all three, with connections to times they or a sibling behaved this way and rich language describing the way their moms reacted.

Michael, the strongest reader, will be reading books with characters that sometimes do surprising things and who sometimes actually change. We would expect him to begin to take this work on independently after the support of read-aloud, shared reading, and possibly some guided reading. Carlie will most likely have made strong progress and be very capable of taking this on too. Although Jeremy will enjoy the read-aloud and benefit from the talk around meaning, he may or may not be ready for this work in his independent reading. If he has not accelerated to a point where his "just-right" books offer this complexity of character and if he has other more crucial needs as a reader, then we will need to consider designing other shared reading opportunities for his needs. Children with needs like Jeremy's are discussed later in the "Small Group Instruction" section.

The progression of work from the read-aloud to shared reading is not always so linear. Often, we notice things in the children's independent reading that need attention, and we take time, with the appropriate approach, to address them. Thinking about moving the focus from read-aloud to shared reading, though, is a good way to get a general sense of where you are going and get some planning done in advance.

## Shared Reading

Your shared reading instructional time will be a mix of teaching children strategies for word and problem solving and teaching them increasingly complex ways to think about their reading. Shared reading can be used for *whole-class* or *small-group* instruction. It provides a safe environment for risk taking, as all readers receive the support of the teacher and their peers. It is a nonthreatening way of strengthening skills and building positive attitudes about reading (Routman, 1991).

During shared reading we ask the children to begin to take on more of the responsibility for reading and making meaning. In classrooms with children in the emergent stage, such as Jeremy, many teachers introduce songs and chants orally first, to build language. Next, they put the printed text in front of the children and begin to work on a mix of meaning-making strategies and skills through shared reading, while focusing on various parts of the text. It is crucial that we always consider reading instruction through the lens of making meaning. Children must approach written text with the expectation that it will make sense.

For this reason we need to teach shared reading as a whole-to-part-to-whole activity. Whole-to-part-to-whole instruction means that we always develop the meaning of the entire text, or a meaningful chunk of text, before we isolate parts. It does not matter whether we are teaching ways in which readers can understand the characters or word-solving strategies: We begin with the text (or large meaningful section of text) as a meaningful whole, then isolate the portion necessary for in-

struction; we next consider the part as a means of getting to the whole, and, finally, we rethink the whole.

For example, when we are using the shared reading approach to teach our students that readers use pictures to make meaning and problem solve the print, we go through a process that's based on the meaning of the text. We carefully select a text for shared reading at a level that meets the needs of the children instructionally and will hold their interest over several rereadings. On the first day we read the text in its entirety, building meaning as we go.

Then we revisit the text, perhaps the next day, perhaps at a later date, moving from the meaningful whole to a piece or pieces we want to focus on instructionally. When using meaning and pictures to problem solve at the word level, we cover a few key words in the text with sticky notes and have our readers use meaning from the picture and the text itself to predict what the print might say. When we are sure our predictions make sense, based on the picture and the accumulated meaning of this text, we reveal the word (or maybe start with the beginning sound) to cross-check, using graphophonic information.

Consider a shared reading lesson from the book *Our Favorite Food* by Anna Porter. The children read this leveled text and came to the conclusion that it was about the fact that we all have our food likes and dislikes. The teacher had decided to focus on using the meaning of the text and the picture on the page to problem solve at the word level. The page the children were working on showed a photograph of a girl with a piece of pizza. She is tearing off a bite, with the cheese all strung out. The text says: "I don't like pizza," said Emma. "The cheese is too messy."

The teacher had covered the word *messy* with a sticky note. The children used the meaning of the text to anticipate that the covered word might be *hot*, *gooey*, *messy*, or *yummy*. Of the four, *yummy* did not make sense when the meaning of this page was considered, as it says "I *don't* like. . . ." So *yummy* was discarded, and the other possibilities remained. The teacher then revealed the first letter, and it was decided that *messy* was the only choice that made sense and matched.

Our conversation then focuses on the way problem solving these words in the text supports our ability to work with the author to make meaning. Here, we are moving from the whole, pulling out a part for instruction, then returning to the whole. Reading is not about the parts, it is about the whole—the meaning. Yes, the parts help us to get there, but looking at parts void of meaning separates reading from the act of making meaning, and we begin to create readers who no longer expect reading to make sense.

For children like Jeremy, the work could have focused on phonics as well:

"Who can find the word *pizza* on this page? What do we hear at the beginning of pizza? Yes, a *p*."

"What does a *p* look like? Point to it, write it, now find it . . . "

If you consult a continuum of reading behaviors for emergent and early read-ers, such as the First Steps continuum (Education Department of Western Austra-lia, 1994), you will be able to anticipate some of the work your children will need to take on with the support of shared reading. The possibilities include:

➢ Oral language development

➢ Concept about print issues

➢ Letter–sound match

➢ Using meaning and beginning letters to predict a word

➢ Looking through the word for more information

➢ Using parts of a word to get at the whole

➢ Cross-checking

➢ Reading beyond an unknown word (end of sentence, end of paragraph, end of page, etc.) to gain more meaning, then returning to the word to solve if neces-sary

➢ Strategies for deepening comprehension

➢ Citing evidence (text, picture)

Focusing again on the three *Gingerbread Man* readers, we know that Jeremy needs more shared reading for connecting meaning with print. Carlie's next step for shared reading may be using more complex strategies, such as looking through the word. Looking through the word is looking beyond the beginning sound to be sure there are matches all the way through. "*Messy* starts with an *m*, and I see an *m*. Let's look through the word to see if the other sounds match."

Michael may need more reading work in the area of strategies for deepening comprehension. So how do you teach shared reading with this range of needs in your classroom? All three children would benefit from the work Michael is ready for, because all readers should be taught to think strategically at all times. But we need to be aware that we have students like Carlie and Jeremy, who might need more small-group opportunities.

Shared reading is also an excellent time for fluency practice. Reading fluency refers to "effortless automatic word recognition with appropriate phrasing and expression" (Lapp & Flood, 2005). As the children read with us, they work to match their voices to ours, practicing over and over with the same phrasing and expressiveness. Then they practice on their own, imitating the fluent reading. We have our students do this because we want to hear their comprehension in their voices while reading. Their reading should be well phrased and expressive.

However, fluency is not synonymous with comprehension. If you have ever watched the Book TV channel, then you have listened to authors read their texts aloud. Now, who should better comprehend a text than its author? Yet some of these authors' oral readings are dreadful. It's not that they don't understand their own work, they're just not good at reading aloud.

Research, though, has shown that developing the ability to read in meaningful phrases supports comprehension, as there is more meaning in phrases than in words. Fluent readers are able to decode well and chunk words in ways that make its meaning more accessible (Rasinski, 2003). So, do we work with children on fluency? Absolutely. How much time do we spend with it? The answer lies in how much it is helping the individual child with his or her comprehension.

Rereading known text, such as chants, poems, and rhymes, is a fun way to practice. Some teachers have fluency warm-ups before their instructional shared reading. Others have a separate period of time for this rereading. Using books on tape and engaging in Readers' Theater are also great ways for children to practice their fluency.

## Small-Group Instruction

Small-group reading instruction is just that—pulling together a small group of children (usually no more than four to six) with similar needs for instruction. The children's instructional levels must be close enough that you can choose one instructional text that works for the entire group. Most often, your small-group instruction will be guided reading, but it can be shared reading as well.

Guided reading is the last instructional step before independence. We use text just slightly above the child's independent reading level, choose one focus that seems to be the children's greatest need, and design lessons with just enough support to ensure success with the print and meaning making.

Among the *Gingerbread Man* readers, Carlie has enough understanding of using pictures to support meaning making and accessing print to take the work into guided reading, in which she will be responsible for making meaning and using pictures to problem solve as she reads the text on her own.

Again, Jeremy needs more shared reading experience with using pictures to support meaning making and accessing print. He could be included in a small group of children with similar needs for this additional shared experience. He can also be placed in a guided reading group with a different instructional focus, such as work needed on aspects of concepts about print (CAP). As an emergent reader at the beginning of first grade, Jeremy needs these multiple small-group instructional opportunities to accelerate his reading development.

Michael has developed an understanding of many reading strategies. His most immediate need for guided reading is to use all strategies in concert to make meaning and access print. He should be placed in a different group than Carlie, with a slightly more difficult level of text.

As detailed in Chapter 5, grouping children based on assessments and needs is an ongoing process. At any given time, you will have a varying number of groups to plan for and schedule into your day. A planning grid can help you to decide which groups you will meet with when. It's important to meet with your most struggling readers daily (or twice a day) in small groups. Other groups might meet for a few days in a row, then have a few days of uninterrupted choice time to practice. Note that even though their guided group is not meeting on a given day, these children still receive reading instruction through read-aloud, shared reading, and conferring.

A guided reading planning grid (Figure 2.3) can be used to plot a week of guided reading, organized in a way that makes sense for you and your students. Consider a mark such as an X to indicate which days you plan to meet with the group, then write the title of the texts you plan to use in the grid, so that the text for any given day of instruction can be identified at a glance. (A blank reading plan grid is provided in Figure 2.4.)

| Group names | Focus | Monday | Tuesday | Wednesday | Thursday | Friday |
|---|---|---|---|---|---|---|
| Jeremy Amy Janette Leonard | CAP—using pattern to predict | X _The Birthday Cake_ | X _The Beach_ | X _Going to School_ | X _My Dog_ | X _Hello!_ |
| Carlie Donny Jared Anthony | Meaning and pictures to problem solve | X _In the Fall_ | X _Water, Water_ | X _Feet_ | X _The Mail Carrier_ | |
| Kate Consuelo Juan Carlos Tanisha Eric | Cross-checking meaning and graphophonic cues | X _The Escalator_ | X _Mr. Grumpy_ | X _Lucy's Secret_ | | |
| Michael Marie Sabrina Kevin | Orchestration of strategies | X | X | X | | |
| Dee Ann Manuel Joanna | Use predictions to anticipate, monitor and modify if necessary | | X | | X | |

**FIGURE 2.3.** Sample guided reading planning grid.

| Group names | Focus | Monday | Tuesday | Wednesday | Thursday | Friday |
|---|---|---|---|---|---|---|
| | | | | | | |
| | | | | | | |
| | | | | | | |
| | | | | | | |
| | | | | | | |
| | | | | | | |
| | | | | | | |
| | | | | | | |
| | | | | | | |

**FIGURE 2.4.** Guided reading planning grid.

From *Teaching Literacy in First Grade* by Diane Lapp, James Flood, Kelly Moore, and Maria Nichols. Copyright 2005 by The Guilford Press. Permission to photocopy this figure is granted to purchasers of this book for personal use only (see copyright page for details).

It is quite possible to meet with three guided reading groups a day. The days with four are a little more difficult. We often need to be flexible with time to meet with one of the groups on these days, gathering the children during independent reading or any other time during the day when we can meet with them for 15 minutes of supportive, explicit instruction.

To support your planning time, consider each group as an inquiry into some aspect of reading. As a general rule of thumb, if the instructional focus is mastered during just one or two lessons, it might have been better addressed in a reading conference. Guided reading groups should be formed with the understanding that they will be ongoing for 1, 2, or possibly even 3 weeks. Some members, however, may exit a group sooner if they progress at a faster rate than others.

Once you decide on an instructional focus for a group, gather enough texts for several lessons. These lessons can all be planned while previewing the books and thinking about the children's literacy needs. As you get a sense of a group's progress toward the focus, you can choose the next batch of texts as you make decisions about individual members.

### Independent Reading

Independent reading is a time for children to practice strategies for independence in a text at their independent levels. The amount of time allowed for independent reading at the beginning of the year depends on your children. Your goal by the end of the year should be at least 30 minutes of self-sustained reading time, and the sooner you get there, the better.

To help increase the length of time your children self-sustain their reading, you may want to use partnerships. Little by little, have the children spend more

time reading independently before they move into their partnerships for more interactive reading and conversing.

The children's book choices during independent reading should enable them to take on the work from the mini-lesson. Not every reader will implement every focus each day, but if the class is studying characterization and one child is reading nonfiction dinosaur books, it's a good bet that readers will not be practicing thinking about characters at all during the workshop. (Yes, the dinosaur lover can still read dinosaur books. See the section ahead on allowing more time for reading.)

Independent reading works best if children have selected their texts prior to the workshop. Time spent in selecting books means less time reading books. And selecting becomes a great avoidance technique for some readers. Your students should have a tray, bag, or other means of keeping a collection of books for their independent reading.

At first, children will need to change books every day or so because texts at their independent levels are very short, quick reads. As they progress as readers, they should be putting together a collection that will last them several days. How many books they collect will, again, depend on their levels. Emergent and early readers, such as Jeremy, will need more books, picture book readers, whereas Carlie will need just a few. As children like Michael progress to early chapter books such as Cynthia Rylant's *Mr. Putter and Tabby* or *Henry and Mudge* series, they will need fewer books.

Having too many books encourages quick, surface-level reading and hopping from book to book. Over time, we want to teach children to linger, reread parts, and think about their books.

As children are reading independently, you are conferring with them. Remember, this is a time to talk reader-to-reader. As you chat, you check for how well the child is making meaning by asking questions. As holes in understanding become apparent, choose one way of thinking about reading that you can teach the children.

During a conference, you might have children read part of the text to you, but it is not always necessary. When you are checking on progress with problem solving at the word level, such as with Jeremy, or if you have concerns about the level of the text, have the child read a little out loud. At other times, you can assess the children's accuracy by having them locate evidence or other special parts in the text. Most often, a conference is a quick, 5-minute exchange. Using a form to help you to track a reader over time is helpful as you plan for that reader's small-group instruction. When a form is filled out, it may look something like Figure 2.5. (A blank conferring guide is provided in Figure 2.6.)

Notice that conferences (in Figure 2.5) were about a week apart. Depending on your class size, you should be able to confer with each reader approximately once a week. Keeping notes like these enables us to plan Carlie's guided reading according to her most crucial need. We can also go back to our notes as Carlie gains independence with this focus and is ready for the next.

| Reading conference notes for *Carlie*                    .                                             |                                                                                                                                    |                                                                                                                                      |
|------------------------------|----------------------------------------------------------------|------------------------------------------------------------|
| **Date/text**                | **What I notice**                                              | **What was taught**                                        |
| 9/05 <u>No, David!</u>       | Text at an easy level<br>All CAP in place?<br>Expressive reading<br>Talks about what David did<br>    wrong event by event | All of those things can help us<br>    to get a sense of a<br>    character—talk about<br>    David—what is he like? |
| 9/12 <u>Our Favorite<br>Food</u> (read once<br>whole class) | Chats about her own food likes<br>    and the text<br>Yes on CAP<br>Makes meaningful substitutions<br>    at tricky words | Cross-checking—idea needs to<br>    make sense and match the<br>    print<br>Reteach this in guided reading<br>    groups |
| 9/23 <u>Tough Boris</u>      | Mix of reading and memory—<br>    little too challenging<br>Meaningful substitutions<br>Used pirate schema to<br>    understand Boris | Getting at tricky words using<br>    meaning—scary<br>Reteach this in guided reading<br>    groups |

**FIGURE 2.5.** Sample conferring guide.

# HOW CAN YOU HANDLE OTHER CONSIDERATIONS SUCH AS DESIGNING THE DAY SO CHILDREN HAVE TIME TO READ AND HEAR TEXT READ ALOUD?

In classrooms that are recognized as being most effective in literacy instruction, teachers allow children more time to read and write than allowed in other classrooms, some of them allotting as much as half the school day or 50% of instructional time for reading and writing. In comparison, less effective classrooms had children reading and writing for as little as 10% of the day (Allington, 2002; Avery, 1993).

What this means is that our instructional reading time is never enough. We need multiple opportunities throughout the day, in many contexts, for children to read and be read to from a range and variety of texts. And we need to read more complex text to them as often as possible. How does this all fit into the day?

## Time for Reading

Think about how you might organize some free choice reading opportunities similar to those afforded to Carlie, Jeremy, and Michael. If you were able to scan their classroom, you would see the teacher with a small group, and other children spread out, engaged in reading in a variety of ways (Chapter 6).

Reading conference notes for _____.

| Date/text | What I notice | What was taught |
|---|---|---|
| | | |
| | | |
| | | |
| | | |
| | | |
| | | |

**FIGURE 2.6.** Conferring guide.

From *Teaching Literacy in First Grade* by Diane Lapp, James Flood, Kelly Moore, and Maria Nichols. Copyright 2005 by The Guilford Press. Permission to photocopy this figure is granted to purchasers of this book for personal use only (see copyright page for details).

A pair of children have small books that go with a Big Book the class has read and revisited for strategy lessons. They are taking turns reading the text out loud, supporting each other with print-related struggles, and pausing to discuss photographs and ideas. "I like this picture—it's all of Big Bear's books. Look at how many he has. It says he loves to read!"

Two girls are rereading/retelling *Wolf!* by Becky Bloom. They, too, are moving back and forth between the pictures and the print, relying heavily on the pictures for support. They are having fun with the font variances in the text, talking about the wolf's progress as a reader, and they are marveling at the realization that none of the humans in the school or bookstore or elsewhere in the book seem much concerned with a wolf being in their midst. "A wolf could eat them. Story wolves do that!"

A group of three children has a tub of Jim Arnosky books. Their teacher has read a few of the books out loud and given book talks on the other titles to entice the children. Their talk about the title they are reading moves from the text itself to the way Jim Arnosky uses what he sees in nature to write his books. "We know there's raccoons—they ate the corn. There must be deer there too. Look, it has the footprints like the raccoons. That's how he knew . . . "

Three boys have a tub of books about cars. They are searching out the models they are familiar with. "Hey, my uncle has this car. It's a Mustang. Let's see . . . yeah, here, see . . . Ford Mustang. His is green, kinda like this one. Yeah, it goes fast, like this one . . . "

Two more children are sitting with a globe and an enormous book of animals from around the world. They are moving back and forth between the pictures of the animals and maps in the text and the globe, trying to figure out exactly where these animals live. "Penguins! It's cold. They live in the white places. It's snow and stuff . . . "

We believe that the most valuable thing children can do while the teacher works with small groups is to read. The teacher in this room has used read-aloud to produce familiar texts and has taught ways to reread, retell, and rethink them purposefully, so the children know how to engage themselves in powerful reading experiences independently. Ideally, this should be free-choice time, when children partner and cluster around texts that engage them.

If completely free choice sounds a little worrisome to you, you might consider reading centers to scaffold the time by adding some structure. Reading centers are addressed as a means of propelling children's oral language development in Chapters 6 and 7. There are other possible centers that can be added to the list.

## Environmental Text Center

Most emergent readers can benefit from the support of a print rich environment. Collections of environmental print may be on a bulletin board. Or an even better choice may be a collection of class-created books. One book might be about favorite restaurants, filled with pieces of text such as a McDonalds bag or an advertisement for Chuck E. Cheese. Another might be about favorite places to go, with logos from Disneyland, area theme parks, or entertainment centers. Ads for favorite toys and games would make an entertaining book as well. All of our readers, and, most important, our emergent readers, will be capable of making meaning and reading these texts.

## Favorite Character Center

Any type of text or way of thinking about reading you are addressing with your students can become a center. Do your children love Franklin books? How about a tub of Franklin books, some known and some new, for children to read and discuss? Have you been studying a variety of characters? Consider putting three of the children's favorite character books such as *Chrysanthemum* by Kevin Henkes, *Harriet, You'll Drive Me Wild!* by Mem Fox, and *No, David!* by David Shannon for children to reread or retell, and talk about and compare the characters in the stories. After reading one of these books, students might fill out the following form:

| Who do you think is the naughtiest character? | | |
|---|---|---|
| Readers' names | Naughtiest character | Evidence |
| | | |
| | | |
| | | |

## Favorite Author Center

A tub of books by a favorite author can be a great scaffold for reading and book talk. This works best when children have some sense of the author's body of work and tendencies as a writer. Early in the year, consider authors such as:

➢ Frank Asch: *Mooncake; Happy Birthday, Moon; Moonbear's Shadow*

➢ Jim Arnosky: *Raccoons and Ripe Corn; Every Autumn Comes the Bear; Deer at the Brook*

➢ Eric Carle: *The Very Hungry Caterpillar; The Very Quiet Cricket; The Very Busy Spider*

➢ Donald Crews: *School Bus; Freight Train; Flying*

➢ Martin Waddell: *You and Me, Little Bear; Good Job, Little Bear; Can't You Sleep, Little Bear?*

➢ Rosemary Wells: *Bunny Cakes; Goodnight Max; Max's Chocolate Chicken*

### Research Center

As you study author's purpose and structures in nonfiction, you will be reading and learning about many topics. Children naturally latch onto these topics, wanting to read more about them. A tub of texts about a favorite topic will entice many children. As real-world nonfiction includes a variety of materials, try to do the same with this collection. Newspaper articles, brochures, maps, field guides, and the like will help children develop a sense of this variety. If this center is paired with the Computer Center, the computer can become a tool for research too. You will need child-friendly websites to make sure the children don't stray into dangerous territory. Two websites to get you started are *www.timeforkids.com* and *www.kids.discovery.com*.

### Library Center

The Library Center, can be used as a place to look for independent reading texts too. Most important for your reading centers is that they engage the children in the real world of reading. Aim for a mix of leveled texts that offer more practice for fluency and complex, engaging materials to challenge readers (remember, they have the support of their peers while at a center).

Over time, with support, your students will begin to define their own purposes for reading and engage in planning their reading time. One day, a child will beg to stay in the Library Center because he wants to learn about all the things sharks eat. Another won't want to tear herself away from the collection of travel brochures, because she is sure she can talk Mom and Dad into a vacation. When this happens, give these children permission to pursue these passions in reading. Suggest that they keep their collections of texts on a corner of their desks so they can get right back to them tomorrow. Highlight this practice for other readers. This is the real world of purposeful reading. What we read forms the passions, interests, and hopes that fill our lives.

These children may no longer need the scaffold of centers to stay engaged with reading. When children are able to set their own goals for reading based on interest, they are ready for true free-choice reading time. Remember, centers do not have to be an all-or-nothing venture. You can keep centers available for children who still need their time scaffolded while you allow others to structure their own time.

### Home Reading

As discussed in Chapter 10, home reading is another way to add reading time to a child's day. Many parents need support in rethinking their vision of what "reading for homework" should look like and sound like.

Back-to-School Night is a wonderful time to discuss home reading with parents. They need to understand that their children need to be reading a wide range of materials, some of which can be read to them, such as newspaper articles, some of which they will read together such as favorite storybooks, and some of which their children will be able to read on their own.

Depending on the economics of the school's population, you may have to support home reading with classroom book checkouts. If so, buy sturdy zip-lock bags and write the children's names and room number on them. This will boost the possibility of having a book returned if it is lost. You may want to send home a parent letter before beginning checkouts, letting parents know that the books have come from the classroom and are needed for classroom instruction. Asking parents to help their children be responsible for the books is a good idea.

Reading does not always have to be separate from the usual activities of the evening. A child may help by reading directions for making dinner with the parent or by reading the pizza delivery menu to the family so everyone can decide what to order. Special time to read is the goal for all of us, but reality sometimes gets in the way. That's okay, because reading is a part of the real world. Consider using a homework recording sheet, such as the one in Chapter 10, so that children can record their home reading daily.

## HOW CAN YOU ENSURE THAT CHILDREN ARE READING A WIDE RANGE OF TEXTS?

Texts that children are actually able to read successfully are crucial to their progress as readers (Allington, 2002). A large amount of our students' reading time should be spent with text at an appropriate developmental level. But a steady diet of "just-right text" is not enough. Children need to explore authors and favorite characters, read and engage in conversations about ways of thinking about reading, read about the passions in their life, and get into the more complex books that just call to them. They need to spend more time reading real books (Daniels & Bizar, 1998). Studies have shown that narrative text tends to dominate elementary instruction. Most children come to school with a sense of narrative structure. However, both the real world and standardized tests are dominated by nonfiction. In short, we need more nonfiction in the classroom (Duke, 2003).

Centers and free-choice reading help us to get real books into children's hands. Consider sources for compelling and beautiful nonfiction text for emergent and early readers to use during this time. Many authors specialize in nonfiction, and some publishers have series for young readers. A few of the many possibilities are listed here:

*Authors*

➢ Joanna Cole: The *Magic School Bus* series

➢ Gail Gibbons: *The Moon Book; Bats; The Reasons for Seasons*

➤ Ruth Heller: *The Reason for a Flower; How to Hide an Octopus and Other Sea Creatures; Animals Born Alive and Well*

➤ Bruce McMillan: *Nights of the Pufflings Growing Colors; Eating Fractions*

➤ Ann Morris: *Houses and Homes; Bread, Bread, Bread; Hats, Hats, Hats*

*Publisher series*

➤ Pebble Books published by Capstone Press

➤ National Geographic's *Jump into Science* series

➤ Discovery Library published by Rourke Enterprises

➤ Rookie Read-About Science published by Children's Press

➤ Lifecycles series published by Franklin Watts

➤ Let's Read and Find Out Science Stage 1 published by HarperCollins

➤ A First Discovery books published by Scholastic

Magazines such as *Your Big Backyard* are also a wonderful addition to the classroom library. It contains a mix of fiction and nonfiction articles, stories, puzzles, and projects.

To fill the need for both more time with real books and a variety of texts, many teachers have additional read-alouds during the school day. It's a smart idea to have a chapter book read ongoing. A few chapters read after lunch each day refocuses the children and teaches many of the more complex reading behaviors they will need, such as visualization, holding onto a story line over time, thinking about more complex characters, and considering cause-and-effect issues as characters change. Titles might include:

*Charlotte's Web* by E. B. White
*The Mouse and the Motorcycle* by Beverly Cleary
*Freckle Juice* by Judy Blume
*Charlie and the Chocolate Factory* by Roald Dahl
*Mr. Popper's Penguins* by Richard and Florence Atwater
*The Stories Julian Tells* by Ann Cameron (short stories)

If your readers' workshop focus is fiction, you may want another time to read nonfiction aloud to the children, or vice versa. Children need many models of fluent reading during the day.

Reading instruction is a complex orchestration of text, instructional approaches, grouping, and time, all in service of children's assessed needs. The challenge can leave you feeling more than a little apprehensive. But there is also much joy in watching the world of reading open up to a child. Most important is that you just get started. You will make mistakes with text selection and grouping. We all do. If a text is too challenging, offer more support and rethink your selection for tomorrow. If it's too easy, then the children get some extra fluency practice. Again, rethink your selection for tomorrow. If a child doesn't fit as well in a group as you thought he or she would, move the child the next day.

You will learn more about your children and their needs, texts, and instruction as you go. Differentiating instruction for children like Carlie, Jeremy, and Michael will get easier. Remember to rely on the plan, teach, and reflect cycle, and watch for your students' success. They will make many little steps forward and some great leaps. Enjoy these changes, as they are a direct result of your hard work. You will find that these successes help to build your confidence in planning and teaching reading each day.

# SUPPORTING FIRST-GRADE WRITING

n *Writing Through Childhood*, Shelley Harwayne (2001) speaks of helping children to find a place of honor for writing in their lives. As goals go, this one is huge. But, as with all goals, when broken into baby steps, it is achievable. To be strong, capable writers, children need a substantial amount of time to write daily, just as they need time to read daily to become strong, capable readers (Flood, Lapp, & Fisher, 2005; Graves, 1994, Calkins, 1986). Writing, like reading, must be perceived as a joyous, real-life experience. If children are to honor time to write, writers' workshop must be a positive, successful experience for children.

To this end, we want our children to view writing as an extension of living. "If you experience your days with wideawake eyes," we say to our children, "If you see the extraordinary in the little moment-to-moment events, wonderings, reflections, and interactions with others, then you write as you live!" Children must not be made to feel that they have to have amazing adventures to have the fuel to write. You don't need to go to Disneyland, have outlandish birthday parties, or win awards. Writers' workshop is a time to get what's already happening in your head onto paper.

As the children develop this understanding, we support their efforts to get it all on paper through our workshop instruction. We begin by using the children's ability with oral language as a bridge to written language. Then we ensure success by sharing with them the ways authors craft their ideas, offering support through a variety of instructional approaches. We develop structures for support as we create a safe environment in which children feel free to be risk takers (Fletcher, 2001). And we make sure the workshop is organized so that time is well spent (Farnan & Dahl, 1998).

## THE WRITERS' WORKSHOP

In this chapter we explore the writers' workshop, looking first at organization, then at supports for writers. From there, we move into workshop content and the instructional approaches used for teaching. Always, we keep in mind our goal, our vision of children who write daily because they understand the power of writing in their lives.

## MATERIALS AND ORGANIZATION

For writers' workshop, you will need an assortment of materials.

➢ Several kinds of paper

➢ Pencils

➢ Erasers

➢ Markers and/or crayons

➢ Scissors

➢ Stapler

➢ Date stamp

The only paper you will need to get started is primary lined paper with space for pictures, because many young writers will draw as a support for or in place of putting print on a page. For this reason, some teachers prefer paper without lines at first. Only you can decide which is best for your children. Eventually, you may need:

➢ Paper without picture space, as you move toward drafting first, illustrating to add details later.

➢ Smaller-ruled paper, if you have students whose handwriting develops to a point where this is more comfortable for them.

➢ Spelling paper for poetry (long and thin).

➢ Paper you design for particular purposes, such as a page with a picture space and a speech bubble to encourage adding dialogue (see Figure 3.1), or a page formatted for letters, and other kinds of pages.

**FIGURE 3.1.** Dialogue writing.

From *Teaching Literacy in First Grade* by Diane Lapp, James Flood, Kelly Moore, and Maria Nichols. Copyright 2005 by The Guilford Press. Permission to photocopy this figure is granted to purchasers of this book for personal use only (see copyright page for details).

These items should be kept in a place where children can access them on their own. Passing out single pieces of paper at the beginning of the workshop limits the children. Some may have more to write and need more than one sheet of paper, some may need to finish a piece, and others may need a different type of paper. A shelf dedicated to writers' workshop supplies is an ideal solution. Teach the children to keep the piles neat, return items if they find them lying around, and use them freely without wasting.

## KEEPING TRACK OF MANY PIECES

Writers need the freedom to choose, to write about the things that matter most to them (Graves, 1994). A writer may be developing a piece around one idea, when another event, thought, or feeling tugs at them. When this happens to a writer, the piece in progress is often abandoned, temporarily or not, for the new idea. This reality of the writing life means that children may be juggling many different pieces at once.

For the children, this means flexibility and choice. For us, it means an organizational nightmare. We suggest using folders to organize children's writings. The best folders for the job have a pocket on each side to hold papers.

To prepare the folders, label the pocket on one side "working on," and the pocket on the other side "resting." All pieces started within a unit of study are kept on one side or the other. A child may have two or three pieces that are important to them on the working on side, and many they have started but not pursued on the resting side.

One helpful tool for assessing how individual children are juggling their pieces and making choices about which to work on is a date stamp. At the beginning of each workshop, set the date stamp and pass it around the room. The children stamp whichever piece they are working on. The date stamp is then placed in the Writing Workshop materials area. If a child changes pieces during the workshop, the child gets the date stamp and stamps the date on the piece he or she switched to, or the new piece of paper.

One piece with many dates stamped on it tells you that this child is sticking with a single piece over time. You may want to count the number of days the piece was stamped and compare it against quality, depth, and length of writing. Is time spent on the piece productive, or is this child stuck?

A great many pieces with little evidence of sustained effort and only one date stamped tells you that this child may be jumping from idea to idea without focusing on and developing any one of them. Both of these scenarios, and every possibility in between, will surface in your workshop, so be prepared to teach in these situations.

# SUPPORTS FOR WRITERS

### Talk Partnerships

In Chapter 7, we discuss the fact that children at this age use their oral language to make sense of their world. By talking about their ideas, children gain clarity in their own understanding and in how well they are communicating their thinking.

As children prepare to write, they also need to use their oral language to rehearse their ideas (Graves, 1983). By talking with partners, children are able to:

➢ Gather the language they will need to articulate, and eventually encode, their thinking

➢ Structure their ideas

➢ Begin the writing process with an idea at least partially formulated (thus never having to stare at a blank page with the feeling of having nothing to write)

➢ Develop a sense of audience

➢ Grow in clarity through feedback

➢ Add details based on questions and reader (listener) confusions

➢ Develop flexibility with the written word by rereading and continually discussing their developing pieces with their partners

Partners must be selected carefully and maintained over time. We teach partners how to listen to each other carefully, act as a keeper of the partner's story, ask sincere questions, and push for clarity.

Every day, before children get out their writing folders, they spend time in their partnerships, talking about their ideas, rereading their pieces, and comparing them with the ideas they originally articulated to their partners. Partners then write in close proximity to each other so they can chat as they write, rethink their ideas, and receive feedback and support. A partner who has heard an idea rehearsed orally can support the encoding process by listening to the author think about and reread his or her piece. "Hey, you forgot the part about . . . " or "I don't get this part . . . "—we hear partners saying to each other.

## Model Texts

The more children read, the more they learn about writing (Smith, 1988; Avery, 1993; Ray, 1999). After children have had time to process the meaning of a piece, they can study the way the author crafted this meaning (see "Careful, Deliberate Crafting of Ideas" in this chapter).

Texts with excellent examples of craft moves, or ways authors work with words and/or structures, can serve as models, or mentors, for the children. Excerpts of these texts can be used for shared reading within the writers' workshop for the purpose of analyzing and discussing the way certain authors worked. Consider having a special place in the classroom for these mentor texts, perhaps near the writing materials. Along with charts from writers' workshop, this can create a comfortable writing corner in the classroom. The following is a list of possible texts and just a hint of what they have to offer. The more you reread and study a text, the more you will see in the words and structures. You'll find more possibilities in the section of this chapter titled "Careful, Deliberate Crafting of Ideas."

*Crossing by Philip Booth*

➢ Text written as one long list

➢ Use of italics and bold print

➢ Startling beginning

*Grandad Bill's Song by Jane Yolen*

➢ Text seesaws between child asking questions and other characters answering

*When I Was Five by Arthur Howard*

➤ Seesaw text structure

*Shortcut by Donald Crews*

➤ Use of italics

➤ Use of sound words

*Come On, Rain! by Karen Hesse*

➤ Use of italics

➤ Repetition of phrase throughout the text

*Butternut Hollow Pond by Brian J. Heinz*

➤ Use of a structure from nature

# CHARTING

As each unit of study in the writers' workshop develops, the ideas explored should be charted and available for the children to consult. For instance, if the class is working on voice (more on this in a later section), the chart may look like Figure 3.2.

Charting such as this not only reminds children of the writing moves (use of structure or ways with words) or strategies they might try, but helps them to remember a specific example of how this move or strategy was used by others and what the result was. Model using the charts yourself as you write to ensure that the children will use them too.

| Authors make their pieces come alive by . . . | Who tried this? What did it sound like? | How did it help? |
|---|---|---|
| Writing like they talk | Connor in his video game piece *My mom blew her sock off* | We laughed because it sounded just like Connor. He always says that! |
| Adding dialogue | Andre in his piece called "Birthdays" *"A scooter . . . YES!" I roared.* | We get excited with him. |

**FIGURE 3.2.** Examples of voice in one's writing.

## MAKING REAL THINGS

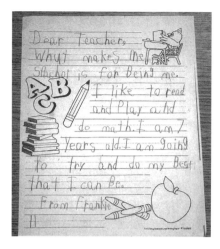

Children delight in making things. When young writers write, knowing that they are making a real product that will live in the world excites and motivates them. It helps them to develop a vision of what might be, motivates them to study others who write, and helps them to plan for their writing (Ray & Cleveland, 2004). The things children make in the writing workshop can vary from elaborate to simple. Among the possibilities, consider such things as:

➢ Simple books
➢ Books designed according to genre needs
  ■ How-to books
  ■ Expository books
➢ Pop-up books
➢ Letters
➢ Lists

## WHAT SHOULD YOU TEACH?: THE CONTENT OF WRITERS' WORKSHOP

The content possibilities for writers' workshop are seemingly endless. Writers do so many things that children can study. Vicki Spandell (2004) offers a description of what she calls the "Six traits," or qualities, of good writing: *ideas*, *organization*, *voice*, *word choice*, *sentence fluency*, and *conventions*. Spandell points out that these traits are not new; they are simply what good writers have been doing for as long as they have been writing.

This chapter offers a number of possibilities to get you started. These possibilities are a mix of strategies and techniques, including the six traits, and product work. To explore them, you will need to develop a repertoire of favorite authors to whom you return again and again to study, and real-world text by a variety of authors who utilize the genres you will be exploring. You will need to use all instructional approaches, releasing responsibility and giving children ample time to immerse themselves in the work.

## Moving from Drawing to Written Text

To support their efforts to record ideas on paper, children need to continually grow stronger in their understanding of spelling and writing conventions. Interactive writing and word study offer separate blocks of time to build spelling knowledge, using an inquiry process, and to develop an understanding of spelling strategies.

### Interactive Writing

During interactive writing, both the responsibility for composing the text and the construction of the text are shared by the teacher and the students. The children are involved at specific points in the construction process, according to the decisions made on the basis of assessed needs and goals. The point of involvement may be instruction on letter formation, sound–letter correspondence, spelling pattern, words that can be spelled strategically, using knowledge of other words, or print features such as punctuation (McCarrier, Pinnell, & Fountas, 2000).

When engaged in interactive writing, the children gather around an easel or another means of displaying a piece of chart paper. Each should have a white board, pen and eraser, or other tools for writing the focus sound, word, phrase, or other element. First the children are engaged in conversation about composing a message of importance to the group (either whole class or small group). The teacher alternates between accepting the message as suggested by the children, and pushing and pulling at it to raise the level of language and vocabulary, thus stretching the children's own natural language.

The teacher acts as scribe for all words with which the children are fairly fluent. When the construction process comes to a word that offers an instructional focus, the teacher pauses and involves the group in problem solving. This problem solving may consist of supporting the children in feeling like writers, taking the first steps to get sounds, words, and/or sentences on paper. Interactive writing can be used to practice letter formation, encourage "getting what you know how to do" on paper, and increase self-esteem (Lapp, Flood, Frey, Moore, & Begley, 2004). It can also be used as an opportunity to teach spelling and conventions, such as punctuation.

When you have chosen a place in the encoding to stop and involve the children, begin by asking them what should be done. The group strategizes out loud, then the children try out the letter or word themselves on their white boards, as one student goes to the chart to write. The children hold up their white boards with their attempts, so the teacher is able to check and teach to what he or she sees. This checking is done through the lens of what is right. The process of noticing what is right might sound something like this:

TEACHER: I see the word *play* spelled *pla*. What parts did this writer get right?

CHILDREN: He got the *p*! And the *l*—he had *pl*! And the *a*!

TEACHER: Yes, this writer got most of the word correct. He doesn't have to learn the whole word, he just has to remember the *y* at the end. The *a* sound in *play* is spelled the same way Kay spells it in her name.

This process encourages the writer. First, the writer realizes that he or she has some control over the difficulty. Then, the child is given specific feedback about the chunk of the word he or she needs to work on and, if possible, a tool to help the child remember. "Remember, the end of *play* is spelled just like the end of Kay's name."

What you focus on during interactive writing will depend on the needs of your students. When working on word solving, the developmental spelling levels of the children and their assessed needs will help you to make decisions (see Chapter 2).

## Rereading

As children begin to lengthen their written pieces, rereading what they have written becomes crucial. Rereading enables them to check and rethink many aspects of their pieces. When we reread, we do so to achieve clarity and meaning, not to correct errors in conventions (Fletcher, 2001). But it is not easy for children to develop the habit of rereading. Rereading must be modeled for children, with explicit language about how it is helpful to pause to reread a piece during its construction.

## Lengthening Pieces

"I'm done! Teacher, I'm done!" We hear this in our sleep, and you will hear it too. We hear little Alex, on the carpet, give a 5-minute dissertation to his partner on his trip to the zoo; then he goes to his desk, writes "I went to the zoo," and he's "done"! Obviously, there is more Alex must commit to paper, either through drawing or writing. This is where we take Alex's piece, study it, turn it over, furrow our brow in confusion, and begin a process that goes something like this:

TEACHER: But, Alex, I thought you saw monkeys.

ALEX: I did!

TEACHER: Hmm—I don't see that here . . . ?

ALEX: Oh, I forgot.

TEACHER: You better go add it!

Alex goes off to add the monkeys to his piece, and 2 minutes later, he's back.

ALEX: I'm done!

TEACHER: (*taking the piece and modeling the same confusion*) Hmm . . . I'm sure you talked about doing more. Where's the part about the elephants?

ALEX: I forgot that too!

Off he goes, and—you guessed it—2 minutes later, he's back. So now we call in the big guns and enlist the aid of his partner. What else did Alex forget? And how can we help him and others to get all of the important parts of their ideas on paper?

This is the beginning of teaching children to lengthen their pieces. Note that a long piece in and of itself does not equal a good piece, but we do need to help children get more of the story on paper. There are many ways to support this effort, such as:

- ➤ Using partners to help the children remember the whole story
- ➤ Talking about filling the whole page while sticking to one idea
- ➤ Stapling pieces of paper together and talking about filling many pages while sticking to one idea
- ➤ Studying favorite books as mentor texts, talking about ways in which authors stick to one idea but add lots of details
- ➤ Zooming in on feelings
- ➤ Slowing down events and really describing them step-by-step
- ➤ Adding characters' voices (conversation)

We do not mean to suggest that this is your writers' workshop curriculum for the first month. When you tackle these ways of lengthening text, and how many you teach at once, will depend on your students. You may revisit lengthening many times during the course of the year.

### Author's Purpose

Whether we are writing a letter to a dear friend or making a shopping list, our writing has purpose. As writers, considering our purpose for writing helps to focus our piece. Fiction pieces may be written to entertain or to convey a lesson on life. In nonfiction writing, six purposes seem to surface most often: to describe, to explain, to inform, to persuade, to retell the past, and to communicate with others (Stead, 2002).

Consider the topic of soccer as an example. We could write everything we're thinking about soccer on four pages, and have no focus, and probably put the readers to sleep. Or we can think about why we need to write about soccer and include just the information that goes with our purpose. We can write to describe our teammates because they're such characters, and just tell about them. We can write to explain why we lost last weekend, and include details about everything that went wrong. We can write to inform you of the rules, to persuade you to join our team because we need more players, to retell the events of the championship game, or to write a letter to the coach thanking him for all he has done to help us. Each of these pieces would have different information, based on the purpose, and the crafting of each would be much easier as the writer's skill increases. Modeling writing the same topic for different purposes makes this very clear. Then, with every piece we write, we model a consideration of purpose before we begin.

### Structure

Very closely related to purpose is structure. Children will retell the events of their lives using the narrative structure common to the storybooks they most often hear.

We must also expose children to and teach them to use the most common text structures for nonfiction, including narrative, sequential, descriptive, cause and effect, problem and solution, compare and contrast. Each of these structures has key words or phrases that help the reader to identify them (Hoyt, 2003). Once writers know their purpose, they can choose the structure that best conveys their ideas. How many of these structures you actually teach to first graders will vary. Certainly, they will use narrative, descriptive, and sequential structures. Some writers may be ready to attempt others.

The accompanying piece by Teddy on the topic of water cycles illustrates a consideration for both structure and audience.

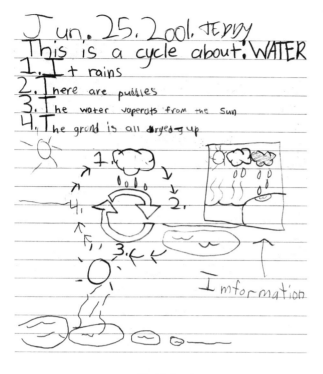

Teddy's piece.

## Audience

With purpose comes consideration of audience. If I am writing to inform my reader of all the rules of soccer, the piece needs to be very different for a kindergarten audience than for an adult audience. Just as we model writing the same topic with different foci, we must model writing the same topic for different audiences to give the children a feel of what needs to be different. And just as we always consider purpose when modeling, we include a consideration of audience.

Teddy uses a mix of running text and diagramming to write about the water cycle, which had been studied in science. Her writing is structured sequentially and supports the reader (audience) by being numbered. Teddy said she was writing the book for kindergarteners, which is why she used the numbers for the steps in the cycles instead of a lot of words.

## Voice

Getting a sense of voice in a piece means that the reader actually hears the author through the words. Sentences are written the way the author would say them. The author's own expressions are used. Donald Graves (1994) describes voice as "the imprint of ourselves on our writing."

Voice is very difficult to separate into discrete elements, but a reader knows when he or she is reading a piece with voice versus a piece without. To illustrate, compare the pieces by Connor and Ryan.

B Connor

I rember wen I got
Punish I was playing
my game Boy to moch

My mom siad I was Pusest
watever That mens
an ☐ Kuded Play
It For a Day isinit
horubul I was about
to bad and cRY I gept

on askin askinan askin
my mom Blooher sooks
ooF I had a hard Feaing

That Day was going
To Be Bad

Connor's piece reads:

I remember when I got punished. I was playing my game boy too much. My mom said I was possessed, whatever that means, and I couldn't play for a day. Isn't it horrible? I was about to beg and cry and cry. I kept on asking and asking and asking. My mom blew her socks off. I had a hard feeling that day was going to be bad.

Ryan's piece.

Do you hear Connor's voice in this piece? Connor uses his own way of talking to write. This creates more complex sentence structure and draws in richer vocabulary. You can tell that he is a child who adds much life and laughter to the classroom.

The reader does not come away from Ryan's piece with a sense of the person behind the story. The reason is not just that it's shorter, but that we don't hear emotion as we did in Connor's piece. The sentences are of simple structure with safe vocabulary.

### Careful, Deliberate Crafting of Ideas

Right from our first modeled writing, we let the children see us in our role as author, struggling to find just the right word, or phrase, to convey meaning. "I like . . . no, not like—I love, well, not really love, hmm, how should I say it . . . ?" This is an author at work. Authors continually craft their language until a piece sounds and feels as they envisioned. As children develop as writers, they can study favorite trade books and take on the ways of crafting used by their favorite authors (Ray, 1999).

"Did you notice," we say to our students, "how in *Can't You Sleep, Little Bear?* Martin Waddell wrote the word **DARK** in bold print and capitals on this page? I wonder why? What other authors do we know who do this? Why? Can we try it?" Who has a word in his or her piece that could be in bold print? What would it do to this part of your piece?

Destiny carefully chose the words she wanted to emphasize and used bold print and enlarged size to do the job.

Or you might say to the children, "Did you notice that in *Do Like Kyla* by Angela Johnson, there's a pattern? First the sister does something, then the narrator does it too? What could we call that? Could that pattern work for you? In *When I Was Young in the Mountains* by Cynthia Rylant, the author used a phrase over and over. Why? How does it help the piece?"

Brea has tried many craft moves within this very short piece. She has written through the voice of a narrator, played with ellipses and parentheses, and used font to emphasize words as Destiny had. She learned about repetition from Cynthia Rylant, this time repeating a single word through her piece rather than a phrase.

Children need to see this crafting of words and structures in modeled writing from teacher and touchstone texts. They need to try it with support during shared writing, and they need time to play with it in their independent writing. Allow the children the freedom to try various craft moves, even if success is not immediate. Their attempts will improve over time, and in the meantime they are building the understanding that authors make choices as they write, and that authors need to be flexible and willing to change if the words don't come out just right. This, of course, is the essence of revision

## Genre

In addition to sharing what is near and dear to them in a narrative structure, expository nonfiction and poetry are genres first graders find enticing.

Destiny's piece reads:

Powerful thinking can make your brain **huge!** So when everybody hears it, it grows **bigger!**

### EXPOSITION

As children study expository text, its features, and its range of topics, they can begin to write about the things they know best. Note that writers' workshop time should not be used for research. Until children are taught to do topical research, they copy facts from books onto their own papers. Even when research is taught, the research is the work of the readers' workshop.

This page from Jeianne's "All-About Dolphins" book uses a mix of running text and visual features to convey information. The class had studied diagrams, maps, and flowcharts as readers to get a sense of how authors use them. The children were then given opportunities to explore these tools as writers when making nonfiction books.

Brea's piece reads:

Ouch, Zachary!!!! Breanne was mad at her brother, Zachary. She had to play with him, so she did. But . . . he punched her (so she said) . . . I will ouch never ouch play with you **AGAIN! OUCH!!**

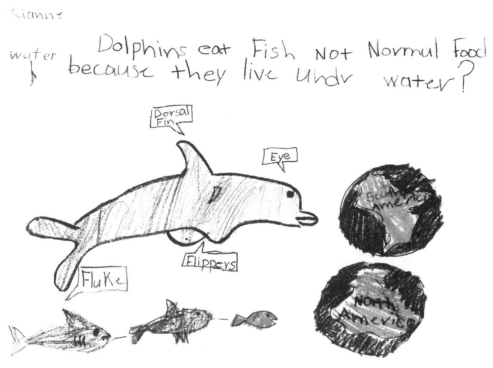

Jeianne's piece reads:

Dolphins eat fish, not normal food, because they live under the water.

## POETRY

Reading and writing poetry should be approached as playfulness with language and discovery of the power of well-chosen words. Groupings of words expressing power or other emotions need to be explored.

We used long, skinny spelling paper for poetry to encourage children to think about line breaks. Jeianne wrote a stunning piece, but still had difficulty with the breaks.

During publishing, you can word process a piece with the child sitting next to you and play with the line breaks electronically, allowing the child to instantly experience the power of moving lines, phrases, and words around. Victoria chose this arrangement, which was different from the arrangement on her unpublished paper.

To support the study of genres, such as poetry, in writing (Harwayne, 2001):

➢ Gather a range of examples for children to read over and over.

➢ Use the examples as mentor pieces.

➢ Allow children to save their favorites.

➢ Teach techniques for the genres.

➢ Allow the children's work to be celebrated.

Oct 2001 9          Jeianne

Cats
Cats eyes gloe on
The night when
you cant see
there Bodys you
will see lights in
the darck a
cats teeth almost
looks like
Vanpier teeth!

Jeianne's piece reads:

Cats

Cats' eyes glow
in the night
when you can't see their bodies.
You will see
lights in the dark.
A cat's teeth
almost look like
vampire teeth!

Your Heart          By Victoria

Your heart is the one.
The one that helps.
The one that helps you to be you.

I'm me"

### Taking Special Pieces through the Writing Cycle

Writers need the freedom to decide what piece or pieces they will stick with, but they then need to be taught strategies for sticking with these pieces by taking one through the entire writing process many times during the course of the year. A general rule of thumb is to take one to two pieces per study through the process, or approximately 10–12 pieces a year.

When it is time to publish, we take the time to allow children to sit, spread out their pieces, and read through them. They should select one that they feel strongly about in order for the revising, editing, and publishing to feel important.

What's often hard for us is that children do not always select what we consider to be their strongest pieces to publish. Remember, the learning was in the act of doing. Even if the amazing piece you were hoping for is not chosen, the author still learned by going through the process of writing it.

At the end of a study, we ask children to clean out their folders. Make sure to keep or copy any pieces you need for evidence of growth; then send the rest home. With new study will come many new pieces, and the process will begin again.

## INSTRUCTIONAL APPROACHES

Just as with reading, there are a range of approaches for teaching writing that differ in the level of support offered to the writer.

### Interactive Writing

As discussed earlier, interactive writing is a time when children and teacher compose and scribe the text together. It is used for phonics and spelling support or to support children as they learn to get words on paper, use punctuation, and to feel confident about writing in general.

### Modeled Writing

Modeled writing is the most supportive of the instructional approaches. During modeled writing, the teacher serves as both composer and encoder. Just as we think aloud in a read-aloud, we think aloud during modeled writing. Our out-loud thinking gives children a chance to listen to the decisions a writer makes about topic selection, word choice, text structure, and other crafting choices.

We model taking memories, thoughts, happenings, and wonderings and finding just the right words to share them on paper. We model our struggles at getting words on paper, our confusions, and the joy of the power of our own language. We reread as we go, rethink an idea, and model flexibility with the written word by changing our minds about words, phrases, or even the inclusion or exclusion of specific information.

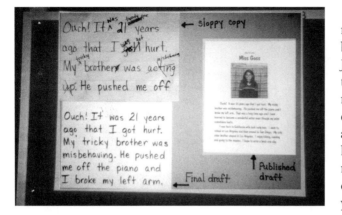

Pieces produced during modeled writing do not have to be finished in one mini-lesson. Just as the children return to their pieces over time, a piece of modeled writing may be developed over time, and returned to again and again for further learning opportunities. How much of a piece you develop in one mini-lesson depends on your instructional purpose.

## Shared Writing

Shared writing removes some of the support offered by modeled writing, as children are encouraged to enter into the composing process. In shared writing, the students and teacher share responsibility in composing a message. The teacher controls the pen, fully supporting the encoding, so that all of the children's efforts are on focused on the actual composition of the message.

Shared writing can help children to understand that writers work to craft what they say very carefully. To reinforce the understanding of how writers compose, we ask the children how we might express the thoughts we want to get on paper. No matter what the children say, we then say, "Yes, that's one way. Who has another way? Which way sounds more powerful (or funnier, or scarier, etc.)?"

Shared writing also offers an opportunity to model flexibility with the written word. As the text is composed and encoded, the teacher and children constantly reread, listening for the way the message flows and how the meaning builds. We show no fear, boldly crossing out and changing sentences, phrases, or words to make our message clearer and stronger.

Through this procedure, the children come to see each of their written texts as a process rather than a product that, once on paper, stays unchanged forever. They also develop a strong understanding of the importance of rereading as a tool for ongoing revision.

Like modeled writing, shared writing can also be used to create pieces of text to which the class returns for extended learning opportunities.

## Independent Writing

Time for independent writing is crucial. Researchers have repeatedly impressed on us the importance of giving children time to write (Ray, 2004; Smith, 1988). Ideally, writing workshop should be a daily, predictable event, with a portion of time for independent writing that continually stretches the children's ability to stay engaged with writing independently. An hour-long block for writers' workshop, with most of the time spent with children writing, should be your goal.

Independent writing time offers children the opportunity to take on the identity of writer, experiencing the joy of the process. It enables children to engage in the ways of writing discussed earlier in "Modeled Writing" and "Shared Writing," to refine their understanding of the encoding process, and to develop the identity of "writer."

This independent time is not silent, all-by-myself work. Writing at this point should be a very social experience. The children can learn to use the support of their partners and others around them to stretch their ability to sustain effort independently. The children learn from each other as they puzzle over spelling difficulties, word choice, and refining their ideas.

Independent writing time is assessment time for you. As the children write, you are moving from writer to writer, engaging them in conversations about their pieces. Our job is to teach the writer, not the writing. This means that we are not so much concerned with making this particular piece of writing better. Rather, we want to teach our writers strategies for writing that they will carry with them from piece to piece (Calkins, 1986).

Assessment can also take place after the workshop. A good habit to develop is to read through two children's folders each day. Look at numbers of pieces, quality and quantity of the writing, range of topic choices, and progress with encoding and writing conventions. Depending on your class size, if you read through two folders each day, you will be assessing each child's body of work twice a month. What you notice through conferring and reading the children's work will fuel your minilessons and decisions about units of study.

## Guided Writing

As you assess, you will find small groups of children with common needs in regard to idea development, craft decisions, and/or writing conventions. Just as with reading, you can form small groups during the workshop to teach whatever is needed to help the children's progress as writers.

Groups can be called during independent writing time, but be careful to leave yourself time for conferring as well. These groups, like guided reading groups, are flexible. They may be considered mini-study groups that will focus on an identified need for a number of lessons and are then disbanded. How often you work with guided writing groups depends on your children's needs. This small-group experience may also be used for extra modeling or shared time for children who need more support.

## ASSESSING

### Assessing to Identify Individual Instructional Needs

To know how our children are progressing as writers and what their next steps are, we must read their work. One piece can be read quickly during a writing conference. But we also need time to read through the child's body of work contained in his or her folder and really consider that child's needs on the basis of multiple pieces of evidence. This is a time-consuming procedure, but it can be done smartly.

When we read our children's writing, the general focus is on what they are doing well, where they are wobbling, and how we might guide them through these "wobbles."

Joshua's piece: September.

Early in September, you will find a developmental range of writers, just as you found with readers. Consider three pieces produced in the first few weeks of independent writing in one first-grade classroom. We discuss what each writer is doing well and how we can plan differentiated instruction based on this information.

Joshua's writing shows a wonderfully creative, artistic child. This piece is about a game he was playing with his brother. He told his story to his teacher thus: "We played fighting men. My guy beated him. It's our best game. We're playing today, too. We do it in the garage so my mom doesn't get mad." The story would have gone on and on if the teacher hadn't gently stopped him to refocus on his piece. The conversation that then took place illustrated that

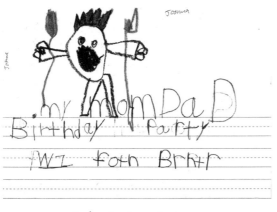

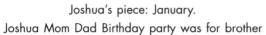

Joshua's piece: January.
Joshua Mom Dad Birthday party was for brother

Joshua's piece: June.
I played a basketball game. But my team was losing. I made the ball go in the basket.

Joshua knew more than was initially apparent about writing. When asked about the picture, Joshua was able to point out details and connect them to the story he had told orally. Joshua knows that print conveys meaning and used random letters to represent these ideas. When asked what the letters said, Joshua retold his story in a briefer version, with simpler sentences, as if he were reading.

Watching Joshua write confirmed that he moved left to right on his paper indicating that he had return sweep under control. Joshua's piece was created in a picture first; then the print was added, using the picture for support. Joshua's rich sense of story will help him greatly in his development as a writer. Interactive writing will be essential for helping Joshua to build letter–sound relationships, asstrategies for spelling unknown words, and sight vocabulary. You can see his progress in the next example. In January, he was crafting simple ideas using the sight vocabulary he had developed. By June, he was creating sentences without needing a picture first to fuel his writing.

Adrian carefully chose his topic based on his favorite experiences. He talked very little about his piece, generally giving one-word answers or nods to questions. Although he had strong control over the encoding process, he wrote the minimum necessary to convey the message. Adrian was developing an understanding of conventions such as capitals and periods. Notice that he capitalized I when it was the first letter in a sentence, but not in mid-sentence. He gave evidence of some sight vocabulary and strategies for more complex words.

Although gaining such information from a single piece probably isn't possible, time spent with Adrian confirmed that his needs lay in the area of oral language development. Adrian was very quiet, both at home and in school. He needed to feel more comfortable with talking through his ideas so that his oral language could further develop and begin to fuel his writing. A carefully selected partner, patient and coaxing, would be a must for Adrian.

Adrian's piece reads:
I went to the roller coaster. I went fast and I went upside down.

Isabel chatted about her ideas as she wrote and captured her own language as she went. She had a sense of sentence structure and punctuation. She was playing with capitals, still unsure of where to use them. Isabel began to insert her own voice into the piece. As she chatted, she said things such as, "Then I said. . . . " Why not put this dialogue into the writing? Modeled writing and interactive writing could be used to show Isabel how to do this.

The needs you notice in your writers when you read their work can be addressed individually in a writing conference. If you notice many children with the same

Isabel's piece reads:

I went to my Auntie's home. She has a little dog. The little dog's name is . . . Mece. One time, I was scared. Then, I am not scared. I got to touch him. I play a lot with him. He barks a little when I come in. I loved that day, and I love Mece a lot. I love Mece to be happy!

needs, a small group may be formed for guided writing, or the work may become a whole-class series of mini-lessons.

## Rubrics

There are times when we need to assess for the purpose of reporting children's progress to others. Rubrics support such a reporting effort. With each unit of study, you may want to design a rubric that reflects the work. Consider the rubric in Figure 3.3 for a nonfiction study.

This rubric is not perfect. It was created collaboratively and is a negotiation between what the teacher felt was important and what the children thought was important. At times, you may want to devise more formal rubrics on your own.

This rich mix of instructional approaches, content, and supports to ensure success and develop positive attitudes around writing will take us far in our goal of encouraging children to create a place of honor in their lives for writing. To accomplish this in a world where time to write, and time to read must compete with video and computer games, TV, DVD's, and endless other distractions will be no small feat. With your well planned instruction, a literacy rich classroom filled with enthusiastic writers and readers can become a reality.

|  | **Excellent** | **Getting there** | **Hmm . . .** |
|---|---|---|---|
| The writer chose a topic they knew well. | • I had lots of interesting information and thoughts. | • I didn't know enough to write on this topic. | • I didn't really tell anything new or interesting. |
| The writer communicated information and ideas with text and features. | • Many organizing features. <br> • Many supporting features. | • Only one organizing feature. <br> • One or two supporting features. | • Not enough features to help my audience. |
| The writer hooked the reader. | • Great lead. <br> • Audience laughed, gasped, or enjoyed. | • Just facts. <br> • Audience learned new information. | • My audience was bored. |

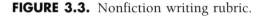

**FIGURE 3.3.** Nonfiction writing rubric.

# CHAPTER 4

# EXCITING DAY 1
## Instruction Begins

E ach year, it's the same. As the first day of school draws near, teachers are filled with nervous anticipation. All too soon, first-grade classrooms will be blessed with 5- and 6-year-olds who feel the same way. The job of every teacher is to craft a day that will leave both children and teacher feeling successful, wanting to come back for more. Careful planning can ensure your success; what you plan will help the children feel successful too!

When planning for the first day of school, we have found that the following four broad goals for literacy instruction (and all instruction in general) help to make that day a successful first encounter.

1. Build a community of learners.

2. Create excitement about learning.

3. Create an expectation of rigor with the security of knowing there will be support and success.

4. Create the belief that reading, writing, thinking, and talking about our thinking are what we do together at school.

These four broad goals, which share the common thread of building a literacy community, are developed through continuous observation/assessment of your students. During every interaction on the first day and thereafter you will be gathering information that will help in designing instruction to meet the needs of this new group of students, as well as the needs of individual students within the group. How to assess literacy development for the purpose of planning instruction from the first day is briefly discussed in Chapter 1 and detailed more fully in Chapter 5.

# BUILDING A LITERACY COMMUNITY

From the moment they enter the classroom, the children and you need to take the first steps toward drawing together as a group who develop, celebrate, and share a passion for learning, within a supportive environment that promotes each child's literacy growth. This co-created community will be the foundation for all learning during the year.

Begin building this community by greeting the children at the door on the first morning of school with a selected book in your hand. "I'm so glad you're *finally* here!" you will say. "I've been waiting for you because I want to share this great book with you. I just know you'll love it as much as I do!" Of course, you will say this in your own way, but the message will be loud and clear: "I love books, and I know you do too!"

As we suggested in Chapter 1, you might find it helpful to prepare a collection of books of varying complexity that deal with many topics. For the first-day read-aloud, focus on some aspect of living a literate life. You might want to label books in this collection as the "Reading, Writing, and Feeling Proud" set. The set may include texts such as *Wolf!* by Becky Bloom, a fictional story about a wolf who wants to learn to read so he will fit in with a group of farm animals, or *More Than Anything Else* by Marie Bradley, the very real story of a young Booker T. Washington's quest to become literate. A few other texts that might be included in such a set are:

*A Story for Bear* by Dennis Haseley
*Amber on the Mountain* by Tony Johnston
*Babu's Song* by Stephanie Stuve-Bodeen
*Edward in the Jungle* by David McPhail
*Jeremiah Learns to Read* by Jo Ellen Bogart
*My Great-Aunt Arizona* by Gloria Houston
*Papa's Mark* by Gwendolyn Battle-Lavert
*Santa's Book of Names* by David McPhail
*Thank You, Mr. Falker* by Patricia Polacco
*The Day of Ahmed's Secret* by Florence Perry Heide and Judith Heide Gilliland
*The Girl Who Hated Books* by Manjusha Pawagi
*The Hard-Times Jar* by Ethel Footman Smothers
*The Library* by Sarah Stewart
*The Lion's Share* by Chris Conover
*The Old Woman Who Loved to Read* by John Winch
*The Wednesday Surprise* by Eve Bunting
*Tibili: The Little Boy Who Didn't Want to Go to School* by Marie Leonard
*Tomas and the Library Lady* by Raul Colon
*Read for Me, Mama* by Vashanti Rahaman

Your choice for the first-day read-aloud will depend on the expected listening comprehension level of your students. You may want to start with one of the less complex texts, one that will appeal to the children and allow for conversation about the desire to learn. Then you can work your way through other texts in the set that are appropriate during the first weeks of school.

As children gather on the rug for the first read-aloud of the book, begin by asking questions carefully designed to build talk around the importance of reading, writing, or how the particular character became smarter or developed a love of learning. As you and the children talk, you can make an assessment by determining which children recall literal events from the story, who is able to move beyond, and who has difficulty focusing during the read-aloud.

As the read-aloud draws to a close, move the conversation from the characters' literate life to our own. "Just by chance," right by your chair, you have some books you are reading. Again, the message you are sending is clear: I am a reader.

Share just two or three texts that tell the children a little something about you. A book about teaching and how it is guiding your work in the classroom, perhaps a book of poetry that makes you wonder and think of beautiful things in nature, or the directions to something you are working on and thinking about.

Then it's the children's turn. Look at the children and say, "Tell us about your reading." What they share will tell you who they are. Explain that what we read tells other people about our interests. You will, we hope, hear about bedtime stories, favorite fairy tales, sharing special time with family members, reading cereal boxes in the morning, and so on. Unfortunately, though, you should be prepared for the fact that some children will be at a loss to share evidence of reading in their lives. This information is also essential to your goal of ensuring that a love of literacy is part of each child's life. This is another very important time for assessment. After this conversation you'll know who among the children have favorite books, who can name titles, authors, and characters, who seems to read, but doesn't have a clear recall of what has been read, who does not participate in the conversation. As the children talk, be sure to jot notes on a form, such as that included in Chapter 5, or on Post-it Notes, that can be placed in individual student folders.

# CLASSROOM ROUTINES, PROCEDURES, AND RULES

A big part of building a community of learners is establishing classroom routines, procedures, and rules. Children must know what is expected of them in the classroom environment. Your discipline plan must be one that identifies expectations, rules, and consequences. By clearly stating these, and returning to them often, you provide children with an understanding of the clear parameters within which they can function. When parents buy into the plan, you have a stronger foundation for the child's success in school. As you focus on the classroom goal of working together to *get smarter*, it's important to help the children understand that there are positive and negative consequences to every behavioral choice they make. Children may need to be reminded of the specific classroom guidelines and consequences each day until they own the rules. Even though you may have specific behaviors in mind, you'll want the children to participate in the creation of them. Discuss how you and the children want the classroom to function. Try to summarize their responses into a few rules that can be easily read and posted on a chart. You might want to establish a general classroom tenor based on the motto "Being Smarter Is Our Goal." Discuss with the children, while making the chart, that to reach this goal, everyone will have to do what is printed on the chart (see Figure 4.1).

Once you have made and discussed this chart, everything that happens in the classroom can be addressed in the light of how it affects learning, which is the reason children come to school. You don't have to pass judgment—this is good, that is bad—it's simply a question of whether or not a certain behavior is helping learning. If it's not, then there is no time for it—the students need to get back to learning! As you discuss more specifically with the children *what to do when the bell rings, when your pencil breaks, when you finish your work early, have a question, need to use the bathroom, or are interrupted by an off-task friend*, you can ask the children to refer to the "Being Smarter" chart to answer the question with you.

The hand signals listed in Figure 4.2 can be easily learned and will also encourage the children to communicate independently without causing an interruption to learning.

---

### BEING SMARTER IS OUR GOAL
Let's:

think and learn together

help each other

be respectful of each other's ideas

put forth our best effort

make sure everything we do is
helping us to learn, not getting
in the way of being smarter

---

**FIGURE 4.1.** "Being Smarter" chart.

From *Teaching Literacy in First Grade* by Diane Lapp, James Flood, Kelly Moore, and Maria Nichols. Copyright 2005 by The Guilford Press. Permission to photocopy this figure is granted to purchasers of this book for personal use only (see copyright page for details).

| Hand signal | What it means |
|---|---|
| Index and middle fingers crossed in the air | May I use the bathroom? |
| Index finger in the air | May I get a drink of water? |
| Pinky finger in the air | I have a question. |
| Fist in the air | I have the answer. |
| Right hand index finger and thumb linked with left hand index finger and thumb | I can make a connection using the text. |

**FIGURE 4.2.** Hand signals.

From *Teaching Literacy in First Grade* by Diane Lapp, James Flood, Kelly Moore, and Maria Nichols. Copyright 2005 by The Guilford Press. Permission to photocopy this figure is granted to purchasers of this book for personal use only (see copyright page for details).

The concept of consequences as a result of choice can be continually reinforced. Positive consequences can include free time activities like extra time at the computer, working with a partner of your choice, special responsibilities like taking the daily attendance folder to the office, feeling good about yourself, getting praise from teacher and friends, sharing a treat, conversation, and an extra read-aloud on Friday afternoon. Negative consequences can include a gentle reminder, time out, feeling bad about yourself, wasted learning time, calls home. Once the chart is complete, ask everyone to sign the bottom and then hang it in the room. Although this will suggest ownership by all, some children will test the rules to see if you enforce the consequences. If you do not, more children will test more of the rules because they believe that you won't enforce the consequences. A letter should be given to parents at the beginning of the school year, describing your classroom routines, rules, schedule, and primary goal. You may want to include a copy of Figure 4.1 (which you can adjust to fit your goals) with your letter.

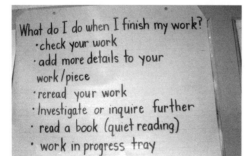

There are many things to consider as you get your classroom up and running. Frey (2004) encourages teachers to think about the following questions when engaging students in learning:

➢ What is your classroom management plan?

➢ How will you involve your students in creating and sticking to classroom rules?

➢ How will you take attendance in a timely fashion?

➢ How will students know what to do after an absence?

➢ How will you signal the class when you need to get their attention?

➢ How will you distribute and collect materials?

Thinking about these questions and ensuring that all students know the classroom procedures will make for a smoothly run environment.

## How Can You Introduce Daily Routines?

This may be the first time that some of your students have spent time in a classroom. They may not be familiar with sitting cross-legged on the carpet, or why it is important to raise hands rather than shouting out. Even if your students have had formal kindergarten experience, reminding them of what you expect will be beneficial. Here are a few suggestions:

### Practice! Practice! Practice!

Although it may seem silly to you, have your students practice lining up at the drinking fountain, walking from literacy center to literacy center, locating a book in the library and returning it to the right book basket, turning in papers at the proper place, using the cassette player at the listening post, and the like. Taking time now to have students practice these routines and procedures will save you time in the long run as instruction will not be interrupted by students exclaiming, "But I didn't know where the papers were supposed to go!"

### Talk about It

You may have an idea of how you want to go about sharpening pencils, but one of your students may have a better idea that can save time. Listen to your students as they share their thoughts about the classroom environment. We are not suggesting that students have the answers to all of the complications of setting up a classroom, but you will want their input on some issues. For years, a certain teacher we know spent 10 minutes walking around the room collecting homework every morning. One of her students suggested that homework should be placed in a basket located by the door as the children entered the room. This was quite an enlightenment for the teacher, as it saved her almost an hour a week (that's 30 hours over the course of the year!). She used this time instead to greet students, talk with parents, and take attendance.

### Environment Experts

Identify several classroom environment experts. These are students who know all the routines, procedures, and rules and can teach them to the new students who will undoubtedly show up after the first week of school. What a great way to empower students who have been in your classroom all year and make later-arriving new students feel welcome—not to mention that it frees you to continue your daily instruction.

## BUILDING EXCITEMENT ABOUT LEARNING

The second broad goal for the first day is to build excitement about learning. This goal, which is important for all of the children, is particularly essential for those whose home reading experiences seem lacking. You can create a sense of excitement about learning by telling the children, "We're going to learn amazing things this year, Reading, writing, thinking and talking will be so important for this learning. If you read a lot already, great! You're going to get to read even more. If you haven't been reading a lot yet, then you're lucky, because you're going to start today. Just look at our library—it is full of our books! Here's how we'll be using it, and the best part is, you'll get to take books home, too."

Then, with the children explore the library to find books the children are familiar with from kindergarten or their home reading. Again, watch and assess. Who goes immediately to favorites and begins chatting about authors, titles, characters, and even the story itself? Who picks up a "favorite," but recalls very little about the book? Who does not seem to recognize these books? Who sits and begins to read?—alone or socially? Who resists the lure of great books and wanders without focus?

Some engaging activities you can introduce on this first day are included here. They will let your students know that your classroom is fun, an exciting place to learn. It will also give you even more information to add to your ever-growing student assessment files. These files, whether mental or anecdotal, grow very quickly in the first few hours of the first day of school.

## FIRST-DAY ACTIVITIES

### A, B, C . . . 1, 2, 3

Write each letter of the alphabet on an index card, assigning a point value to each card. Some teachers use the letter values from the Scrabble game. Place the letter cards on the floor in rows. Make six beanbags by filling socks with sand, beans, or pebbles and tying them shut. Ask students to stand in a line and throw a beanbag onto the letter cards. Beginning students may throw one beanbag onto a letter and say a word that begins with that letter. More advanced students may throw several beanbags onto the letter cards to build a word. Points can be assigned for each letter used. Your students will love this interactive game, and you will come to know more about your students' letter–sound knowledge and their math sense (can they add up their points?).

## "I Spy"

Select an object in the room and tell students its initial letter (or sound). Students then take turns guessing what the object could be. Once a student guesses the correct object, he or she can be the next person to select an object. Be sure to have the student tell you the object to ensure that he or she names the correct letter (or sound) and doesn't change the object in the middle of play. Students with more literacy proficiency may be able to identify the object from such clues as "I spy something in the room that begins with the sound /sh/, ends with the sound /f/ and has one syllable (answer: *shelf*). Think of all you will learn about your students phonemic awareness and how well they will get to know your classroom environment.

## Letter Pretzels

Cluster students into groups of five or six. Say a letter. The groups of students must arrange themselves to create the shape of the letter. For more literacy-proficient students, you can say a word and they must create the letter that represents the word's initial sound. You can also say a two- or three-letter word and see if the class can build the word together. This will tell you a lot about the students' knowledge of letter formation and will be very engaging for your kinesthetic learners.

## Lost Letters

Have students form a circle; then place letter flashcards outside the circle behind the students. Teach students the tune of "The Farmer in the Dell":

Where is the *t*?
Where is the *t*?
(Sing the sound "t" to the tune of "Heigh, ho, the derry oh!")
Where is the *t*?

Students take turns walking around the circle looking for the lost letter. When located, students place each flashcard in the middle of the circle until all the letters have been used. Vowel sounds or blends can be used with advanced students. Again, this activity will get your students excited about learning and will inform you about their knowledge of letters and sounds.

## Scavenger Hunt

After introducing and practicing routines and procedures, you can engage your students in a fun scavenger hunt. Write the letters of the alphabet on index cards and give pairs of students 10 index cards. Be sure to give each pair a plastic grocery bag as well. Students circulate around the room to find the objects that begin with the letters on their index cards. For example, students may put a *book* or a *box* of crayons in their bag for the letter *B*. Remind students to pay careful attention to where they found the objects so that all items can be returned to the proper places. For more literacy proficient students, write words on the cards and have them find objects such as dictionary, lined paper, or an eraser. This will help them to become familiar with their classroom environment and help you to assess their letter–sound and word knowledge.

# BUILDING A SENSE OF RIGOR ABOUT LEARNING

Along with excitement about learning, you'll need to create a sense of rigor about learning, along with the security of knowing there will be both support and success. "Yes, the work we do here will be hard. We're going to need to be big thinkers. But you are smart, we'll be working together, helping each other, and you can do it!"

A first step here is some reading work that requires strong thinking and produces something the children can then read with some degree of immediate success. A Big Book used for shared reading with the whole class is appropriate. The text you use and the focus you choose for instruction depend on your population and your yearlong daily instructional plan.

If available, you might consider a title such as *Moonbear's Books* by Frank Asch to continue the conversation on literate lives. Or you may want to consider using a nonfiction Big Book, with a focus on the wonder and questioning that must go on in a reader's head when reading nonfiction. The most important considerations for your choice is that the text is engaging and at a level just slightly beyond independent for the majority of your readers. You want the children to feel challenged, but successful because of the support offered.

The focus for instruction may range widely, from using pictures (meaning) to think about a story, to getting a sense of the character in a fiction text from what he or she does. In nonfiction, your focus may range from the role of wonder to questions about the content that will drive further reading.

It is important that your instructional focus be some aspect that readers take on to help them better understand their reading. It will be challenging, but with the group working together and your support, it can be successful. Be very explicit with the children about this. "That was really hard! But what good thinking! Because you stuck with it, now we . . . [know that Bear is a real reader who loves learning, or have so many questions to answer about our nonfiction topic . . . ]. I knew you were smart learners! This is what our year will be about—taking on big thinking all together."

And as you teach, you assess. Who is reading along, talking, and listening? Who is attentive, but voiceless? Most first-grade children need continued instruction about strategies for word solving. You can return to the text in the days to come to work on these strategies, but for now continue assessing their engagement with and general understanding of the text.

Whenever possible, have small copies of the Big Book available so the children can group together to reread and think more about the book. Because, after all, "that's what we do in first grade." And, yes, you will continue to assess. Who can read the little book on their own? Who can read with peer support? Who listens to the others read? Looks at the pictures and talks? Seems uninterested in the book? Answers to these questions will help you to plan the next steps in each child's literacy instruction.

## BUILDING A COMMUNITY OF READERS, WRITERS, SPEAKERS, THINKERS

Right from the first moment you need to communicate that reading, writing, talking, and thinking will be a part of the learning every day: "It is what we do in this classroom. In fact, we don't just do it in here; this is a way of living in the world. We have already planned for reading, talking, and thinking. Now add writing to your first day. From day one, writing needs to be a part of classroom life. Remember, writing is also what we do here!" As discussed in Chapter 3, consider introducing the writers' workshop as a special time each day for capturing thinking to hold onto and share. This will create excitement around the workshop, which is your second goal for the day.

Your first mini-lesson will depend on your population and how much writing experience the children had in kindergarten. Most first graders are comfortable with drawing a story but need to work on adding text to expand on an idea. A mini-lesson focusing on just this might be a great way to start.

Begin the lesson with a modeled writing of some thinking you want to share. By using modeled writing, you are showing the children that your are a writer too and giving them a greater sense of you as a person. This helps with the building of community, which is our first goal for the day. Modeled writing also supports rigorous work, and enabling children to be successful with rigorous work is goal 3 for the day.

You will need a large piece of paper on an easel. Make sure the paper has space for a picture, and space for writing. Tell the children that something exciting happened last night, or you have been thinking about something exciting, and you just can't wait to get it on paper to capture it and share it with them by letting them read it.

Begin to draw quickly, without a lot of explanation, except to keep saying how amazing this thing was and that they will be so excited to read it. Purposefully draw something that will have several possible interpretations. For example, you may draw yourself in the kitchen with pots and pans. The story could be about making spaghetti, or cooking a great meal, then burning it and having to go to McDonald's for dinner, or making a meal that tasted terrible, getting a new cookbook to try, or thinking about a new recipe that will make your family happy. As you finish drawing, say to the children, "So here's my story to share . . . can you read it?" They will begin to guess, and with each guess you become more frustrated because they don't get it. "Hmm . . . ", you say. "I captured my story, but you can't read it. Something must be missing. . . . " Inevitably, a child will finally say, "Maybe it needs words!" If not, ask the children, "Would words help?"

Add words as labels, or a sentence (or two, depending again on the population), to give an idea about the picture they didn't guess. Then talk about the process and come to a collective realization that writers need a picture and words or a sentence(s) on a page to capture a story and share it. Be sure to have recipes or a cookbook handy so they can see that you read many types of books.

Now it's their turn. Give the children time to talk with a partner to form an idea. We always like the first draft to be an oral draft. As they talk, circulate among them, listening to and, of course, assessing their ideas and participation for the purpose of differentiating future instruction. Ask a few children to share their ideas with the whole group. Then pass out paper, and off they go to write. As they begin, move from child to child and continue assessing and teaching.

Observe and note: Which children are still unsure of what to do. Which have drawings with amazing details? Which have drawings that are difficult to decipher? Who adds words or sentences on his or her own, who can do so with support, and who has difficulty even with support? Who uses temporary spelling, who has some conventional spelling? Who won't write unless you spell the words for him or her? You won't get to every child the first day, but you will get a general sense of the children's abilities. You can make your way to every child over the course of the week.

And, most important, you have taken the first step in helping the children to define themselves as writers as well as readers. You have set a rigorous standard and have supported it with modeling, talk, and one-on-one instruction.

## COLLECTING INFORMATION ABOUT THE CHILDREN

In discussing the content of the first day of school, we hinted at the ways assessment weaves through every aspect of the day as a common thread. This does not happen on just the first day or just during your literacy time block. As detailed in Chapter 5, assessment must thread through every moment of your work with your children.

Your first day with the children will be filled with rich opportunities for anecdotal assessment, which is learning about your children based on observation. This must begin as the children walk through the door. In addition to having a book in

your hands, you should also have a clipboard. The types of materials used to document what you see is a very individual decision. Choices include:

➢ Blank paper on a clipboard
➢ Formatted paper on a clipboard, with a place to make notes on each child
➢ 20 pages of paper on a clipboard, one for each child
➢ 20 sticky notes or labels, one for each child, that will be placed in a folder or binder section for each child

There are countless other possibilities.

You will most likely try many methods for taking and organizing notes before you decide on one that works for you. What is most important is that you are wondering about your students and finding a way to record what you see and hear. This section will help to fill you with questions that you might hold onto as a means of starting your wondering and observing. They are not intended to suggest everything you will need to know about each child, nor should you expect to gain a full understanding of each child through considering these questions on the first day, or even necessarily in the first week. They are simply a means of helping you to get a start in a never-ending assessment process.

We begin by revisiting what we've suggested should occur on the first day. But this time, we include the opportunities for assessment, and a better sense of what you will be watching for and why.

First, observe each child as he or she enters the room.

➤ Is this child drawn to the library or the desks, or does the child investigate learning tools such as paper, pencils, crayons, and the like?

➤ Aside from first-day shyness, does this child seem to know what is expected in this place, and is he or she eager to get started?

A good way to get a first sense of the children is to create a "getting started" opportunity for them to engage in as you meet and greet them. This can be as simple as providing pieces of paper for the children to "write" about themselves on the first day of first grade. You will need to have crayons or markers and pencils available, and watch to see how each child gets started.

➤ While working, does the child chat about what he or she is doing, or work quietly?

➤ Does the child draw, write, or both?

➤ How much detail is in either the drawing or the writing?

➤ Where on the paper does the child add writing, and why? This can give you an insight about prior book reading.

➤ Did the child start on his or her own or require support, such as by watching others, asking others, or requesting help from the teacher? These behaviors provide clues about independence.

They may also offer some sense of the child's comfort and confidence, the child's sense of the social aspects of learning, and his or her experience with writing. But remember, what you see is not absolute. These are very young children coming into a new environment, which may skew what you see. Make several observations of the children in various situations before drawing any conclusions, and always err on the side of the child.

You may also want to have books available for browsing when the children have finished the first task. You might watch to see:

➤ How long does the child stick with the "getting started" piece before abandoning it for a book?

➤ Who chooses a book purposefully, and who just grabs any book available?

➤ Who uses the books in a social way?

➤ Who picks up a book simply because others are doing so, but seems unsure?

Again, you are collecting preliminary information about attitude, risk taking, and literacy.

As you design instruction, you will continue to watch and wonder about each child. Over the course of the week, you will gauge each child's interest and ability to attend to a read-aloud. Questions to ask yourself include:

➢ Does this child appear eager to engage with a text?

➢ Does this child hold an expectation of what's to come during a read-aloud?

➢ Was this child able to attend throughout the read-aloud? Passively or actively?

➢ Did this child participate by questioning, sharing his or her thinking, listening to others?

The answers to these questions will help you to get a sense of how the child views reading. A lack of interest *may* indicate that the child has not yet discovered the excitement that reading can contribute to his or her life, nor found anything that interests him or her as a reader. Or it may be that the child is distracted by the new environment. You will need more observations over time to be more sure.

During individual conversations and group sharing, you will be looking for and listening for evidence of the children's comprehension through their ability to think about reading and articulate their thinking. But be careful. Lack of articulation of thought does not mean that a child is not comprehending. Some children are shy at first and may not speak out. Others need longer to process their thinking and lose out to those quick thinkers who blurt out ideas immediately. English language learners may be translating their thoughts into English or may be searching for a way to express their ideas. Some children may keep their thoughts to themselves because they have not come to realize the importance of sharing thoughts and talking about reading. So you will need to consider the many ways children show that they understand text. As you observe, there are a few things to look for that can give you insights about the children's comprehension and enjoyment of text:

➢ Children who laugh at the funny spots, show surprise, or exhibit other appropriate emotions through the read

➢ Children who inch closer at the "good parts"

➢ Children who seem to be using the pictures and don't want to miss one

Then listen to the children's talk, both in the whole group and in partnerships. As you listen, hold onto questions about each child and note the way the child thinks and talks, or attempts to think and talk, about the text. Very often, it is what a child is attempting to do that will have the greatest implications for the next steps in instruction. The following are questions about a reader that you may be considering:

➤ Does this child have a literal understanding of the text?

➤ Does the talk reflect a sequential understanding of important details, or a sense of random miscellaneous details?

➤ Does this child have an understanding of cause and effect in the literal details: "This happened because . . . "

➤ Does this child summarize or see the bigger picture in all the little details?

➤ Does this child think beyond the literal, showing evidence of making connections, questioning, predicting, inferring?

➤ Does this child initiate ideas, piggyback on another child's ideas, or repeat what he or she has heard others say?

➤ Does the child's talk stay connected to the text or lose focus?

Again, the information you gather will not be absolute. It is a snapshot of what a child does with only one text. You will need data over time, drawn from experiences with many texts, to truly get an accurate picture of the child's literacy behaviors. However, this will give you a starting place as you consider instruction for the next days and weeks. As children begin to become more independent readers and they then move into the library to explore, the questions previously mentioned drive your observation and continuous assessment. You can continue to ask yourself the following questions about your students:

➤ Is the child able to name favorite books and authors?

➤ Does the child have a favorite character in fiction?

➤ Does the child talk about fiction or nonfiction text?

➤ Does the child recognize books but have difficulty recalling the story or content?

➤ Does reading seem to be a part of the child's family routine?

➤ Does the child see reading as a social activity or sit alone with a book?

➤ Does the child have a sense of what might be too easy, too challenging, or just right for independent reading?

➤ Does the child not seem interested in the particular books available?

Among the many things to consider as you watch the children is how much each child reads outside school. Do the children value talking about books as a means of deepening enjoyment and comprehension? Have they developed a sense of themselves as readers? All of this has implications for building a community of learners and establishing the climate of the classroom. It helps you to know how much you need to teach as you circulate and confer with children during their independent reading time.

As you move into shared reading, you will have to listen closely as well as watch. During shared reading with the Big Book, ask yourself:

➢ Does this child engage in the bigger conversations about meaning?

➢ Does this child read with me, lag slightly behind me, or not read at all—at least out loud?

➢ Is this child showing any engagement in word work as I discuss the pictures and text?

The answers may give you a beginning sense of the child's interest and ability at problem solving at the word level, as well as his or her willingness to take risks.

Once the little books are passed out, watch to see:

➢ Does this child take a leadership role within the small group or partnership?

➢ Is this child able to reread some or all of the text?

➢ Is this child able to tell or talk about the story? Using the pictures, or not?

➢ Does this child listen to others reread the book to him or her?

➢ Does this child show little interest in the whole experience?

➢ Does this child reread several times, or read once and yell, "I'm done!"

The answers should help you to again consider attitude about learning, ability with a certain level of text with support, and social interactions.

During writers' workshop, your greatest wondering will be about each child's ability to use writing as a tool for purposeful communicating. As soon as you bring up writing, you will watch and listen to gauge attitudes about writing. As you watch and listen, ask yourself: "Does this child seem happy, apprehensive, or confused that it is writers' workshop time?" This will help you to get a sense of the children's development as writers in kindergarten or at home. Your first graders may have had varying amounts of exposure to writing, with varying levels of emphasis on correctness versus effort and understanding of writing as a tool. This is important to know as you design your first weeks of mini-lessons.

As you model writing, watch and listen for engagement.

➢ Does this child work to "read" my story as I draw?

➢ Does this child attempt to help me with the words as I add writing?

➢ Does this child shout out help for spelling or punctuation?

➢ Is this child attentive but quiet?

And as the children move from the mini-lesson to independent work, you continue to wonder, watch, and assess:

➤ Is this child starting right away, or does he or she need support?

➤ Does this child need support with an idea, or does the child have an idea but isn't sure of how to begin getting it on paper?

➤ Does this child have detail in his or her drawing?

➤ Does this child add print on his or her own? How much?

➤ How much letter–sound correspondence does he or she have under control?

➤ Does this child know and use sight words?

These observations will help you to understand each child as a writer. You will come to know how each child sees writing in his or her life, who views his or her life and the world as the impetus for ideas, and how far each child has come in his or her control of conventions.

Do not restrict this wondering process to the literacy portion of your day. Wonder, watch, and listen during mathematics, social studies, and science. Most important, do not limit your note taking with a "can or can't" way of thinking. *Do not make these questions into a checklist.* Rather, as you wonder, watch, and listen, record what you see and hear, even if you are not sure of its importance or relevance at the moment. Often, in reflection, we are able to see importance or sheer brilliance in something a child said or did that escaped us as it was happening.

You will not, of course, come away with a strong sense of every child after just the first day. This process of inquiry must be repeated each and every day over the course of the year. It will support an ever-changing understanding of what each child can do, and is trying to do, which will continually guide your planning for instruction.

As we discuss in Chapter 5, you will spend more time during the first weeks with individual children, using more formal assessment tools. What you learn about the children during these opportunities along with your recorded observations, will help you to develop a more comprehensive sense of each student and will assist in planning for whole-class, small-group, and individual instructional needs.

Remember that the first day of first grade is a memory that children will have forever. They may not be able to recount the specifics of the day, but it is reflected in their attitudes about themselves as learners throughout each day that follows. Do your *best* to make it the *best day* of their school lives.

# CHAPTER 5

# DIFFERENTIATING INSTRUCTION
## Using Assessment Information Wisely

As you have probably realized from your teaching experiences and from reading the previous chapters of this book, assessment of your students is a continuous daily process that will help you to gather insights about each child's literacy development and the next instructional steps as they move toward proficiency as speakers, readers, and writers. The information you collect about their literacy performance will inform your instruction and grouping practices. By observing the literacy growth you see in your students, you will be able to make decisions about the effectiveness of your instructional approach.

You will realize very quickly during the first day of school that not all children in your first-grade class are reading with the same degree of proficiency. Proficiency among your students at the beginning of the school year will probably range, on average, from emergent readers to those who can read at the mid-second-grade level.

## WHERE/HOW TO BEGIN?

Many teachers attempt to gain insights and an understanding of the early literacy experiences of their students before they meet them on the first day of school. Studying the portfolios of those who have attended kindergarten at your school can help you ascertain their prior schooling and literacy expertise. As you read this information, jot notes about:

1. The primary language spoken in the home.
2. Each child's proficiency speaking in English.
3. The child's performance on early literacy tasks (phonemic awareness, reading, and writing).

For easy access to this information, you can compile a chart similar to that in Figure 5.1. Because not all children attend kindergarten, reviewing students' folders will probably not give you a complete preview of the class, but you will have started to gain information that will help you to plan instruction for your students.

## EARLY LITERACY ASSESSMENT BATTERIES

Several states have developed early literacy assessments that reflect current research on essential domains of early reading and that are accessible for use electronically. Those noted in the following list are batteries of standardized, individually administered measures of early literacy development for grades K, 1, and 2. They consist of brief measures of performance, which can be used to regularly monitor the development of early literacy skills. The measures were developed to reflect the essential early literacy domains discussed in best practice research in early reading (Kamil, 2000; National Reading Panel, 2000; Snow, Burns, & Griffin, 1998).

➤ Phonological Awareness Literacy Screening (PALS), designed at the University of Virginia; *pals.virginia.edu*

➤ Illinois Snapshots of Early Literacy (ISEL), is designed at the National College of Education of National-Louis University, Chicago, IL; *www2.nl.edu/reading_center/ISEL2004.html*

➤ Texas Primary Reading Inventory (TPRI), designed by the Texas Department of Education; *www.tpri.org*

➤ Dynamic Indicators of Basic Early Literacy Skills (DIBELS), designed at the University of Oregon; *dibels.oregon.edu*

These measures can be used to assess such areas as alphabetic knowledge, listening to and talking about stories (ISEL), phonological awareness, letter–sound knowledge, developmental spelling (ISEL and PALS), word recognition out of context, passage reading accuracy and comprehension, vocabulary, and fluency. ISEL-2 also assesses written constructed responses to reading. These assessments are intended to be used to help identify students in need of specialist support and for planning instruction.

## ON THE FIRST DAY OF SCHOOL

As suggested in Chapter 4, your first assessments will be informally conducted as you do a lot of "kid watching" while building a classroom community. The following ideas for initial assessments measure the natural behaviors that are exhibited by the children as they participate in authentic literacy tasks. Read-alouds and sing-alongs allow you to teach and assess your students quickly and easily to find out a

| Child's name | Language spoken in the home | Phonemic awareness knowledge | Can identify letters? Which letters? | Analysis of reading sample |
|---|---|---|---|---|
| | | | | |
| | | | | |
| | | | | |
| | | | | |
| | | | | |
| | | | | |
| | | | | |
| | | | | |
| | | | | |
| | | | | |
| | | | | |

**FIGURE 5.1.** Literacy information: Before meeting the children.

From *Teaching Literacy in First Grade* by Diane Lapp, James Flood, Kelly Moore, and Maria Nichols. Copyright 2005 by The Guilford Press. Permission to photocopy this figure is granted to purchasers of this book for personal use only (see copyright page for details).

great deal about their oral language development, understanding of story structure, and reading, writing, and listening proficiencies.

## Read Aloud

Gather your students on the rug and introduce yourself. The students will undoubtedly be feeling a range of emotions. For some, this may be the first time they have been in a formal classroom. Other students may be very confident because they have attended preschool and kindergarten. Still, the majority will be anxious about their new environment, their new friends, and *you*.

Read one of your favorite books, such as *First Day Jitters* by Julie Danneberg, or a book listed in Figure 5.2. Pay close attention to your students throughout this experience.

Once you've *selected the best book* to share with your students, *set the purpose* and ask students to pay attention to their favorite people (characters) in the story. Ask them to see if any of the characters in the story are like themselves or anyone they know. This is a good introduction to having students make connections with characters as they read and listen to texts. After you read, remind the students that they will have a chance to draw or write about their favorite characters. As you read, *observe your students*. Who's listening? Who can't wait to make a connection with the book? When you stop to ask a question, encourage partner talk. Are students eager to share? Who talks too much? Who is shy? Who is using a language other than English to communicate? You can tell much about your students after reading one book. Figure 5.3 is an example of how you might compile some of the emergent literacy behaviors exhibited by students during their early days of instruction.

Children can be listed by name, or each child can be given a number that you use throughout the year. It's easier for you and the children to remember the numbers if they refer to their first names in alphabetical order and if you write those numbers on their name tags, which you can use for their seat placement. These numbers can also be used for lining up, partner work, book boxes, materials, and folders. Class work can also be numbered for ease in sorting, organizing, and locating missing items. Children's names and numbers can also be written on popsicle sticks and placed in a container. It's easy to form heterogeneous groups or to call on children to respond by pulling sticks from the container.

Complete the checklist as you observe behaviors throughout the day. You can do this while students are drawing and/or writing about their favorite character in a book. Be sure they write or tell you (or a partner) why they chose to write about a specific character. As your students continue to work, you can confer with each of them to learn a little bit more about their literacy proficiencies. As you converse, ask questions and observe their work. Ask questions such as: Why did you choose to write about this character? How is this character at all like you or anyone you know? Can you say some of the sounds you hear as you write the words that tell about this character. By recess you will already have a good idea of your students as literacy learners. Be careful not to ask questions that can be answered with yes or no responses.

*Amazing Grace* by Mary Hoffman—This story of a young girl can teach your first graders the power of determination, hopes, and dreams.

*A Chair for My Mother* by Vera Williams—Your first graders are sure to make connections to this text about a loving family who work together.

*Duck on a Bike* by David Shannon—This is a great text to teach emotions and highlight differences among your students.

*Joseph Had a Little Overcoat* by Simms Taback—Teaching prediction to your first graders will be easy with this text as you explore the theme of "making something from nothing."

*The Lorax* by Dr. Seuss—Want to teach your first graders about pollution and the environment? This is a great text for Earth Day!

*Where the Wild Things Are* by Maurice Sendak—First graders will let their imaginations go *wild* after listening to this classic.

*Wilfrid Gordon McDonald Partridge* by Mem Fox—This wonderful story explores the relationship of a young boy and an elderly woman as they talk about what it means to have a memory.

*Diary of a Worm* by Doreen Cronin—This hilarious text is a great way to teach your students about writing . . . and worms!

*Grumblebunny* by Bob Hartman—Students will learn what it means to be both optimistic and grumpy as they find out what happens to four little bunnies caught in a pot of soup.

*I'm Mighty!* by Kate McMullan—Want your first graders to chime in with you as you read? This is a great text that will have your students choral reading and learning about taking charge!

*Click Clack Moo: Cows That Type* by Doreen Cronin—You will want to read this hilarious book to your first graders while introducing the ideas of cooperation and peaceful protest at the beginning of the year.

*Giggle, Giggle, Quack* by Doreen Cronin—This book offers a great way to teach the importance of written communication and how sometimes following the wrong instructions can lead to disaster.

*Enemy Pie* by Derek Munson—This is a great book to read to your first graders at the beginning of the year as you discuss friendship and making good choices.

(continued)

**FIGURE 5.2.** Read-alouds for first grade.

From *Teaching Literacy in First Grade* by Diane Lapp, James Flood, Kelly Moore, and Maria Nichols. Copyright 2005 by The Guilford Press. Permission to photocopy this figure is granted to purchasers of this book for personal use only (see copyright page for details).

*The Recess Queen* by Alexis O'Neill—You will want to pull this book out and share it with your students when trouble erupts on the playground and bullying is prevalent.

*Hooway for Wodney Wat* by Helen Lester—Read this wonderful story to your students when you want to teach them how *everyone* can be a hero—especially those children who get teased and harassed.

*The Secret Shortcut* by Mark Teague—This book tells the story of two children who are notoriously late to school and the wild adventures they have on their way to school.

*Goldie and the Three Bears* by Diane Stanley—Looking for a great book on friendship? Here's a new twist to the old favorite and how one girl wants a friend who's *just right*— not too bossy, not too boring, not too rough!

*Tera, Star Student (First Graders from Mars)* by Shana Corey—You will want to read this book to your students and teach them the importance of working together on group projects.

*The Problem with Pelly (First Graders from Mars)* by Shana Corey—This book is great for the beginning of the year as you discuss with your first graders the value of accepting and appreciating differences.

*Horus's Horrible Day (First Graders from Mars)* by Shana Corey—Need a book for the first day of school? This book is sure to please all your students as it discusses how different first grade can be from kindergarten.

*Jimmy's Boa and the Bungee Jump Slam Dunk* by Trinka Hakes Noble—Need a hilarious book to read after recess? This book is sure to make your first graders laugh as they learn about a snake's way of playing basketball.

*The Three Pigs* by David Wiesner—This twist on the classic offers a great way to teach perspective, dialogue balloons, and different illustrative styles.

*Thank You, Mr. Falker* by Patricia Polacco—If you have students who are struggling to read, this great book is sure to inspire them.

*Mr. Lincoln's Way* by Patricia Polacco—In this book, Mr. Lincoln is the "coolest principal in the whole world" and teaches students about intolerance, ethnic slurs, bullying, and the importance of differences.

*Pigsty* by Mark Teague—Students will enjoy listening to this book about pigs who have worn out their welcome in a young boy's bedroom.

**FIGURE 5.2.** (*continued*)

| Behaviors | 1 | 2 | 3 | 4 | 5 | 6 | 7 | 8 | 9 | 10 | 11 | 12 | 13 | 14 | 15 | 16 | 17 | 18 | 19 | 20 |
|---|---|---|---|---|---|---|---|---|---|---|---|---|---|---|---|---|---|---|---|---|
| 1. Can identify subject matter through title and illustrations. | | | | | | | | | | | | | | | | | | | | |
| 2. Listens attentively. | | | | | | | | | | | | | | | | | | | | |
| 3. Can retell big ideas of text. | | | | | | | | | | | | | | | | | | | | |
| 4. Uses sequencing in retell. | | | | | | | | | | | | | | | | | | | | |
| 5. Can identify story elements: setting, problem/solution. | | | | | | | | | | | | | | | | | | | | |
| 6. Understands concept of character. | | | | | | | | | | | | | | | | | | | | |
| 7. Makes connections between self and characters. | | | | | | | | | | | | | | | | | | | | |
| 8. Refers to pictures/illustrations to explain text. | | | | | | | | | | | | | | | | | | | | |
| 9. Makes text-based predictions. | | | | | | | | | | | | | | | | | | | | |
| 10. Makes connections between self and story theme. | | | | | | | | | | | | | | | | | | | | |
| 11. Understands that meaning is coming from words. | | | | | | | | | | | | | | | | | | | | |
| 12. Recognizes high-frequency words. | | | | | | | | | | | | | | | | | | | | |
| 13. Can read repetitive words or phrases. | | | | | | | | | | | | | | | | | | | | |
| 14. Has sufficient language to convey text ideas. | | | | | | | | | | | | | | | | | | | | |
| 15. Participates well in partner talk. | | | | | | | | | | | | | | | | | | | | |

**FIGURE 5.3.** Emergent Literacy Behaviors Checklist. Use ✓ to indicate very well, + for adequate, – for needs help.

From *Teaching Literacy in First Grade* by Diane Lapp, James Flood, Kelly Moore, and Maria Nichols. Copyright 2005 by The Guilford Press. Permission to photocopy this figure is granted to purchasers of this book for personal use only (see copyright page for details).

By now you've begun to teach about characterization and how students can make connections to the characters in a story. You have also observed and assessed your students quickly. Calling them back to the rug for sharing time will give you more information for your notes. Once they are on the rug, ask them to cluster into groups of four to share their pictures or writings. This will help to lower their anxiety about group sharing and will give you a chance to visit with each group, paying attention to the communication that is occurring. Observe their participation. Ask yourself questions such as: How well are my students communicating in English? How well do they understand the text and pay attention to characterization? Why is this so? How do students do while listening to their peers? Do they take turns? Do they listen? Do they ask questions and share? When this activity is finished, randomly select one child from each group to share with the larger group. Remember to consider what was shared by whom in a small group but not in a larger group. These observations can help your continuing assessment of your students. Remember to add information to the checklist as you learn more about their literacy behaviors.

## Sing a Song

A second way you can learn about your students in a nonthreatening manner is by singing a song with them. Display a songbook or a piece of chart paper on which you have written the words you're going to teach the children to sing. As you read and sing, point to the words. Observe the students' behaviors. Which students are chiming in? Which are tracking the print? Which students seem to know the next rhyming word in the song even though you have covered it with a sticky note? Sing the song several times and see who is singing along. If you have musical instruments, share them so those who are not singing and reading the words can feel as though they are part of the community of learners. If no instruments are available, have students clap along to the beat (that's a good way to get all involved, and it's free!). The idea is to observe what your students can and cannot do in terms of language arts, not to isolate and alienate those who do not have the needed skills or are not yet comfortable in participating in the activity.

Remember, during the first day of school you will be learning a lot about your students. Continue to observe them during the course of the whole year. Students in first grade are developing at very different rates. Some are ready and willing to speak academic English from day one. Some students need much more time. Ongoing assessment tied closely to instruction will ensure that you do not overlook your students' strengths and needs throughout the year. Throughout the first day, as you ask questions and encourage responses to the whole group or to a partner, children are able to share feelings and experiences, build relationships, or respond to a read-aloud. During this time you'll be making mental notes or jotting them on Post-it Notes that are later added to your informational chart or folder on each child.

# DURING THE FIRST WEEK OF SCHOOL

As suggested in Chapters 4 and 6, the entire class of children can be randomly assigned to literacy center groups. Because you won't yet know the exact reading levels and capabilities of all your students, the literacy activities should be designed so that each student can feel successful. The idea is to get the students into cooperative groups quickly so that you can begin more thorough individualized assessments.

Using each child's folder from kindergarten, you will have a place to start instruction. However, with new students, for whom you have no data, you'll need to collect all of the information needed to design their instruction. The following process is a more detailed example of how you can assess a child who comes to your classroom with no kindergarten records.

## San Diego Quick Assessment

*Administration*

While the others are working at literacy center activities, you meet with the new student and administer the San Diego Quick Assessment (SD Quick; LaPray & Ross, 1969), which is a graded list of sight words. A child's resulting score provides information related to his overall knowledge of sight words ability as related to word knowledge. Children who are good at sight word reading are also often very good at using word-attack skills to read words not in their sight vocabulary. Remember this is an assessment of sight-word recognition not comprehension. This just gets you started understanding the child's reading proficiency.

Although the words on the SD Quick are out of context, they do tell you a bit about the child's sight word vocabulary and knowledge of sound–letter correspondence. It is important to have this information so that sight word and word study instruction can be planned on the basis of these findings. As a result, you'll have a place to start assessing the child's reading of connected text.

By analyzing the child's performance on the SD Quick or other graded word lists (Botel, 1978; Dolch, 1942; Durr, 1973; Ekwall, 1986; Fry, 1980; Harris & Jacobson, 1982; Hillerich, 1974), you'll have a starting point for instruction and a place to begin assessment of the child's reading of narrative and nonnarrative passages. Later in the year you may compile a graded word list from the basal reader, social studies, and science books your school has adopted, because the words in these books are usually from a controlled list developed by the publisher. We find this to be a very useful practice, as these are the books the children will be reading.

When asking children to read any list of words, remember that you will have found a child's instructional reading level when he or she has correctly read 95% of the list. A sample of the SD Quick is presented in Figure 5.4, including a word list, directions for administering, and analysis.

## Decision Point

If the child is able to read eight or more of the words on the preprimer list of the SD Quick, continue until an approximate reading level has been determined. If the child is unable to read seven or more of the words on the preprimer list, you would conclude that this is where his or her sight word study instruction should begin. The example shown in Figure 5.5 illustrates the performance of one child, Malik, on the SD Quick and his teacher's analysis.

## Analysis of Malik's Performance on the SD Quick

Malik's teacher, Ms. Williams, began assessing Malik using the SD Quick. She started with the preprimer word list because it was 2 years below Malik's grade-level assignment. As Malik read the words, Ms. Williams made a checkmark (✓) for each word that was read accurately. She wrote in the word or words that Malik read incorrectly. By doing so, Ms. Williams was able to see the kinds of errors he was making. You can see from her comments that Ms. Williams recommended more vowel instruction with Malik as he attempts words out of context. Remember, though, this assessment is meant to give the teacher an approximate reading level. These words are out of context and bear no meaning. Now that Ms. Williams knows that Malik's approximate reading level *may* be at the primer level, she can choose a book that Malik is likely to read successfully.

## Alphabet and Sound–Letter Identification Assessment

If Malik had missed three or more words on the preprimer list, Ms. Williams would have asked him to identify the letters of the alphabet and to complete a sound–letter identification assessment. When you need to do the same, ask the child to identify each letter of the alphabet, its sound, and a word that begins with that letter. A sample of a sound–letter identification assessment is included here for your use. The child's performance on this assessment indicates which letters and sounds he or she knows. This is important information as you plan subsequent phonics instruction and select texts that include words containing familiar and unfamiliar sound–letter correspondence. The Sound–Letter Assessment shown in Figure 5.6 was designed by the faculty at the Zamarano Fine Arts Academy in the San Diego Unified School District and is based on research conducted by Durrell and Catterson (1980). This measure can be used to assess the following skills: letter recognition, letter sounds, beginning picture sounds, and word recognition.

## Administering the Reading Assessment

Each section of the assessment is administered individually. The assessment should be administered three times a year, once at the beginning of the year, once at the middle, and once at the end.

The teacher uses the summary sheet for all assessments. Each assessment is color coded, the first assessment in red, the second assessment in green, and the third assessment in purple.

## Word List

| PP | Primer | 1 | 2 | 3 |
|---|---|---|---|---|
| see | you | road | our | city |
| play | come | live | please | middle |
| me | not | thank | myself | moment |
| at | with | when | town | frightened |
| run | jump | bigger | early | exclaimed |
| go | help | how | send | several |
| and | is | always | wide | lonely |
| look | work | night | believe | drew |
| can | are | spring | quietly | since |
| here | this | today | carefully | straight |

| 4 | 5 | 6 | 7 |
|---|---|---|---|
| decided | scanty | bridge | amber |
| served | business | commercial | dominion |
| amazed | develop | abolish | sundry |
| silent | considered | trucker | capillary |
| wrecked | discussed | apparatus | impetuous |
| improved | behaved | elementary | blight |
| certainly | splendid | comment | wrest |
| entered | acquainted | necessity | enumerate |
| realized | escaped | gallery | daunted |
| interrupted | grim | relativity | condescend |

| 8 | 9 | 10 | 11 |
|---|---|---|---|
| capacious | conscientious | zany | galore |
| limitation | isolation | jerkin | rotunda |
| pretext | molecule | nausea | capitalism |
| intrigue | ritual | gratuitous | prevaricate |
| delusion | momentous | linear | risible |
| immaculate | vulnerable | inept | exonerate |
| ascent | kinship | legality | superannuate |
| acrid | conservatism | aspen | luxuriate |
| binocular | jaunty | amnesty | piebald |
| embankment | inventive | barometer | crunch |

*(continued)*

**FIGURE 5.4.** San Diego Quick Assessment. From LaPray and Ross (1969). Reprinted with permission from the authors and the International Reading Association.

## ADMINISTRATION

1. Type out each list of 10 words on an index card.

2. Begin with a card that is at least 2 years below the student's grade-level assignment.

3. Ask the student to read the words aloud to you. If he or she misreads any words on the list, drop to easier lists until he or she makes no errors. This indicates the base level.

4. Write down all incorrect responses, or use diacritical marks on your copy of the test. For example, *lonely* might be read and recorded as *lovely. Apparatus* might be recorded as *a per' a tus.*

5. Encourage the student to read words he or she does not know so that you can identify the techniques he or she uses for word identification.

6. Have the student read from increasingly difficult lists until he or she misses at least three words.

## ANALYSIS

1. The list in which a student misses no more than one of the 10 words is the level at which he or she can read independently. Two errors indicate his or her instructional level. Three or more errors identify the level at which reading material will be too difficult for that student.

2. An analysis of a student's errors is useful. Among those which occur with greatest frequency are the following:

| Error | Example |
|---|---|
| reversal | *ton* for *not* |
| consonant | *now* for *how* |
| consonant clusters | *state* for *straight* |
| short vowel | *cane* for *can* |
| long vowel | *wid* for *wide* |
| prefix | *inproved* for *improved* |
| suffix | *improve* for *improved* |
| miscellaneous | (accent, omission of) |

3. As with other reading tasks, teacher observation of student behavior is essential. Such things as posture, facial expression, and voice quality may signal restlessness, lack of assurance, or frustration while reading.

**FIGURE 5.4.** (*continued*)

```
Name: Malik                Date: 10/15          Teacher: Williams

        PP                  Primer                1                    2
see  ✓              you  ✓              road  ride rid        our _____
play ✓              come  came          live  ✓              please _____
me   ✓              not  ✓              thank  ✓             myself _____
at   ✓              with  ✓             when  went           town _____
run  ✓              jump  ✓             bigger  ✓            early _____
go   ✓              help  hop           how  ✓               send _____
and  ✓              is  ✓               always  away         wide _____
look ✓              work  ✓             night  ✓             believe _____
can  ✓              are  ✓              spring  ✓            quietly _____
here ✓              this  ✓             today  ✓             carefully _____

Comments:  Malik's instructional level is primer. He accurately identifies beginning
        sounds but needs more instruction w/ vowels. Will begin w/ beginning of 1st grade
        text for running record.
```

**FIGURE 5.5.** Malik's reading of words on the SD Quick.

### Letter Names and Sounds

The teacher points to each letter and asks the student if he or she knows the name of the letter. If the student knows the name of the letter, the teacher, using the correct colored pen, circles that letter on the summary sheet. Next, the teacher asks the student if he or she knows the sound that letter makes. If the student knows the sound the letter makes, the teacher puts an X through that letter on the summary sheet.

### Beginning Sounds

The teacher names the object in each picture and asks the student if he or she knows what letter the name of the object begins with. Using the correct colored pen, the teacher writes a check next to each correct response on the summary sheet.

### Word Recognition

The teacher points to each of the 20 words. The student has 10 seconds to respond. Using the correct colored pen, the teacher writes a check next to each correct word on the summary sheet.

## Informal Reading Inventory

An informal reading inventory (IRI) which is a series of leveled/graded passages with comprehension questions, was first developed by Emmet Betts in 1946. Since then many other very comprehensive IRIs have been developed (Bader, 2002; Beaver, 1999; Shanker & Ekwall, 2000, 2003; Johns, 1994; Silvaroli & Wheelock, 2001). Your goal in administering an IRI is to determine a child's reading level so that you can

**Directions:** Teacher points to each picture and says its name. The teacher then asks the child to say what letter the picture name begins with.

**FIGURE 5.6.** Sound–Letter Assessment. Reprinted with permission of the San Diego Unified School District Literacy Department.

(continued)

# Reading Assessment Summary

Name _____   Teacher _____

Date _____   Date _____   Date _____
        (red)                       (green)                    (purple)

Letter Names (Circle letters when recognized)

(Capitals)              Total _____  _____  _____

S  M  O  T  P  N  E  X  C  K  R  B  J

U  F  G  H  D  I  Z  W  V  L  Y  A  Q

(Lowercase)            Total _____  _____  _____

j  u  f  g  h  d  y  a  q  i  z  w  v

l  e  x  c  k  r  b  s  m  o  t  p  n

Beginning Sounds        Total _____  _____  _____

S___ M___ O___ T___ P___ N___ E___ X___ C___ K___ R___

B___ J___ U___ F___ G___ H___ D___ I___ Z___ W___ V___

L___ Y___ A___ O___

Beginning Picture Sounds     Total _____  _____  _____

sun____  boots ____  goat ____  turtle ____  hat ____  dog ____  fish ____

kite ____  net ____  pencil ____  monkey ____  leaf ____  apple ____

zebra ____  rabbit ____  yarn ____  watermelon ____  violin ____

jump rope ____  quarter ____

Word Recognition         Total _____  _____  _____

A____  will____  I____  can____  go____  to____  see____  we____

The ____  not ____  red ____  yellow ____  blue ____  green ____

orange ____  brown ____  purple ____  black ____  white ____  pink ____

**FIGURE 5.6.** (*continued*)

plan subsequent instruction. The levels include the *independent level*, which is reached when the child can comprehend *90% of the information and instantly recognize 99% of the words*, and the *instructional level*, which is reached when the child has *75% comprehension and 95% word recognition*. The instructional level identifies the text that can be read with help from the teacher (book difficulty). Anything more difficult is at the reader's frustrational reading level. On the basis of a child's performance on the IRI, you can plan the specifics of the needed instruction.

During an IRI the child orally and then silently reads graded passages and retells the text, and answers questions asked by the teacher, who also has a copy of the text and is recording oral reading errors, fluency rate, and comprehension. Commercial IRIs include graded passages, questions, and a code for marking the errors. We have found that any series of graded passages or leveled books can be used for an informal reading assessment. As the child reads orally, you can keep a running record to determine the types of errors made.

## Running Record

Once you have information about a child's ability to read sight words, name the letters of the alphabet, and identify corresponding sounds, you will want to assess his or her ability to read and comprehend connected text passages by keeping a running record (Clay, 1972, 2000) as the child reads graded passages, retells what he or she has read, and answers comprehension questions. Although a running record can be easily kept for any book or passage the child is reading, we find that it is time-efficient to keep the initial running record for a graded passage you believe may be at the child's instructional level, because when you have finished you will know the literacy strengths and needs of the child as well as the level of text the child can read independently or with instructional help from the teacher.

The initial running record can be kept as the child reads a series of leveled classroom readers or graded passages from an IRI. As a child is orally reading a graded/leveled passage of 100–200 words, you record words read correctly with a checkmark (see Figure 5.7). Errors include word insertions, omissions, deletions, repetitions, substitutions, reversals, refusals to try or to pronounce a word, and appeals for help. Record self-corrections, but don't record them as errors. As you analyze these errors, you'll be able to note problems with graphophonics, semantics, and syntax. Graphophonics refers to sound–symbol relationships (V), semantics refers to the meaning children make with respect to their reading (M), and syntax refers to knowledge about the structure of the language (S) (see Figure 5.8). While analyzing a student's reading, it is very important to pay attention to the cues he or she is using or not using.

Gathering information from a running record directly affects what the focus will be for future individual or small-group lessons in which the child is a participant. You can also see patterns that are emerging amosng readers and can plan lessons based on similar needs.

How do you know which graded passage to start with? On the basis of the child's performance on the SD Quick, you know where to begin his or her reading of the graded passages of the IRI. For example, the level of the list in which a student misses no more than one of the 10 words is the level at which the child can read independently. Two errors indicate his or her instructional level. Three or more errors identify the level at which reading material will be too difficult for the child. If the child misses two words in the primer list, you know that your instruction should begin here; further assessment should begin on a passage that is less difficult so that the child can begin with a feeling of success.

Your purpose in using the graded passages of an IRI to keep a running record is to determine the child's ability to recognize and analyze words and understand their meaning within a connected text. Once you've carefully selected a leveled passage that you think will be at his or her instructional level, begin by asking the child to

| Type of error or miscue | Code | Description |
|---|---|---|
| Accurate reading | ✓ ✓ ✓ ✓ | For each word read correctly, a check or dash is placed above the word. Some prefer no marking to mean accurate reading. |
| Self-correction (not counted as an error) | his / her   sc | Child reads the word incorrectly, pauses, and the corrects the error. |
| Refusal to pronounce Told word (counted as an error) | — / table   T | The student neither pronounces the word nor attempts to do so. The teacher pronounces the word so that testing can continue. |
| Insertion (counted as an error) | at / — | The student inserts a word or a series of words that do not appear in the text. |
| Omission (counted as an error) | — / rat | The student omits a word or a continuous sequence of words in the text, but continues to read. |
| Repetition (not counted as an error) | The horse ran away | The student repeats on or more words that have been read groups of adjacent words that are repeated count as one repetition. |
| Reversal | he\said wĂƒas | The student reverses the order of words or letters. |
| Appeal for help (counted as an error) | — App / house   T | Child asks for help with a word he or she cannot read. |

**FIGURE 5.7.** Running record coding system. From Morrow (2005). Copyright 2005 by Pearson Education. Reprinted with permission of the author and publisher.

| Name: | | Age: | Date: | | Teacher: | |
|---|---|---|---|---|---|---|
| Title: | | | | | Level: | |

| # of words | # of errors | Error rate | # of self-corrections | Self-correction rate |
|---|---|---|---|---|
| | | | | |

Accuracy rate and reading level: _____

Comments: _____

_____

_____

ANALYSIS OF CUES USED
M = meaning
S = structure
V = visual

| Page # | # of errors | # of self-corrections | Text | Errors | Self-corrections |
|---|---|---|---|---|---|
| | | | | | |
| | | | | | |
| | | | | | |
| | | | | | |
| | | | | | |
| | | | | | |
| | | | | | |
| | | | | | |
| | | | | | |
| | | | | | |
| | | | | | |
| | | | | | |
| | | | | | |
| | | | | | |
| | | | | | |
| | | | | | |
| | | | | | |
| | | | | | |
| | | | | | |
| | | | | | |
| | | | | | |

**FIGURE 5.8.** Running record form. This form should be used to help you analyze and summarize the child's performance. On the basis of these data, you can plan appropriate instruction.

From *Teaching Literacy in First Grade* by Diane Lapp, James Flood, Kelly Moore, and Maria Nichols. Copyright 2005 by The Guilford Press. Permission to photocopy this figure is granted to purchasers of this book for personal use only (see copyright page for details).

look it over and read it to him- or herself. Observe closely. Did you make a good selection? Does it appear that the child can read it? If so, ask the child to do so while you record his or her performance on a separate sheet (Figure 5.8). When finished, ask the child to retell what he or she has read. Probe with a few additional questions to assess the child's comprehension. Continue until you have identified his instructional level. Next, have the child silently read a passage at the same level. When he or she finishes, invite a retell (Figure 5.9) and probe with questions. Do so until you have reached the child's instructional level. Once you have found his or her instructional level, analyze the types of errors made during oral reading and then plan appropriately.

### Analysis of Malik's Performance on the Running Record

Because Malik missed three words on the first-grade list, Ms. Williams continued his assessment by having him read a book intended for beginning first-grade readers: *Baby Bear Goes Fishing*, Level 7. While Malik read, Ms. Williams codes his reading and asked for a retell when he was done. His performance is shown in Figures 5.10 and 5.11.

#### RECOMMENDED INSTRUCTION AT THE WORD LEVEL

Malik's performance on the running record gave Ms. Williams a fair amount of insight into his reading development. After analyzing his miscues, Ms. Williams concluded that this text was at Malik's instructional level because he had read it with 92% accuracy. Malik self-corrected one in every three words he read. This meant that he monitored his own reading. Malik did well at attempting unknown words as he used his knowledge of beginning sounds. Many of the errors Malik made while reading fit with the meaning of the story and the structure of the sentence. We know this because Ms. Williams coded M (meaning) and S (structure) many times in the Errors column while analyzing his cueing systems. However, Malik needs additional instruction on *reading through words*. When Malik is stuck on a word, Ms. Williams will also encourage him to *reread and repeat phrases*. He attempted this only once during the reading of the text. *Fluency* instruction will also be a target of instruction for Malik inasmuch as he read most of the text word by word. Through *repeated readings, choral readings,* and *neurological impress* Malik will become more fluent in his reading.

#### RECOMMENDED COMPREHENSION INSTRUCTION

Based on his retelling of the story, Ms. Williams knows that Malik needs further instruction in *connecting the events of the story*. He was able to tell the gist of the story but left out some important *minor ideas*. Ms. Williams recommends working on retelling, using a *beginning, middle,* and *end graphic organizer* as a guide for Malik. By *modeling* how this could sound during read-alouds and shared reading whole-group instruction, Ms. Williams can think aloud and explicitly teach Malik how to retell a story more completely. She will also spend time during small-group guided reading to teach Malik and others how to retell a story using index cards as visuals labeled *who, what, where, when, why,* and *how*. Ms. Williams will also work with Malik to *add more detail* to his retell. His vocabulary will be strengthened through conversation, listen-

Student _____ Date _____

Book Title and Author _____

Check each skill as: (1) weak, (2) average, (3) very good, (4) superior

|  | 1 | 2 | 3 | 4 |
|---|---|---|---|---|

1. The student comprehensively retold the story
2. Comprehended the story line and plot
   - Understood the roles played by the various characters
   - Understood implied as well as stated meanings
   - Comprehended author's intention
3. Understood the major ideas
4. Understood the minor ideas that built to the major ideas
5. Brought a background of information to the selection
6. Analyzed and made judgments based on facts
8. Retold the selection in sentences that made grammatical sense
   - predicates (verbs)
   - adverbs
   - adjectives
   - phrases
   - compound sentences
   - conjunctions
   - complex sentences

9. Used a rich and meaningful vocabulary:

   Example: _____

   _____

10. Overused, slang, and colloquial expressions:

   List: _____

   _____

11. Summary of retelling:

   Comprehension: _____

   Sentence structure: _____

   Vocabulary: _____

12. Proposed instruction: _____

   _____

   _____

   _____

   _____

**FIGURE 5.9.** Story retelling guide. This chart will help you in assessing a child's proficiency at retelling after reading.

From *Teaching Literacy in First Grade* by Diane Lapp, James Flood, Kelly Moore, and Maria Nichols. Copyright 2005 by The Guilford Press. Permission to photocopy this figure is granted to purchasers of this book for personal use only (see copyright page for details).

| Name: _Malik_ | | Age: _5_ Date: _10/5_ | | Teacher: _Williams_ |
| :-- | :-- | :-- | :-- | :-- |
| Title: _Baby Bear Goes Fishing_ | | | | Level: _7_ |

| # of words | # of errors | Error rate | # of self-corrections | Self-correction rate |
| :--: | :--: | :--: | :--: | :--: |
| 112 | 9 | 1:12 | 4 | 1:3 |

Accuracy rate and reading level: _92% instructional_

Comments: _Malik is mostly reading word by word. Attempts unfamiliar words_
_with initial sounds_

ANALYSIS OF CUES USED
M = meaning
S = structure
V = visual

| Page # | # of errors | # of self-corrections | Text | Errors | Self-corrections |
| :--: | :--: | :--: | :-- | :--: | :--: |
| 3 | | 1 | $\frac{I\ am}{I'm}$ / sc ✓✓ | MS | V |
| | | | ✓✓✓ <br> ✓✓✓ | | |
| | 1 | | ✓ $\frac{brown}{baby}$ ✓ | MS | |
| | 1 | | ✓ $\frac{wish}{will}$ ✓✓✓ | | V |
| | 1 | | ✓ $\frac{h\ ...}{help}$ ✓ | | V |
| 5 | 1 | | ✓✓✓ $\frac{I\ ...}{little}$ / T | | |
| | | | ✓✓✓ <br> ✓✓✓ | | |
| | | 1 | ✓✓ $\frac{no}{not}$ / sc ✓✓ | MS | V |
| | | | ✓✓✓ <br> ✓✓ | | |
| 7 | 1 | | ✓✓✓ $\frac{\quad}{baby}$ ✓ | | |
| | 1 | | $\frac{walked}{went}$ ✓✓✓✓ | MS | |
| | | | $\lvert$✓✓✓$\rvert$ R | | |

(continued)

**FIGURE 5.10.** Malik's running record.

| Page # | # of errors | # of self-corrections | Text | Errors | Self-corrections |
|---|---|---|---|---|---|
| | | | ✓✓✓ | | |
| 8 + 9 | | | ✓✓✓✓✓✓✓✓ | | |
| 11 | | | ✓✓✓✓✓ | | |
| 13 | | | $\frac{L\,...}{Look}$ ✓✓✓ | V | |
| | | | ✓✓ | | |
| | 1 | | ✓ $\frac{am}{at}$ ✓✓ | V | |
| 15 | | | ✓✓✓✓✓ | | |
| | | 1 | $\frac{walked}{went}$/ sc ✓✓✓✓ | MSV | V |
| | | | ✓✓✓✓ | | |
| | | | ✓✓✓ | | |
| | | | ✓✓✓✓✓✓✓ | | |
| 16 | | 1 | $\frac{I\ am}{I'm}$ sc ✓✓✓ | MSV | V |
| | 1 | | ✓ $\frac{brown}{baby}$ ✓ | MS | V |
| | | | | | |
| | | | | | |
| | | | | | |
| | | | | | |
| | | | | | |
| | | | | | |

**FIGURE 5.10.** (continued)

Student _Malik_____ Date _10/5_____

Book Title and Author _Baby Bear Goes Fishing_____

Check each skill as:  (1) weak, (2) average, (3) very good, (4) superior

|  |  | 1 | 2 | 3 | 4 |
|---|---|---|---|---|---|
| 1. | Comprehensively retold the story | | ✓ | | |
| 2. | Comprehended the story line and plot | | | ✓ | |
|  | • Understood the roles played by the various characters | | ✓ | | |
|  | • Understood implied as well as stated meanings | | | ✓ | |
|  | • Comprehended author's intention | | | ✓ | |
| 3. | Understood the major ideas | | ✓ | | |
| 4. | Understood the minor ideas that built to the major ideas | | | ✓ | |
| 5. | Brought a background of information to the selection | | | ✓ | |
| 6. | Analyzed and made judgments based on facts | | ✓ | | |
| 7. | Retold the selection in sentences that made grammatical sense | | | ✓ | |
| 8. | Retold the selection in sentences that include correct usage of: | | | | |
|  | • predicates (verbs) | | ✓ | | |
|  | • adverbs | | ✓ | | |
|  | • adjectives | | ✓ | | |
|  | • phrases | | ✓ | | |
|  | • compound sentences | | ✓ | | |
|  | • conjunctions | | ✓ | | |
|  | • complex sentences | | ✓ | | |

9. Used a rich and meaningful vocabulary:

   Example: _Used appropriate grade level vocab._____

   _____

10. Overused, slang, and colloquial expressions:

   List: _None used_____

   _____

11. Summary of retelling:

   Comprehension: _"Mama bear thought he was too little but he did it"—average retell_

   Sentence structure: _Uses mostly simple phrases_____

   Vocabulary: _Knew the meaning of "river" though he read "water"_____

12. Proposed instruction: _Will work on minor ideas & events leading up to major ideas._

   _Use graphic organizers to organize thoughts._____

   _____

**FIGURE 5.11.** Malik's story retelling guide.

ing to read-alouds, and word study activities similar to those that can be found in Chapter 6. Ms. Williams will *preteach vocabulary* words prior to reading, *discuss the meanings of words*, use *visuals and realia*, and have Malik *write*, using his new vocabulary words. With the use of these instructional strategies, Malik's vocabulary is sure to increase and help him with his overall understanding of the story.

Spend approximately 20 minutes formally assessing each child during the first week. However, you can gain additional information by observing each child at the centers and during all of the whole-group, small-group, partner, and individual learning times. Be careful not to frustrate the children by giving them too many formal assessments. The information you gather the first week is enough to get started. You will learn a lot more about the students once you have them grouped homogeneously for small-group explicit instruction. You can usually assess all students within the first week of school and be ready for small-group instruction beginning at week 2.

# ONGOING ASSESSMENTS

After the first week of school you can continue to assess during small-group instruction. You'll want to learn more about each students' knowledge of the concepts of print, phonemic awareness, fluency, and comprehension. This information can be acquired through observations, questioning, and interactions with them during daily literacy instruction. If you feel the need to assess the students in a more formal way, you may administer other assessments. Figure 5.12 provides an example of how to keep track of student performance throughout the year. It shows information gathered about the reading ability of a student, Anna, throughout the year. This one-page form is helpful in maintaining a picture of each student's reading progress. It is helpful to show parents and administrators as well. More detailed assessment information (running records, comprehension tests, phonemic awareness, oral language, and writing assessments) can be kept in the child's portfolio.

Figure 5.13 shows how students can be grouped according to needs and instructional levels. After initial assessments are made in September, the students in this class are grouped into five small homogeneous groups during guided reading interactions with the teacher. Continuous assessment ensures that groups are ever changing and meeting the needs of the students.

These initial and continuous assessments, which take approximately 5–20 minutes, will prove invaluable as you plan instruction for each child because they help to identify the reading strategies a child is using and those that are needed. As your students gain proficiency with reading, you can assess individual students through *conferencing* as they participate in independent reading. Sometimes you can sit with a reader for as much as 15 minutes as you note information about the child's fluency, comprehension, and decoding. To get a quick picture of what your students look like as readers, use a one-page form such as that shown in Figure 5.14. You will be able to capture a little information about each student's reading behaviors using this form.

Student: _Anna_　　　　Teacher: _Harrison_　　　　School: _Main_

D.O.B.: _10-27_　　　　Grade: _1_

Instructional Reading Level:

| Preprimer | DRA–8 (Kindergarten) | DRA–16 (First) |
|---|---|---|
| September | February | June |

| | **September** | **February** | **June** |
|---|---|---|---|
| Letter–Sound Assessment | Knows most consonant letters and sounds; confuses short vowel sounds. | | |
| SD Quick | Knows "at, go, can." Did not attempt initial sounds on most words; said "my" for "me." | | |
| IRI-DRA | | Can decode most passages at level 8; comprehension good; needs a lot of prompting at level 10. | Level 16—fluent reading, decoding well; retell is accurate, including main idea and details. |
| Other (CORE, Observation Survey, SOLOM, etc.) | Knows book-handling skills; has some phonemic awareness, limited ability to rhyme. | | |

**FIGURE 5.12.** Individual student assessment form.

For a more in-depth picture of the students' reading behaviors, use a 4 × 6 index card for each student, which can be held together by a brass ring. You can take more detailed notes about the students' reading using individual student cards. You can still note strengths, areas for improvement, text read, and plans for future instruction on each individual index card. This is a nice way to capture reading over time and will be helpful when conferencing with parents and administrators about your students' progress. Remember that careful and continuous assessment ensures that each child will take the appropriate next steps that will promote his or her literacy success.

Keeping running records on your students daily during guided reading time will help you to have a very accurate picture of how your students are progressing in reading. We recommend spending 5 minutes at the beginning of each guided reading lesson with one student, taking a running record, while the other students are warming up with familiar texts. By doing so, you will be able to assess each child in your class every 2 weeks. It is imperative that your instruction match the assessment information in order to maximize student achievement. Teachers who have a thorough understanding of the diagnostic/instructional model realize that

| Date: September 2005 | | | | | |
|---|---|---|---|---|---|
| DRA levels | | | | | |
| 14+ | Ricky | Carol | | | |
| 12 | Johanna | Bart | | | |
| 10 | | | | | |
| 8 | | | | | |
| 6 | Michael | | | | |
| 4 | Devin | Shannon | Eric | Jose B. | |
| 3 | | | | | |
| 2 | Darren | Angela | Harrison | | |
| 1 | Jim | Darrell | | | |
| A | Luis | Elizabeth | | | |
| Letters/Sounds | Juan | Miguel | Yesenia | Jose G. | |

**FIGURE 5.13.** Determining groups.

information, continuous process assessment, and instruction support a child's literacy development, which is not static but rather flexible and ever growing (Moore, 2004). Effective reading teachers are those who utilize daily opportunities to observe authentic literacy performances, to talk with their students, and to *plan for tomorrow based on the growth that occurred today.*

| Juan 9/3—Trouble decoding; retell weak | Mary 9/5—Confusing B and D; fluency slow | Anthony 9/5—Needs practice with sight words, phonemic awareness; does well at predicting | AnnaKate | Jose |
|---|---|---|---|---|
| Maria | Marco | Yesenia | Erik | Amanda |
| Terrence | Adrienne | Darrel | Angel | Malik |
| Lajuana | Doumas | Vicki | Rayna | Ricky |

**FIGURE 5.14.** Whole class student/teacher conferencing form.

# CHAPTER 6

# GROUPING FOR DIFFERENTIATED INSTRUCTION AND CLASSROOM MANAGEMENT

One of the most important roles you assume as a teacher is that of the classroom manager who can design and maintain an environment that offers many differentiated, and varied language and literacy learning experiences. The better managed your classroom, the more effective will be your relationships with your students (Marzano, Marzano, & Pickering, 2003) and the greater their potential for learning success (Wang, Haertel, & Wahlberg, 1993). As discussed in Chapters 4 and 10, expectations regarding classroom *rules* and *goals* for student–teacher behaviors, independent and group work, *procedures* for beginning and ending the day, transitioning between and during lessons and activities, using materials and equipment, and *responsibilities* and *consequences* associated with identified behaviors must be thoroughly designed and communicated for effective learning to occur (Glasser, 1969, 1990, 1998).

As described in Chapters 2 and 3, your first graders will learn and grow as readers and writers when you design instruction that includes both large heterogeneous and small homogeneous group settings. You can't possibly teach all of your students at one time all the time. Nor can you possibly fit time into your schedule to teach individuals or small groups of students for 6 hours a day. Realizing this, we've designed this chapter to help you plan a flexible grouping system for you and your students so you can best meet their individual and group needs.

# LARGE HETEROGENEOUS GROUPS

### When Should I Group My Students in Large Heterogeneous (Mixed-Ability) Groups?

A great time to teach all of your students in a large group is when you are introducing a new concept to them, giving direct instruction, or reviewing or reteaching something that isn't quite at their independent level. Gathering students on the rug is an excellent way to have all students within close proximity. Assigning students to spots on the rug where they can share their ideas with a partner is also a good way to develop oral language. Make sure students who may be struggling with the language can hear models of standard English as they turn to their peers to discuss new ideas. You may also need to teach students as a whole group while they are seated at their desks. We recommend seating your students in clusters rather than single rows so that they can share ideas and develop important concepts with their surrounding peers. Arranging desks this way will help when you assign cooperative group activities as well.

### When Are Large Heterogeneous Groups Most Effective?

As discussed in detail in Chapters 2, 3, and 8, working with children in large groups is very appropriate during:

➢ Read-alouds

➢ Shared reading

➢ Interactive writing

➢ Word study

➢ Oral language development

➢ Opening/closing routines

# SMALL HOMOGENEOUS GROUPS

### When Should I Group My Students in Small Homogeneous (Similar-Needs) Groups?

Teachers are able to motivate, instruct, model, monitor, observe, and confirm students' literacy behaviors during small homogeneous group settings. We believe that this is when you will be able to learn a great deal about your students, as you have only a few students to work with at a time.

## When Are Small Homogeneous Groups Most Effective?

As shown in Chapters 2 and 3, small groups with similar strengths and needs are most effective during:

➢ Guided reading

➢ Small-group interactive writing

➢ Small-group shared reading

➢ Word study

➢ Guided writing

A major issue that you must consider when you call a small group of students to work with you at a table or on the rug is, *What are the other students doing while you provide explicit instruction to a small group of students?*

# CENTER ACTIVITY ROTATION SYSTEM

The Center Activity Rotation System (CARS; Lapp, Flood, & Goss, 2000) is a system that accommodates both heterogeneous and homogeneous group instruction. This system is sure to help you meet all your students' needs as they work together in heterogeneous groups until being called to meet with you in small groups of children with similar strengths or needs for explicit instruction. This system avoids labeling and tracking children into static groups. CARS is a flexible method of grouping that encourages children to work in many group configurations throughout the day (see Figure 6.1).

## How Does CARS Work?

The first thing you must do in order to have a flexible grouping system is to get your students into *heterogeneous groups*. This means that each heterogeneous group should consist of four to six students with varying literacy proficiencies. The idea is to create heterogeneous groups that can work independently even when you call the most fluent reader from the group to work with you at the Teacher Center in a *homogeneous group*. When you constitute the groups, be sure to consider behavior issues, gender, ethnicity, and language proficiency in addition to reading levels. To do this you might make a list of all your students' names or numbers, in descending order, from the most to the least proficient reader. As you scan the list, you might select child 2, who is a very good reader

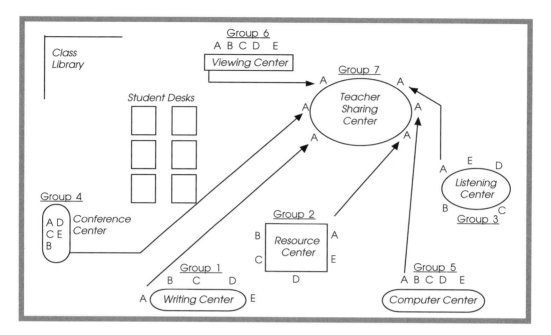

**FIGURE 6.1.** Center Activity Rotation System (CARS). Groups labeled A B C D E are heterogeneous. The group labeled A A A A A A is homogeneous.

and an independent worker; child 4, who is a proficient reader but not an independent worker; child 8, a grade level reader who is less independent; child 13, a slightly below grade level reader who is an independent worker and a friend of child 2; and child 18, who is very well liked but is below grade level because she is learning English as a second language. Think through your groupings carefully. If you don't constitute a group that works well together at first, you can always reconstitute it.

After you have the heterogeneous groups formed, you need to design literacy centers that provide practice for your students to develop reading fluency, comprehension of narrative and nonnarrative text, word study, writing, and conversation proficiency. As you design these weekly literacy activities, you will have to reflect on the broad range of literacy experiences that your students need to develop and how they relate to the district standards. Your students' continuing literacy development must be the focus of all instructional experiences.

Suggestions for these literacy centers include the following.

## Center 1: Computer Station

Students can be involved in comprehension and word study activities as they explore Reader Rabbit or other computer programs. Use a chart like that shown in

Figure 6.2 to allow students to practice making words that are part of word families that are being studied in spelling.

## Center 2: Content Area Connections

Undoubtedly, you will run into difficulty in getting all your content area teaching into your busy day. Make one of your centers a Social Studies/Literacy Center (or Science/Literacy Center) so you can integrate content into reading and writing activities. At this center students can read a range of leveled expository texts and answer "who, what, where, when, why, and how" questions about a topic of study that you may have introduced in an earlier whole-class discussion (see Figure 6.3).

## Center 3: Word Study Adventures

Students can study real and nonreal words as they practice writing and spelling them on a white board (see Figure 6.4). Dictionaries should be available so that they can be consulted if the children have questions about the meaning or authenticity of a word. You can analyze patterns of errors in students' writing assignments in order to plan these word study activities. Having students write high-frequency words at this center is also a good way to increase their sight word vocabulary.

## Center 4: Library Explorations

At this center students can engage in "buddy reading" and discuss books in the leveled library. Encourage your students to read at their independent levels when they are at this center. Figure 6.5 provides a list of leveled readers for first graders.

| Make words that are part of each word family. | |
|---|---|
| *at* family | *an* family |
| _____ at | _____ an |
| _____ at | _____ an |
| _____ at | _____ an |

**FIGURE 6.2.** Word family chart.

From *Teaching Literacy in First Grade* by Diane Lapp, James Flood, Kelly Moore, and Maria Nichols. Copyright 2005 by The Guilford Press. Permission to photocopy this figure is granted to purchasers of this book for personal use only (see copyright page for details).

| | | My answers |
|---|---|---|
| WHAT? | Today is *what* season of the year? | |
| HOW? | How does the sky look? | |
| WHEN? | Summer comes after which season? | |
| WHO? | Which animals are typically born during this time of year? | |
| WHERE? | Where do the animals go during the winter? | |
| WHY? | *Why* do you wear different clothes in winter than summer? | |

**FIGURE 6.3.** Seasons.

From *Teaching Literacy in First Grade* by Diane Lapp, James Flood, Kelly Moore, and Maria Nichols. Copyright 2005 by The Guilford Press. Permission to photocopy this figure is granted to purchasers of this book for personal use only (see copyright page for details).

| Write the words that are real. Use your dictionary to check. Write a sentence using each real word. | |
|---|---|
| he | |
| the | |
| jam | |
| is | |
| ras | |
| pot | |
| skip | |
| nop | |
| egy | |
| big | |

**FIGURE 6.4.** Writing real words.

From *Teaching Literacy in First Grade* by Diane Lapp, James Flood, Kelly Moore, and Maria Nichols. Copyright 2005 by The Guilford Press. Permission to photocopy this figure is granted to purchasers of this book for personal use only (see copyright page for details).

<u>Kindergarten</u>

- *Brown Bear, Brown Bear, What Do You See?* by Bill Martin Jr.—Students can read about different colored animals in this wonderfully illustrated text. A great book to use for prediction.
- *Anno's Counting Book* by Mitsumasa Anno—Students can count along with this book as they learn about a little town and the changing seasons.
- *Eating the Alphabet* by Lois Ehlert—Your first graders will be able to identify numbers and different foods as they eat up the alphabet!
- *Roll Over!: A Counting Song* by Merle Peek—Students will count backward as they read this book about animals who try to make room for each other in a crowded bed.
- *I Eat Leaves* by JoAnn Vandine—Students will enjoy reading about many different animals that eat leaves, such as koalas, giraffes, and caterpillars.

<u>First Grade</u>

- *Bears in the Night* by Stan and Jan Berenstain—Your first graders will enjoy reading this fun book about critters that sneak out of their beds at night.
- *All by Myself* by Mercer Mayer—Students will be able to relate to this book about doing things on their own.
- *Here Comes a Bus* by Harriet Ziefert—Students will enjoy this interactive text as they pull up the flaps to find out where a bus is going.
- *The Day I Had to Play with My Sister* by Crosby Bonsall—Students are sure to connect to this text as they read about two siblings who have different ideas of what it means to play together.
- *We Are Best Friends* by Aliki—Any student who is new to the school or neighborhood will enjoy reading about the characters in this story who have a similar experience.
- *Go Away, Dog* by Joan L. Nodset—Do your students love to read about friendship and animals? If so, they are sure to love this book about two best friends.

<u>Second Grade</u>

- *Henry and Mudge: The First Book* by Cynthia Rylant—A young boy, Henry, befriends a dog, Mudge, and together they have one adventure after another.
- *Arthur's Loose Tooth* by Lillian Hoban—If your first graders are worried about losing a tooth they should read this book. Arthur overcomes his fear, and so will your students.
- *Who's Afraid of the Big, Bad Bully?* by Teddy Slater—Any student who has ever been teased or bullied will enjoy reading this book about overcoming fears at school.
- *Cam Jansen and the Mystery of the Carnival Prize* by David A. Adler—Students will enjoy reading how Cam uses her photographic memory to solve another mystery.
- *Gregory, the Terrible Eater* by Mitchell Sharmat—Students will laugh out loud as they read about a goat who is a very picky eater.

*(continued)*

**FIGURE 6.5.** Leveled readers for your first-grade students.

---

Third Grade

- *The Drinking Gourd: A Story of the Underground Railroad* by F. N. Monjo— This exciting book is sure to captivate young readers as they learn about adventures on the Underground Railroad.
- *How to Eat Fried Worms* by Thomas Rockwell—Students will find this hilarious book irresistible. What young child wouldn't want to learn how to eat 15 worms in 15 days?
- *Amber Brown Is Not a Crayon* by Paula Danziger—When her best friend moves away, Amber is feeling blue . . . just like the color of a crayon. Students are sure to connect to the characters in this story about friendship.
- *Flossie and the Fox* by Patricia C. McKissack—Students can read about a young girl who is on her way to a neighbor's house when a sly fox tries to outwit her.

---

**FIGURE 6.5.** (*continued*)

### Center 5: Listening and Sharing

Students at this center can listen to and read along with cassettes of their favorite books as they increase their fluency. When your first graders finish their reading, they can share their responses to the text and make text connections as they discuss story elements such as plot, character, and setting. Figure 6.6 provides a list of first-grade books on tape.

### Center 6: Authors at Work

Students working at this center can draw and add one line of writing, write letters, diary entries, experiences, responses to literature, and so on, while conferring with their peers. Encourage your students to first share their ideas with a partner, answering such questions as "who, what, where, when, and how" in order to expand what they plan to share in writing. For more detailed ideas about writing, see Chapter 3.

### Teacher Center

As the students work at the heterogeneously grouped literacy centers, you can call students with similar strengths and needs to work with you at your Teacher Center. This is why you want to be sure that you have constituted groups that

- *The Emperor's Egg* by Martin Jenkins—Your first graders will enjoy reading along with this story while learning about the unusual habits of penguins.
- *Come On into the Rainforest* by Judy Nayer—This nonnarrative text is full of vivid photos and interesting facts about the rainforest.
- *The Happy Hedgehog* by Marcus Pfister—Do your students love Marcus Pfister's *The Rainbow Fish*? This book is sure to appeal to students who enjoy a "feel good" story about doing what makes you happy.
- *Never Ride Your Elephant to School* by Doug Johnson—This is a great book and cassette to have at your listening center at the beginning of the year. Students will laugh out loud as they listen to what happens at school when an unexpected guest comes visiting.
- *Officer Buckle and Gloria* by Peggy Rathmann—When your first graders need a lesson on teamwork and cooperation, this is a great book to introduce. Students will enjoy reading along with Officer Buckle and Gloria as they work together and review safety tips.
- *There Was an Old Lady Who Swallowed a Fly* by Simms Taback—If you like the old version by the same name, you will love this newer version, and so will your students. The familiar verse will have your students reading along with the narrator in no time.
- *Zin! Zin! Zin! A Violin* by Lloyd Moss—Want to introduce music into your curriculum? This is a great text to have at a listening post as students explore the vivid illustrations and learn about musical instruments.
- *Brown Rabbit's Shape Book* by Alan Baker—This is a great text to use at the beginning of the year, as students may need to revisit shapes and colors.

**FIGURE 6.6.** First-grade books on tape.

can work independently without any one child. When a homogeneous group meets with you at the Teacher Center, you should be deliberate and explicit in your instruction as you focus on helping them to develop their literacy. You will also have to be flexible about who meets with you at the Teacher Center. For example, some days you may call all five of your students who struggle with characterization to work with you; on other days it may be only three of that original group who have a different need. In addition to working with children in groups, you will meet with children individually when they have a need that cannot be addressed in a group setting.

The chart in Figure 6.7 shows how your students, who are grouped heterogeneously, can rotate from center to center (1–6) approximately every 20 minutes. During this center rotation, you will be calling your homogeneous groups, composed of children with the same needs, from the centers, to work with you at the Teacher Center.

| Student groups | Centers |
|---|---|
| Jose, Hannah, AnnaKate | 1, 2, 3, 4, 5, 6 |
| Jessie, Maria, Zabdy, Sean, | 2, 3, 4, 5, 6, 1 |
| Zoe, Ricky, Michelle, Lynn | 3, 4, 5, 6, 1, 2 |
| Juan D., Devin, Arianna | 4, 5, 6, 1, 2, 3 |
| Maya, Alizay, Joey | 5, 6, 1, 2, 3, 4 |
| Angel, Maricella, Juan G. | 6, 1, 2, 3, 4, 5 |

**FIGURE 6.7.** Center rotation.

# ONE ON ONE

### When Should I Work with Students in Individual Settings?

We know that working individually with students is a time when you can truly meet the needs of your children most effectively. Unfortunately, with all the content that must be taught, the standards that must be met, and the number of children in your classroom, time for individual conferencing is hard to come by. However, we believe you can and *must* find time to meet with as many students as you can daily—both those who struggle with literacy and those who are above grade level.

### When Are Individual Conferencing and One-on-One Direct Instruction Most Effective?

➢ During independent reading

➢ During independent writing

You will need a system for recording student information during individual conferencing. You may get a file folder for each student and jot down notes on pieces of paper. This information can easily be transferred to students' portfolios for parent conferences. You may want to hook a bunch of 5 × 7 index cards together with a metal ring and label each card with a student's name for quick reference.

These cards can easily be unhooked and placed in the child's portfolio as well, at conference and report card times. Another way to chart your students' progress is to use the example provided in Figure 6.8. This may be useful as you jot down students' strengths and needs in each square. It is also a nice reminder as you check to see which of your students you haven't met with in a while.

| Emmanuel | Sarah | Amanda | Hali |
|---|---|---|---|
| 9/27 Fluency has improved; needs more sight word practice (came, said, this) | | 9/27 thorough retell; includes connections to text; slow and choppy reading | |
| Deidre | Richard | James | Michael |
| | 9/28 struggling at level 3; may need to go to level 2 | 10/5 chooses comic books during I.R.; cannot retell | |
| Abdi | Aaron | Darrel | Adrienne |
| | | | |
| Stephanie | Kyle | Jorge | Jasslyn |
| | | | |
| Ezekial | Douglas | Ricky | Dina |
| | | | |

**FIGURE 6.8.** Sample progress chart.

There is a lot to consider as you group your students during the instructional day. However, we believe that the most important thing to consider when grouping students is flexibility. You should assess your students daily so that you can regroup them according to their needs. You don't want to mistakenly keep a student in a homogeneous group that is not meeting his or her needs as a literacy learner.

Teaching children to read is a wonderful opportunity to group students heterogeneously and homogeneously. However, don't forget about all the other times when student grouping is just as important. Remember, your students can learn a lot from each other during cooperative group activities and content area instruction. You can adapt the CARS plan in your classroom during other instructional times (i.e., math, social studies, science) when you want to ensure that students learn *from* and *with* each other in both heterogeneous and homogeneous groups. Children's reading behaviors are individual and ever growing. Your ongoing assessment of their performance will guide your instruction. As you observe your students, you will become aware of the next steps each child must take to become a fluent, independent reader and writer. Because children gain literacy fluency at different rates, regrouping must be ongoing.

## CHAPTER 7

# SUPPORTING ORAL
# LANGUAGE DEVELOPMENT

C hildren become proficient with language by using it in a variety of situations with many different people. Through conversational interchanges children are provided feedback about the clarity of their communication and are exposed to a model of a language structure they will use throughout life. The following examples illustrate how oral language experiences can occur continuously throughout a school day.

## HOW CAN CHILDREN BE INVOLVED IN ENGAGING EXPERIENCES THAT FOSTER COMMUNICATION SKILLS?

### Morning Conversations

As children enter the classroom each morning, it is important to greet them and engage them in conversation about their pets, sports activities, a favorite program watched on television last night, a new outfit or hair-do, sor a family event you knew was to occur. You may choose to use a friendly looking puppet to do the talking. Puppets have a calming effect on first graders, especially those who are shy or scared. Be careful not to ask a question that can be answered with one word. For example, you might say,

138

"Last night I watched [TV program] _____. What did you think about _____ [a character or some part of the plot]?" Once they've answered, give an appropriate response that isn't judgmental, but that invites further explanation, by saying something like, "How interesting, why did you think that?" If

you are having a conversation with a child who is learning English as a second language, the child might give a response to the initial question such as, "The boy bad." Your response could be, "How interesting, what made you think that the boy (name) was bad?" This provides a model of conventional grammatical and syntactical structures (Salus & Flood, 2003) within the context of the topic being discussed.

When engaging children in conversation, be sure to wait long enough to allow them to respond (Otto, 2002). If they need more time than is available at that moment, have the children further elaborate their responses by sharing through journal writing or with a peer. Plan to say something each morning to each child. Although you won't have time for long daily conversations with every student, you can vary the time so that by the end of the week you will have had at least one extended morning conversation with each child. Some children will be easier to engage in conversation than others, because interactive communication patterns with adults may or may not be familiar patterns in their homes. Be careful not to overwhelm children with too much talk. Start slowly, and use short sentences as you build their comfort and trust.

Additional informal conversations can occur during snack time, after lunch, and as the children prepare to leave for the day. Never miss an opportunity for one-to-one conversations with your students, and encourage children to greet and talk to one another for a few moments whenever appropriate. You are the model for the types of interchanges that will occur in your classroom. As children engage in

classroom conversations with you and their peers, they learn to hypothesize, compare, contrast, clarify, classify, and summarize their ideas (Raban, 2001).

Oral language development is not just the domain of language arts and readers' or writers' workshop; it is also the domain of every part of learning throughout the entire day. Although the following examples are drawn primarily from these areas, children need to be developing their oral language skills in social studies, science, mathematics, art, and physical education, as well as in language arts.

## The Literacy Block

Oral language development has a role in every aspect of the literacy block from word study to independent reading. The following sections offer some ideas and examples of how oral language development can be encouraged within the literacy block.

### Word Study

As children engage in word study activities, they naturally talk with one another. It's quite common to hear a child say, "I found three words that rhyme with cat, but this word (chat) has four letters, not three." This easy exchange of an observation between children (even when it's parallel conversation) illustrates the idea that language development occurs all day long. Children use oral language to formulate ideas, organize information, and test hypotheses. In this case the child was observing words like the following:

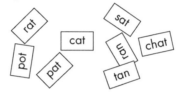

When she found *rat*, *pat*, and *sat*, she classified them as words that rhymed with *cat*. She sounded out *chat* and knew it rhymed, but saw that it had four letters instead of three. At this point, she hypothesized that it also rhymed with *cat*, but she wasn't sure because of the four letters. By stating her hypothesis aloud, she was able to "try out" her idea through oral language.

### Read-Alouds

Everyone has memories of teachers or other adults sharing a wonderful selection through a read-aloud text, which is typically a text that is more difficult for children than their independent reading texts. Teachers use read-alouds to motivate their students to read and to build their topical knowledge about a specific subject (Fisher, Flood, Lapp, & Frey, 2004; Hoffman, Roser, & Battle, 1993). Chapters 1 and 2 explain the procedures for read-alouds and provide excellent titles that you may want to use in your program. The read-aloud experience provides a perfect opportunity for a discussion of the events and themes of the text. Children can be invited to talk with a partner about the text before sharing their thoughts with the whole group. During read-alouds children also learn vocabulary that enhances their oral language skills as well as their comprehension skills (Brassell & Flood, 2004).

## *Storytelling*

Teachers often use folktales for storytelling. When children listen to stories, they experience a "transfer of imagery"(Lipman, 1999) as they visualize their personal images of the story. After modeling students can develop oral fluency and expression as they share a story orally. This experience increases their awareness of vocal pitch and volume, timing, gestures, and audience responsiveness. Children respond well to storytelling because there are no basic rules for the proper telling of a story. Even the greatest storytellers can't agree on a "best set of methods." Each class storyteller should be invited to develop his or her own techniques, style, and selection of stories. As you prepare to tell a story, you might want to think about the following considerations. These can also be shared with children as considerations to guide their storytelling.

1. Who is your audience? The story must be appropriate for them. First graders like simple folktales. They do not understand a story that is too abstract. It must contain some elements with which they can identify. In the story of *The Three Bears*, the beds, chairs, bowls of soup, and grandmother are familiar. Associating them with bears and mystery and adventure allows for a perfect mix of reality and fantasy.

2. Be careful not to select a book that would be better shared as a read-aloud. Stories for telling should be simple and direct. *Winnie the Pooh* and *The Jungle Book* have such rich dialogue that they should be shared as a read-aloud. Books like *The Gingerbread Man*, *The Three Little Pigs*, and *The Three Billy Goats Gruff* have simple clear-cut events that allow the listeners to make distinct pictures in their imaginations. These would be perfect selections for storytelling by first graders because they are short and there are no complexities in the plots. A story that lasts longer than 6 minutes is too long for storytelling.

3. Practice, practice, practice, think about it, and then practice again before telling the story to the intended audience.

4. Be sure that the listeners are comfortable and free of distractions.

Once the story has been told, listeners should be partnered so that they can share a response before the whole class is invited to share.

The following stories from various parts of the world lend themselves to exciting storytelling episodes:

➤ Africa: *Anansi the Spider* adapted by Gerald McDermott

➤ Germany: *The Bremen-Town Musicians* by the Brothers Grimm; retold by Ruth Belov Gross

➤ Israel: *It Could Always Be Worse* retold by Margot Zemach

➤ Nigeria: *Why the Sun and the Moon Live in the Sky* by Elphinstone Dayrell

## Guided Reading

A great deal of oral language development occurs during guided reading. As children discuss the meaning of the text, they have opportunities to ask questions, generate hypotheses and ideas, wonder aloud, predict and interpret (Roser & Martinez, 1995). Guided reading techniques and tips are discussed in more detail in Chapter 2. Frequently, when teachers are working with a small group of children in guided reading groups, the other children are working on group or individual projects at literacy centers or learning stations.

## Learning Centers

As children work together at learning centers, they have opportunities to expand their language proficiency and acquire new topical vocabulary and concepts as they work on themes. While at learning centers, children are independently engaged in teacher-planned activities that support their oral language, reading, and writing development. The goal of learning center activities is to provide opportunities for children to work in small groups at various locations, where they must take responsibility for their own behaviors as they socialize, communicate, and learn. Some of the centers that best accomplish this goal are described in the following paragraphs.

### LISTENING (AND READING ALONG) CENTER

When children are at the Listening Center, they have opportunities to listen to taped versions of stories that they have already read silently, as well as opportunities to read along as new books that are unfamiliar to them are read.

Although the Listening Center is important for all students, it is especially beneficial for students who are struggling with texts. English language learners who listen to texts at their independent level learn how to pronounce words in English and have an opportunity to hear the prosody of the language, including phrasing and chunking parts of sentences. The Listening Center helps children who are having difficulty with decoding because they have an opportunity to listen to texts in their spoken form.

Taped versions of texts include well-read interpretations of texts that emphasize the intent of the author; the speakers on the tape express their characters' intentions through emphasizing various words or phrases. They change their voices to show that different characters are talking; they also show how characters differ from one another in motivation and intent. You can add another dimension to your Listening Center by taping yourself reading your favorite books. You can insert comments and questions throughout the story to make the listening experience an interactive experience like your read-alouds.

### LIBRARY CENTER

At the Library Center, children talk to each other quite easily about their book selection processes. They often tell what they liked about a certain book or explain the kind of book they are hoping to find. The Library Center is a perfect place for both informal and more formal book discussions. In addition to the brief informal discussion they have with one another in the Library Center, you may want to have a "book chat" discussion with a group of children, in which you pose questions and ask them to discuss their answers with one another.

When children begin to participate in discussions, start by asking each of the children to talk with another child before they share with the whole group; that is, they should work in pairs. Working in pairs guarantees that the children will have both speaking and listening experiences.

WRITING CENTER

At the Writing Center, children should begin their writing with an oral "pre-writing topic selection" phase of writing. They might talk through what they want to write about before they begin writing. Oral language is practiced throughout the writing process as children talk about their attempts. They often want to practice their writing by sharing it aloud with their teacher as well as other students who are in the center with them.

COMPUTER CENTER

It is often a good idea to pair children as they work on a single computer. As they share the computer, they use their language to negotiate turn-taking, try to find correct answers, plan approaches to games, and complete the task assigned to them. Children frequently "stray" from the assignment as they talk about related games they have "played on the computer" and as they describe and act out plots of games they've played in the past.

PERFORMANCE CENTER

The Performance Center is the place where children practice for plays, Readers' Theater enactments, and creative dramatic performances. As they practice, they use oral language skills to make meaning of texts and share possible interpretations of texts with one another.

## Independent Reading

Even during independent reading, children have an opportunity to develop oral language skills. Many teachers confer with their children individually during independent reading, or they may use a buddy reading technique. As children read to each other in buddy reading, which is often used as an activity to help develop their fluency, they talk and listen to one another. As one reads, the other reads along and listens to his or her partner. When the child who is reading comes to a difficult word or improperly reads a word, the partner says the correct word. Sometimes they discuss the miscue, trying to figure it out.

This process occurs rather naturally, but you can enhance the buddy reading activity by adding an explicit oral language component. Ask the children to retell the story to the partner as they finish each page (or portion of the page). As they retell the text to one another, they have another opportunity for speaking and listening.

# PRACTICING ORAL LANGUAGE: ACTIVITIES, TECHNIQUES, AND EXERCISES

## Puppetry

Children usually love puppets. Puppetry is an activity in which all children can participate as speakers. If some of your children are very shy or uncomfortable in performing in front of other children, puppetry may offer a way for them to speak to the group through a persona without fear of ridicule or rejection. Puppets can be very primitive or more elaborate in construction; children can create their own puppets from simple brown paper bags. You may select or write (or ask the children to write) scripts for a puppet show. Note that puppetry is closely related to role playing.

## Role Playing

Role playing is important in helping children develop their skills in the following areas:

1. Listening skills
2. Attention/concentration skills
3. Speaking skills
4. Oral interpretation skills
5. Emotive skills
6. Empathy/sympathy skills

You can compose scripts for your children by creating a scene that ends at the point of conflict. The role-playing episode can explore alternative answers for the conflict you have described. Role playing can be used as a motivating activity for a story or text you are reading with the children, and it can also be used to start off a writing activity.

The following procedures will help you "direct" your children's role-playing sessions:

1. Warm up. The audience needs to be warmed up with a situation that is similar to the situation to be enacted. Good beginnings may include, "Has anyone ever been in a situation where . . . ?" or "Have you ever felt . . . ?"

2. Read the actual situation. The situation must have some dramatic sense. Give the characters names, include descriptions (limited), and include dialogue. Continue the story to a crisis point—a point at which a character must either say or do something.

3. Discuss the reading. Ask the students what they would do and what they think about the situation. Ask a prospective player to delineate his or her character. Ask for characteristics and feelings before the role play begins.

4. Select players. Try to have students volunteer, but be selective. Choose someone who has a feeling for a particular character and a point of view.

5. Ask players to describe themselves alone and then in relation to one another. Ask them what they want to be doing, where they want to be standing, sitting, and so forth.

6. Have students who are not players observe a specific player. The net effect of this is involvement.

7. Play the scene. This is the point at which personal taste, choice, and objectives come into view. You may want to play the scene up to a crisis point or until it's played out.

8. Ask the players how they feel about what happened.

9. Ask the nonplayers to respond. If a student has another point of view (and you think it's worthwhile), ask that student to elaborate. Ask students to play the part and to reenact the scene.

10. Select new players. You may choose a combination of old and new players.

11. Play the scene.

The following situation may be used with your first graders:

"Your older brother, Robbie, has made it clear that he doesn't want you to play with his new Game Boy. One day, you take it to school. In the schoolyard your friend Kyle asks if he can play the game by himself. You're not sure what to do, but Kyle says, 'Don't worry. I'm not going to break it.' You protest, but Kyle is already walking away with the game. You run after him, almost tackling him. He drops the Game Boy with a thud, and it's clearly broken. You look up from the ground and see your brother turning the corner with his friends. He is approaching you, but he hasn't seen what just happened. You know he sees you, Kyle, and the broken Game Boy. You say: _____."

## Readers' Theater

Readers' Theater is a form of dramatic interpretation in which children are given an opportunity to read orally. No scenery, costumes, or actions are used in Readers' Theater. The reader must project the story line, or plot, through his or her reading; the reader must also convey mood, emotion, and tone through interpretation of the script.

Readers' Theater helps students in the audience listen attentively, because they do not have scripts in front of them. They have to listen critically to make sure that they are comprehending the story accurately. Readers' Theater also helps the children who are doing the acting to speak effectively. They must read their lines with expression so that the audience can imagine the entire story.

As they read, all the players in the Readers' Theater hold copies of the scripts they are performing. They do not attempt to become the characters; rather, they give the audience an idea of the characters. The audience, the listeners, must use imagination to complete the picture. No actions by the players are introduced; the members of the audience must use their own creative resources to interpret action and to build an inclusive picture of the entire story.

Readers' Theater works extremely well as a speaking and listening activity because it does not require that a student physically portray a character, which can be extremely threatening to children. Children who are acting in the play have an opportunity to practice oral skills without stress; they have the script in front of them. Less able readers can participate in this activity fully because they can almost memorize their lines. Children who serve as the audience have an opportunity to hone their listening skills.

Readers' Theater can integrate a wide range of activities within your language arts curriculum. For example, a group of students may research the life and legend of a historical character and write a Readers' Theater script for presentation to the entire class. This type of format may be especially helpful in having your children interpret the information they find in reference materials. In one classroom, we saw a group of children write a Readers' Theater script using the writings of Martin Luther King Jr. as the basis of drama; a second group used writings about Abraham Lincoln as the source of their script.

The way in which you set up your stage is extremely important in Reader's Theater.

A beloved first-grade script for eight children is included in Appendix 7.1. The script in Appendix 7.2 about the water cycle helps to expand children's understanding of nonnarrative text structures as well as content information.

For ideas on other Readers' Theater scripts, check the websites *www.teachingheart. net/readerstheater*.htm and *www.geocities.com/EnchantedForest/Tower/3235/-3k*.

## Creative Dramatics

Creative dramatics has a place in every classroom. Children need opportunities for performing creative, spontaneous enactments of dramatic materials. You can write the materials yourself or you can select scripts that have been written for classroom acting. Children need to explore the range of their own voices as well as the range of their own abilities to interpret and convey meaning to an audience. Creative dramatics is an excellent vehicle with which to accomplish this.

Before you begin creative dramatics activities, you may have the children do some warm-up exercises such as the following:

1. Facial expressions only: sad, happy, angry, annoyed, elated, frustrated
2. Facial expressions with gestures: sad, happy, angry, annoyed, elated, frustrated
3. Pantomime a simple action: climbing a ladder, washing a window
4. Pantomime a complex action: scoring the winning point in a soccer game or a basketball game

## Choral Speaking/Reading

Choral speaking is an excellent activity for helping children, in a nonthreatening way, to develop oral speaking skills and reading skills. As children read along with the group, they learn the skills of syllabication, pronunciation, prosody (pitch, stress, tone), and interpretation. You (or one of the children) can direct this activity in the role of a conductor. Assign specific lines to individual children and ask them to do something special as they speak their solo lines; for example, ask a child to shout his or her line or to say the line softly or in a staccato manner.

We've included several activities that you can use for developing oral language activities in your classroom.

# ACTIVITIES FOR YOUR STUDENTS

Each of the following activities will help reinforce the importance of oral language skills.

**Name of Activity:** Simon Says.

**Skills Developed:** Naming parts of the body and following directions.

**Materials Needed:** None.

**Procedures:** Students follow direction only when teacher begins the sentence with "Simon says." Otherwise, children disregard the command.

**Name of Activity:** Big Wind Blows.

**Skills Developed:** Naming colors, objects (clothing).

**Materials Needed:** None.

**Procedures:**    1.  Teacher says, "Big wind blows."
                    2.  Students say, "What does it blow?"
                    3.  Teacher says, "It blows those who wear red socks."
                    4.  Students wearing red socks must run.

**Name of Activity:** Opposites

**Skills Developed:** Interpretation of word meaning.

**Materials Needed:** None.

**Procedures:** Teacher says a word and students say the opposite of the word; or teacher says a noun and students say its verb. For example: "Put the book on the *stand*"; "I can't *stand* there."

**Name of Activity:** I Packed My Bag.

**Skills Developed:** Memory.

**Materials Needed:** None.

**Procedures:** Teacher starts by saying, "I packed my bag. In my bag I placed a _____." Students must repeat the previous sentence and add their own words. The final sentence will be built quite long, depending on the number of students in your group.

**Name of Activity:** What Am I?

**Skills Developed:** Drawing conclusions from stated clues; creating definition.

**Materials Needed:** None.

**Procedures:** Teacher reads a four- or five-line description of an object. Students guess the object.

**Name of Activity:** Strip Story.

**Skills Developed:** Logical sequencing and organizing.

**Materials Needed:** Story cut up into sentences, which are written on strips of paper and distributed to students.

**Procedures:** Students have to organize the story. The child who thinks that he or she has the first part, reads it. Other students build on the story.

**Name of Activity:** Building Story.

**Skills Developed:** Developing word phrases, sentences, and logical thinking.

**Materials Needed:** None.

**Procedures**: One student starts the story by offering an opening. A second student repeats the previous sentence and adds his or her own. The activity continues until everyone has contributed a part and ended a story.

**Name of Activity**: Sharing a Message.

**Skills Developed**: Ability to listen to and repeat a sentence without mistakes.

**Materials Needed**: None.

**Procedures**: The teacher may start the message by whispering to a player. The player whispers the message to the next player, and the activity continues until all the players have had a chance to receive and give the message. The last one tells the group what he or she heard and compares it with the original message.

**Name of Activity**: Three Ideas.

**Skills Developed**: Finding the main idea.

**Materials Needed**: None.

**Procedures**: One child is given three ideas such as (1) a trip, (2) a happy day, and (3) a family. He or she is asked to tell a story to the class using these three main ideas. The other children are told to listen for them. As a variation, do not tell the ideas of the story to the children who are listening, but have them guess what they are.

**Name of Activity**: Predicting News.

**Skills Developed**: Making inferences.

**Materials Needed**: Television; paper and pencil if desired.

**Procedures**: After listening to a newscast, the children are asked to predict the outcome of the event. They may also discuss what possible event led to the situation, using the facts supplied by the newscaster.

Each of the following activities will help reinforce your students' speaking skills.

**Name of Activity**: Newscast.

**Skills Developed**: Speaking in the role of someone else.

**Materials Needed**: None.

**Procedures**: Children compose fictitious news stories and report them to the class.

**Name of Activity**: Tongue twisters.

**Skills Developed**: Articulation.

**Materials Needed**: None.

Procedures: Have students write tongue twisters, which are then put in a box. Each child chooses a tongue twister and attempts to recite it.

Name of Activity: Train Game.

Skills Developed: Initial sounds.

Materials Needed: None.

Procedures: One child is an engineer and gives an initial sound. The engineer calls on someone to give the same sound, and if the sound is correct the other children join the train.

Name of Activity: Listen and Remember.

Skills Developed: Listening, remembering, and then restating what is heard.

Materials Needed: None.

Procedures: One child says something. You write it down or record it. The next child then attempts to restate the utterance of the first child. Continue with other children.

Name of Activity: Whose Voice Is It?

Skills Developed: Auditory acuity.

Materials Needed: None.

Procedures: Have five speakers ready to speak. The other children should all be ready to listen, with their heads turned around so that they cannot see the speakers. Ask one of the five children to speak, and ask the listeners to guess who spoke.

Name of Activity: Context Game.

Skills Developed: Ability to figure out context when a word in speech is missing or garbled.

Materials Needed: None.

Procedures: Replace a word in a sentence with a nonsense word. Students guess, through use of context, the meaning of the word. The guesser then creates another sentence.

Name of Activity: Off the Cuff.

Skills Developed: Ability to give an oral speech on the spur of the moment.

Materials Needed: None.

Procedures: Ask students to define words such as *adult, knowledge, family*. Students then give definitions without preparation.

1: Poor old lady, she swallowed a fly.
I don't know why she swallowed a fly.

2: Poor old lady, I think she'll die.

3: Poor old lady, she swallowed a spider.
It squirmed and wriggled and turned inside her.

1: She swallowed the spider to catch the fly.
I don't know why she swallowed a fly.

2: Poor old lady, I think she'll die.

4: Poor old lady, she swallowed a bird.
How absurd! She swallowed a bird.

3: She swallowed the bird to catch the spider.

1: She swallowed the spider to catch the fly,
I don't know why she swallowed a fly.

2: Poor old lady, I think she'll die.

5: Poor old lady, she swallowed a cat.
Think of that! She swallowed a cat.

4: She swallowed the cat to catch the bird.

3: She swallowed the bird to catch the spider.

1: She swallowed the spider to catch the fly,
I don't know why she swallowed the fly.

2: Poor old lady, I think she'll die.

6: Poor old lady, she swallowed a dog.
She went the whole hog when she swallowed the dog.

5: She swallowed the dog to catch the cat.

4: She swallowed the cat to catch the bird.

3: She swallowed the bird to catch the spider.

*(continued)*

From *Teaching Literacy in First Grade* by Diane Lapp, James Flood, Kelly Moore, and Maria Nichols. Copyright 2005 by The Guilford Press. Permission to photocopy this appendix is granted to purchasers of this book for personal use only (see copyright page for details).

1: She swallowed the spider to catch the fly,
   I don't know why she swallowed the fly.

2: Poor old lady, I think she'll die.

7: Poor old lady, she swallowed a cow.
   I don't know how she swallowed the cow.

6: She swallowed the cow to catch the dog,

5: She swallowed the dog to catch the cat,

4: She swallowed the cat to catch the bird,

3: She swallowed the bird to catch the spider,

1: She swallowed the spider to catch the fly.
   I don't know why she swallowed a fly.

2: Poor old lady, I think she'll die.

8: Poor old lady, she swallowed a horse.

All: She died, of course.

**APPENDIX 7.2.** Script for *The Water Cycle*

### Cast:

| | | |
|---|---|---|
| Sun (who is also the narrator) | Snowflake | Reservoir water 1 |
| Ocean water drop 1 | Glacier ice 1 | Reservoir water 2 |
| Ocean water drop 2 | Glacier ice 2 | Tap water 1 |
| Water vapor 1 | Stream water 1 | Tap water 2 |
| Water vapor 2 | Stream water 2 | Water in drainpipe |
| Cloud | River water 1 | Sewage processing plant |
| | River water 2 | |

SUN: Our story begins in the ocean. We are watching two drops of water.

OCEAN WATER DROP 1: It is getting hot here in the ocean. I don't think I can swim any more. I am not feeling well. Oh no! I'm feeling light and airy! I think the Sun is doing this to me.

SUN: I can't help it—I'm very hot and full of energy. That's what I do, and I do it so well, don't you think?

OCEAN WATER DROP 2: Yes, I must say that you do, but I think I'm getting dizzy and there isn't even a whirlpool here. I'm feeling so strange! I think I'll just float for a while—no more swimming for me. I need to take a break.

OCEAN WATER DROP 1: Uh oh! You're not floating in the water anymore, you're floating up in the air—you're not a drop of water either—you're water vapor now.

WATER VAPOR 1: What? What's water vapor? I am confused. Please explain.

WATER VAPOR 2: It's water, but it's a gas. You've evaporated and turned into a gas—and so have I. Let's fly up high! Come on!

WATER VAPOR 1: I feel like joining the others and forming a crowd.

WATER VAPOR 2: I think you mean a cloud, silly, not a crowd. Okay, let's condense.

WATER VAPOR 1: What does that mean? I am confused again.

WATER VAPOR 2: Condensing means that we'll change back into a liquid (water, of course). Then we'll be part of a beautiful cloud.

CLOUD: Okay, now we're a beautiful, fluffy cloud. Let's fly over the land and watch the billy goats. Take a look at those beautiful mountains! But now I'm feeling heavy and cold. I think I'm going to snow!

SNOWFLAKE 1: Hey, here is a riddle. What's got six arms and there's nothing exactly like it in the whole world?

SNOWFLAKE 2: Me—I'm so special. You, too, of course. We're both snowflakes. Hey, where are you going now? You keep changing.

SNOWFLAKE 1: I can't stop falling—you're falling too. But where are we going?

*(continued)*

From *Teaching Literacy in First Grade* by Diane Lapp, James Flood, Kelly Moore, and Maria Nichols. Copyright 2005 by The Guilford Press. Permission to photocopy this appendix is granted to purchasers of this book for personal use only (see copyright page for details).

SNOWFLAKE 2: Down. Down. Down.

SNOWFLAKE 1: Thanks—I knew that. It looks like we're taking a trip to the mountains. I hope you know how to ski. This should be fun!

SNOWFLAKE 2: Well, it looks like we're stuck on a glacier—I wonder why they're called rivers of ice.

GLACIER ICE 1: I'm getting crushed here. Now I'm ice—this is NOT my favorite part of the water cycle. UGH!!!!

GLACIER ICE 2: Believe it or not, we're only moving at about one foot a year. This is going to be soooooo boring—it's a long way to the bottom.

GLACIER ICE 1: You'd better get used to it, we're stuck on this glacier for a while. A long while.

SUN: A long, long, long time later, two very bored drops of water emerge from the bottom of the glacier. I haven't been much help to them lately.

STREAM WATER 1: Wow, I've finally melted!

STREAM WATER 2: Me too—I'm free at last. What a change, we were practically standing still, and now we're shooting the roaring rapids.

STREAM WATER 1: Whoa! Watch out for that rock! Oh . . . and over there. Watch out for that waterfall!

STREAM WATER 2: Ouch! I've had enough of this. Can we please go home now?

STREAM WATER 1: We don't have a home. At least we're out of the mountains. The water's getting so deep. What's going on here?

RIVER WATER 1: You can slow down now—we're in a river. And we're getting warmer and warmer.

RIVER WATER 2: I like this a lot. Not too fast and not too slow. It is just right!

RIVER WATER 1: Let's go down this side stream—it looks very clear and clean.

RESERVOIR WATER 1: Okay. We're in a reservoir now—we'll be flowing through huge pipes very soon—I have been here before.

RESERVOIR WATER 2: Here they are. It's dark and kind of spooky in these pipes. How do we get out of here? Help!

RESERVOIR WATER 1: Just go with the flow.

TAPWATER 1: There's a light at the end of the tap—we're in a sink now. Eew—that kid is brushing her teeth! Do you see her?

TAPWATER 2: I hope she doesn't drink us—it's really weird when that happens. I think it is kind of gross!

TAPWATER 2: Whew, that was a close call. We made it! Looks like we're whirlpooling down the drain. Hold your nose! This could smell pretty bad.

WATER IN DRAINPIPE: More dark pipes—but these pipes are really, really smelly. We must be in the sewer under the big city. Boy, do I need to take a bath now. I feel disgusting!

(*continued*)

**SEWAGE PROCESSING PLANT:** I heard that. I'm a sewage processing plant, you know? You've come to the right place. I'm so amazing that I can even give bath water a bath! Now you're all filtered and clean—just take that pipe to the sea. You look great!

**OCEAN WATER DROP 1:** Thank goodness! We're finally back in the ocean. You know, I've done this trip a million times, and every time it's different.

**OCEAN WATER DROP 2:** I was well water in Washington once.

**OCEAN WATER DROP 1:** Really? I was in a typhoon in Thailand twice.

**OCEAN WATER DROP 2:** I was rain in Rwanda. Lots of rain.

**OCEAN WATER DROP 1:** I was snow in Siberia. Boy, was it cold!

**OCEAN WATER DROP 2:** We've all been snow in Siberia. But I was in a puddle in Pakistan.

**OCEAN WATER DROP 1:** I was in a lake in Utah.

**OCEAN WATER DROP 2:** I was in a swamp in Switzerland.

**OCEAN WATER DROP 1:** No, you were not! There are no swamps in Switzerland. But a long, long time ago, I was sleet that fell on the snout of a T. rex.

**OCEAN WATER DROP 2:** You are a showoff. I rained on a plain in Spain, and I seeped through the soil and went into a cave, and was groundwater for 500 years.

**OCEAN WATER DROP 1:** Booooorrrrrring. Zzzzzzzzzzz!

**Sun:** Hi there! It's me again. Did you miss me? I know you did.

**OCEAN WATER DROP 1:** I feel so hot and dizzy! So, so hot!

**OCEAN WATER DROP 2:** Oh no, it's starting all over again!

**OCEAN WATER DROP 1:** I wonder where we'll go this time? Here we . . . . .

# CHAPTER 8
# TEACHING ENGLISH LANGUAGE LEARNERS

As the demographics in U.S. schools continue to change, there will be very few classrooms where English is the only language of the children (August & Hakuta, 1997; Faltis, 2001). Increasingly, classrooms are filled with children who are becoming literate in two or more languages. Some of the children are already bilingual, and some speak only their mother tongue, which in many cases is not English. As you begin to learn about your first graders, either before the school year begins or during the first few days after their arrival in your classroom, you will realize how important it is to make them feel comfortable from the first moments they are with you. What can you do to make sure they are warmly welcomed? Here are four suggestions:

1. Learn how to say "Hello," "Good morning," and "We are so happy that you'll be in our classroom this year" in the native language of your children. If your children's first language is Spanish, you might greet them with the following words: "Hola." "Buenos días." "Estamos muy contentos que estaras en nuestra clase este año."

2. Learn a song in another language, preferably in the native language of your English language learners (ELLs). During the first days of school you can teach the song to all of the children. "Frère Jacques" and "De Colores" are two favorites of first graders.

3. Have trade books that contain words from other languages ready for the children. You may also want to have books written in both languages in your library. If your children's first language is Spanish, you might have the following books ready: *El gato ensombrerado/The Cat in the Hat, Tren de carga/Cargo Train*; and *Abuelita Fina y sus sombrillas maravillosas/Grandma Fina and Her Wonderful Umbrellas.*

4. Invite the children's parents into your room so that they know how welcome they are. The children will sense that you value their home experiences.

## TIPS TO HELP CHILDREN SPEAK AND READ IN ENGLISH

You're probably somewhat apprehensive at this point, and you likely have many questions about your ability to meet the needs of your English language learning (ELL) students. Your most basic question right now probably is: "Help—what do I do?" We offer many suggestions throughout this chapter, but just remember these three tips and you'll soon have all your children on their way to speaking and reading in English:

1. Provide the children with good models of the English language. Make sure they are frequently paired with native English speakers so that they hear competent English on a daily basis.

2. Talk to your children every day. Make it a point to speak to each ELL child in a one-to-one situation at least once a day. Make sure that they are talking to you, too, as soon as they have learned a few words in English.

3. Use realia everywhere. Your mantra should be "Realia, realia, realia." Realia come in two main forms:

- *Visuals.* Have pictures or real objects of everything possible (bunnies, hot dogs, pizza, soccer balls, dolls, coin collections, playing cards, etc.) so that the children can make sense of the words they're hearing by seeing visuals that represent the vocabulary concepts they're learning.

- *Performance.* Act out all the new vocabulary words for the children. Slither, slide, pirouette, bump, fumble (a ball), tumble, fall, and jump for them.

Before discussing the development of an instructional plan, we offer a clarification of the terminology associated with ELL children (bilingual, immersion, etc.). The following is a brief review.

# TERMS ASSOCIATED WITH ENGLISH LANGUAGE LEARNERS

You'll hear many terms used to refer to English language learners: non-English proficient (NEP), limited English proficient (LEP), fluent English proficient (FEP), and second language learners (Faltis, 2001). We prefer the term *English language learners* because all the other terms, such as NEP and LEP, have negative connotations. Cummins (2000) and Faltis (2001) argue that these terms focus on what children cannot do rather than on what they can do and what they are capable of learning.

### Terms Used in ELL Education

Here's a quick glossary of terms that are frequently used to describe programs and teaching methods for English language learners.

➢ *Bilingualism*—is the ability to function in a second language in addition to one's home language.

➢ *Bilingual education*—is a process by which learning experiences provided in the home enable a person to function in a second language and culture in addition to the home language and culture. Bilingual education programs are usually divided into two types: transitional bilingual programs and dual-language programs. The goal of transitional bilingual programs is to assist the child in adapting to school and progressing with peers in all subject areas while learning English. The goal of dual-language programs is to help children develop competency in the native language as well as in the second language in every subject area.

## Terms and Programs Associated with English as a Second Language Education

> *English immersion*—ELLs are immersed solely in English contexts with no support in their home languages. The goal of English immersion is to develop English language and literacy skills, but the reality is that it is very difficult to learn a new language as well as learn literacy in a new language without support from one's home language (August & Hakuta, 1997).

> *TESOL*—teaching English to speakers of other languages.

> *ESL*—English as a second language. ESL teachers speak only English and work short-term (a year or less) with children who are learning English. ESL instruction frequently focuses on teaching children the basic English that they will need to survive in school and in the community.

# HOW CAN YOU ASSESS ELL CHILDREN'S STRENGTHS AND NEEDS?

Just as you have thought about assessment as the initial step in developing your instructional plan for each of your English-speaking children, so too will you have to think about using assessment data to help you instruct your ELL children. For the children who come to your classroom with no English on the first day they arrive from a country where English is not the native language, it is important to get a sense of what they can do in their first language.

Your judgment will be one of the most important and accurate measures of how well your students' oral language is developing. To obtain this information, you'll have to observe such a child intently, and you'll have to find a speaker of the child's language (perhaps a parent) who can give some insights into the basic skills of the child—for example, does the child know letters of the alphabet (if the Roman alphabet is used in the native language)? Does the child have a sense of story? Has the child begun rudimentary decoding? Does the child draw or write?

## Student Oral Language Observation Matrix

As a first step we recommend using skills and strategy checklists, story retellings, and student self-assessment to better understand each student's language performance. One such measure is the Student Oral Language Observation Matrix (SOLOM; see Figure 8.1), which was developed by the California State Department of Education.

Student's Last Name _____ Student's First Name _____ 0 ___ ID# ___

| | 1 | 2 | 3 | 4 | 5 |
|---|---|---|---|---|---|
| Comprehension | Cannot understand even simple conversation | Has great difficulty following everyday social conversation even when spoken slowly with frequent repetitions | Understands most of what is said at slower-than-normal speed with repetitions | Understands nearly everything at normal speed, although occasional repetitions may be necessary | Understands everyday conversation and normal classroom discussion without difficulty |
| Fluency | Speech is so halting and fragmentary that conversation is virtually impossible | Usually hesitant; often forced into silence by language limitations | Everyday conversation and classroom discussion frequently disrupted by the student's search for the correct manner of expression | Everyday conversation and classroom discussion generally fluent, with occasional lapses while the student searches for the correct manner of expression | Everyday conversation and classroom discussion fluent and effortless, approximating that of a native speaker |
| Vocabulary | Vocabulary limitations so extreme that conversation is virtually impossible | Difficult to understand due to misuse of words and very limited vocabulary | Frequently uses the wrong words; conversation somewhat limited because of inadequate vocabulary | Occasionally uses inappropriate items and/or must rephrase ideas due to limited vocabulary | Use of vocabulary and idioms approximates that of a native speaker |
| Pronounciation | Pronunciation problems are so severe that speech is virtually unintelligible | Difficult to understand because of pronunciation problems; must frequently repeat in order to be understood | Pronunciation problems necessitate concentration on the part of the listener and occasionally lead to misunderstanding | Always intelligible, though one is conscious of a definite accent and occasional inappropriate intonation pattern | Pronunciation and intonation approximate those of a native speaker |
| Grammar | Errors in grammar and word order so severe that speech is virtually unintelligible | Difficult to understand due to errors in grammar and word order; must often rephrase and/or restrict speech to basic patterns | Frequent errors in grammar and word order do not obscure meaning | Occasional errors in grammar and/or word order do not obscure meaning | Grammar and word order approximate those of a native speaker |

**FIGURE 8.1.** SOLOM: Student Oral Language Observation Matrix. The SOLOM was developed by the San Jose Area Bilingual Consortium and has undergone revisions by the California Department of Education. It is in the public domain and can be copied and adapted.

The SOLOM can be easily used throughout the year as you observe students using language in authentic classroom situations. We find the SOLOM quite easy to use and very informative, because the children are not asked to converse in a stressful test-like situation, and cumulative observations can be recorded.

### Steps toward English Language Proficiency

You can use Figures 8.2 and 8.3 to record your children's progress. After assessing with the SOLOM, note where your children are on the developmental chart. It is intended to help you see where your children are currently and where they will be in "no time at all" with your help.

*Overview*

The SOLOM provides five scales for rating key dimensions of language proficiency. Each of these scales may be rated from zero to five, yielding a total score between 0 and 25. The key dimensions are:

1. Comprehension
2. Fluency
3. Vocabulary
4. Pronunciation
5. Grammar

*Administration and Scoring*

Persons who are native speakers of English and who are familiar with the student to be rated should use the SOLOM. Ideally, the classroom teacher will rate the English proficiency of a student after at least a few weeks of instruction. There is no test to administer; rather, the teacher needs a few quiet moments to reflect on the language skill of a given student, selecting the SOLOM description which most closely matches the current listening and speaking proficiency of that student in each of the five language proficiency dimensions.

The number at the top of each column on the SOLOM card determines the point value of each box checked in that column. If a student's English ability is less than the description with a point value of one, the teacher should assign a zero rating for the applicable section. The teacher then enters the score for each category and the total of the five categories on the scoring card of the SOLOM (Figure 8.2). The teacher also must enter the date, school, and his or her name in the corresponding sections on the reverse side of the SOLOM scoring card.

*Required and Optional Uses*

The SOLOM rating (see Figure 8.3) is to be combined with results of measures of English reading and writing proficiency to determine a student's overall English

| Grade | Date | School | Teacher | Comprehension | Fluency | Vocabulary | Pronunciation | Grammar | Total |
|---|---|---|---|---|---|---|---|---|---|
| K | | | | | | | | | |
| 1 | | | | | | | | | |
| 3 | | | | | | | | | |
| 2 | | | | | | | | | |
| 4 | | | | | | | | | |
| 5 | | | | | | | | | |
| 6 | | | | | | | | | |
| 7 | | | | | | | | | |
| 8 | | | | | | | | | |
| 9 | | | | | | | | | |
| 10 | | | | | | | | | |
| 11 | | | | | | | | | |

**FIGURE 8.2.** Scoring card for the SOLOM.

| Total SOLOM score | Speaking/listening proficiency level |
|:---:|:---:|
| 0–7 | Beginning |
| 8–12 | Early intermediate |
| 13–18 | Intermediate |
| 19–22 | Early advanced |
| 23–25 | Advanced |

**FIGURE 8.3.** Rating scale for the SOLOM.

language proficiency level, and whether the student has achieved a "good working knowledge of English." Many school districts require the SOLOM to be administered only once each spring (and the total score entered on the *third* report card scan sheet each year) as part of the English learner annual assessment. Trained teachers have the *option* of using the SOLOM rating at additional times for additional purposes, such as to group or regroup students for English language development (ELD) lessons, to monitor student progress in oral English skills, and to target specific areas for instructional focus.

### English Language Proficiency Levels (Elementary)

On the SOLOM rating scale English learners range in English language proficiency from "beginning" to "advanced." The following descriptions provide general characteristics of students at each stage related to all aspects of language development. The ELD standards provide a more detailed description of expectations for each level. *All* English learner students must be provided with daily English language development instruction appropriate to their respective proficiency levels.

BEGINNING

At the beginning level, students first develop receptive language and demonstrate comprehension using gestures or other physical actions. Students then begin to produce single words or simple, repetitive phrases to communicate basic needs. Students begin to develop early (age-appropriate) literacy skills, such as recognizing the sounds of the English language (e.g., identifying rhyme); reading highly familiar vocabulary presented in the context of a story or game; responding to or retelling familiar stories using gestures, drawings, or simple vocabulary; copying English letters or familiar words (e.g., from word walls or labels); and writing or copying simple sentences related to a group-generated story or a familiar, predictable text. Students at this level must receive focused, small-group ELD instruction that is appropriate to their proficiency level, on a daily basis.

### EARLY INTERMEDIATE

At the early intermediate level, students communicate their basic needs and ideas by speaking in phrases and short sentences. English fluency is increasing, and students are increasingly able to understand and respond to a wider range of questions and interactions; however, speech errors may still be common. Speech may sound "telegraphic" (e.g., "I go home now." or "Teacher, what time lunch?"). Students continue to develop (age-appropriate) early literacy in English. Students continue to develop phonemic awareness in English, and begin to apply understanding of the English language and sound system to literacy activities such as reading and discussing simple patterned and decodable texts. They also begin writing or contributing to highly contextualized self- or group-generated stories. Written language often reflects students' oral language in terms of errors in language usage, structure, or convention, or may include only key known words or phrases. Students at this level must receive focused small-group ELD instruction that is appropriate to their proficiency level on a daily basis.

### INTERMEDIATE

At the intermediate level, Students begin to have a command of conversational English and engage in conversations that produce full sentences and narratives. They exhibit increasing use of English language related to academic tasks and are able to use English to express more complex thoughts. Although students are beginning to sound fluent in English, speech and other grammatical errors may still be common, but they rarely obscure meaning. Students are moving toward grade-level standards in literacy. They are able to produce and identify the sounds of English as well as apply this understanding to familiar, highly contextualized reading and writing tasks. Students are able to read and write with increased fluency on familiar topics. Students at this level must receive focused, small-group ELD instruction that is appropriate to their proficiency level on a daily basis.

### EARLY ADVANCED

At the early advanced level, students have a command of conversational English and are able to produce full sentences and narratives. They are developing close to native-like proficiency with language related to conversational as well as academic tasks. Speech and grammatical errors may still appear, but they rarely interfere with communication. Students are approaching grade-level standards in reading and writing. While relying heavily on context and prior knowledge to obtain meaning from print, students apply, with increasing consistency, an understanding of English language structure and usage in a wider variety of literacy needs. Students at this level must receive early-advanced ELD instruction, including intensive English writing instruction and support on a daily basis in small-group settings.

ADVANCED

At the advanced level, students have full command of conversational English and utilize language related to academic tasks approximating that of native speakers of English. Students approximate grade-level standards in reading and writing. Students participate in age-appropriate, increasingly complex and varied literacy tasks and are able to participate fully in all academic subjects. Students at this level must receive advanced ELD instruction, including intensive English writing instruction and support, on a daily basis in small-group settings until they meet *all* criteria for redesignation and are officially redesignated as fluent English proficient.

## What Other Assessments Can Provide Insights about a Child's Language Development?

We recommend that you keep careful notes on your ELL children's attempts at reading in English. Consult the assessment instruments we discussed in Chapters 2, 3, 4, and 5, including the story retelling guide. Ask your children to draw and write as well as they can so that you can obtain information about their writing skills.

Two other assessments that can provide you with additional insights about a child's language use are checklists and anecdotal records.

### Checklists

Checklists are helpful because you can tailor them to assess whichever factors you wish to evaluate. They are also easy to use because the behaviors can just be checked off. When using them, be sure to include exactly what you wish to observe and to leave space for any descriptions you may want to include. For example, Chapter 1 discusses the functions of language. You may want to include some of this information in a checklist similar to the one shown in Figure 8.4, which can be used during on-the-spot observations of *language functions*, or you may decide to make a checklist for each function. You may also wish to make checklists of *children's language forms*, which include vocabulary, sentence structure, phonology, morphology, and discourse, or their performance in the *social situations* in which they engage in language interchanges (e.g., partner work, centers, group and individual presentations).

### Anecdotal Records

An *anecdotal report*, which requires more time and the noting of more details, is also very helpful in assessing language performance because it allows for an in-depth recording of what you observed during a specific language event. You record as you observe and interpret the flow of the interaction. Transcriptions should include quotes from the participants. An anecdotal report provides a fuller account

Name: _AnnaMaria_

| Function | | Notes |
|---|---|---|
| | | CONTROLLING |
| States wants | | When encouraged |
| Offers assistance | ✓ | Without hesitation |
| Commands | ✓ | Without being offensive |
| Suggests | | Needs to be encouraged |
| Formulates ideas | | Hesitates when speaking with more than one other person |
| Permits | ✓ | |
| States intentions | | Seldom |
| Asks questions | | When encouraged |
| Makes promises | ✓ | |
| Gives warnings | | Seldom |
| Identifies prohibitions | ✓ | |
| Notes conditions | ✓ | |
| Makes contracts | | |
| Agrees | | |
| Refuses | | |
| Rejects | ✓ | |
| Justifies | | |
| Tells jokes | | |
| | | FEELING |
| Rejects | | |
| Exclaims | ✓ | |
| Expresses state of mind/attitude | | |
| Inquires about others' state of mind/attitude | | |
| Taunts | ✓ | Never |
| Challenges | | |
| Approves | | |
| Disapproves | | |
| Cajoles | | |
| Congratulates | | |
| Commiserates | ✓ | |

(continued)

**FIGURE 8.4.** Checklist: Functions of language.

| Function | | Notes |
|---|---|---|
| Offers endearing statements | ✓ | |
| Blames | ✓ | |
| Questions accusations | | |
| Commands | | |
| Apologizes | | |
| Demands apologies | | Nonverbally |
| Disagrees | | Without offending |
| Evades | | |
| Offers justification | | |
| Questions justification | | |
| INFORMING | | |
| Justifies | | |
| States condition | | |
| Rejects | | |
| Evades | | |
| Denies | | When friends do so |
| Affirms | | |
| Responds | | |
| Questions | | |
| RITUALIZING | | |
| Offers greetings | | |
| States farewells | | |
| Takes conversation turns | | |
| Calls to others | | |
| Replies | | |
| Repeats | | |
| Introduces others | | |
| Welcomes | | |
| Acknowledges status | | |
| IMAGINATIVE | | |
| Expressive | | |
| Offers commentary | | |

**FIGURE 8.4.** *(continued)*

of the interaction and of your on-the-spot analysis. This narrative report provides a snapshot of a language interchange that can be reviewed often. Because of the quick pace and the complexity of the interactions, we often tape-record such exchanges. However, if the children become aware of the recorder, their interactions become stifled at first. Over time they get very used to the idea that we are recording so that we can offer them better instruction. They know that we are a community trying to get smarter.

## HOW IS A SECOND LANGUAGE ACQUIRED AND DEVELOPED?

Before we answer this question, you probably should know that some researchers maintain that it takes between 5 and 7 years to function effectively in a second language (Collier, 1995; Perogy & Boyle, 1997); other researchers contend that the figure is really closer to 10 to 12 years. So, take a deep breath, you're not responsible for creating a proficient English language speaker during first grade. But you can certainly get English language learners on the right road to literacy learning.

As children learn a second language, they rely heavily on the store of knowledge in their first language. Children who have rich vocabularies and who have begun to read and write in their first language acquire English language skills relatively quickly. However, children who do not have previous experiences with reading and writing will have to be introduced to the foundations of literacy, including concepts of print, story structures, and the relationship between oral and written language and writing.

It may be helpful to think about the skills of your ELL children and make note of them on a chart similar to that in Figure 8.5, which illustrates the strengths and needs of five students whose native language is Spanish.

|        | **Anna**       | **Hector**         | **Enrique**    | **Lourdes**       | **Leo**            |
|--------|----------------|--------------------|----------------|-------------------|--------------------|
| Speaks | Spanish —      | Spanish English    | Spanish —      | Spanish English   | Spanish English    |
| Reads  | — —            | — —                | Spanish —      | — English         | Spanish English    |
| Writes | — —            | — —                | Spanish —      | — English         | Spanish English    |

**FIGURE 8.5.** Students' language proficiencies.

As you've noticed, Enrique, Lourdes, and Leo have begun reading and writing in at least one language, so their transition to the other language will be quicker than Anna's and Hector's, because they do not have the foundation skills in either language.

All children seem to pass through a period called *interlanguage*, which is an intermediate linguistic stage at which children are acquiring a more formal version of the new language. During this stage they overgeneralize rules from the new language, which can make some of their sentences sound awkward—for example, "He asked me that should he go." This complex idea has been syntactically scrambled as the child is learning about the appropriate ways to use the word "if." His thinking is clear, but his knowledge of English syntax is still developing. The child who uttered this sentence is well on his way to becoming proficient in English; he just needs time, practice, and large amounts of English modeled for him by proficient speakers.

## CULTURAL PATTERNS ACROSS LANGUAGES

Jim Gee (1996) maintains that different cultural groups have unique norms, values, beliefs, behaviors and ways of acting and interacting. Deschenes, Cuban, and Tyack (2001) note that children who come to middle-class schools designed around a set of middle-class Anglo cultural norms often feel uncomfortable and isolated because they do not know the "rules" of the new culture's behaviors. We need to be aware of these differences so that we don't misinterpret or misjudge our ELL students' behaviors or those of our students who come to school as speakers of African American Vernacular English (AAVE). It's important to remember that their literacy-related behaviors are not deficient. Their literacy practices at home just differ from the practices of our classroom. As teachers, we need to patiently help children explore the new environment as they acquire skills that help them to become more literate.

All children who come to our classrooms deserve the potential benefits of high expectations. Our ELL and bidialectic students who speak AAVE need to be held to high expectations in their journey to English proficiency.

## HOW CAN YOU TEACH YOUR ELL STUDENTS TO READ AND WRITE ENGLISH?

As we answer this question, "the big question," we discuss the physical classroom environment, materials, grouping, and lessons.

## Physical Classroom Environment

As discussed in Chapter 1, just as the classroom must be physically and emotionally comfortable for a native speaker, it must also be comfortable for ELL children. Your room should be filled with print, books, and artifacts that are familiar to the ELL child.

### Labeling Objects in Two Languages

Objects in your room should be labeled in English and in the first language of your students. For example, Figure 8.6 lists in Spanish and English the names of common objects you may have in your room.

### Posting Guidelines, Rules, and Directions in Two Languages

The rules and routines of the classroom should also be posted in both languages to help students and parents. It is not rare for a parent to be reticent to ask teachers for clarification of directions/instructions for an assignment or a time when something will occur, such as the departure time for a field trip. When this information is posted in both English and the parent's language, it helps avoid confusion, and it shows respect for the parents.

### Creating Word Walls in Two Languages

Some first-grade teachers have found it very effective to post their word wall list in both languages, especially in biliteracy classrooms. In addition to word study word walls, you may want to include word walls for common words that children will need throughout the year. In Figures 8.7–8.9, we have included words for the days of the week, months of the year, and numbers from 1 to 50 in English and Spanish.

```
the chair—la silla
the table—la mesa
the desk—el pupitre
the door—la puerta
the window—la ventana
the overhead projector—el proyector
the transparency—la transparencia
the marker—el plumón
the pencil—el lápiz
the pen—la pluma
the backpack—la mochila
the board—el pizarrón
the clock—el reloj
the paper—el papel
the play area—el área de recreo
recess—la hora de recreo
the centers—los centros
the classroom library—la biblioteca de la clase
the painting/art area—el área de la pintura/del arte
the paint brush—el cepillo de pintar
the stage—el ataje, El teatro
the bookcase—el estante
the teacher's desk—el escritorio
the easel—el caballete
the book—el libro
the folder—la carpeta
the eraser—el borrador
```

**FIGURE 8.6.** Classroom items/Objetos de la clase.

From *Teaching Literacy in First Grade* by Diane Lapp, James Flood, Kelly Moore, and Maria Nichols. Copyright 2005 by The Guilford Press. Permission to photocopy this figure is granted to purchasers of this book for personal use only (see copyright page for details).

```
Monday—el lunes
Tuesday—el martes
Wednesday—el miércoles
Thursday—el jueves
Friday—el viernes
Saturday—el sábado
Sunday—el domingo
```

**FIGURE 8.7.** Days of the week/Días de la semana.

From *Teaching Literacy in First Grade* by Diane Lapp, James Flood, Kelly Moore, and Maria Nichols. Copyright 2005 by The Guilford Press. Permission to photocopy this figure is granted to purchasers of this book for personal use only (see copyright page for details).

| | |
|---|---|
| January—enero | July—julio |
| February—febrero | August—agosto |
| March—marzo | September—septiembre |
| April—abril | October—octubre |
| May—mayo | November—noviembre |
| June—junio | December—diciembre |

**FIGURE 8.8.** Months of the year/Meses del año.

From *Teaching Literacy in First Grade* by Diane Lapp, James Flood, Kelly Moore, and Maria Nichols. Copyright 2005 by The Guilford Press. Permission to photocopy this figure is granted to purchasers of this book for personal use only (see copyright page for details).

| | | |
|---|---|---|
| One—Uno | Twenty-one—veintiuno | Forty-one—cuarenta y uno |
| Two—dos | Twenty-two—veintidós | Forty-two—cuarenta y dos |
| Three—tres | Twenty-three—veintitrés | Forty-three—cuarenta y tres |
| Four—cuatro | Twenty-four—veinticuatro | Forty-four—cuarenta y cuatro |
| Five—cinco | Twenty-five—veinticinco | Forty-five—cuarenta y cinco |
| Six—seis | Twenty-six—veintiséis | Forty-six—cuarenta y seis |
| Seven—siete | Twenty-seven—veintisiete | Forty-seven—cuarenta y siete |
| Eight—ocho | Twenty-eight—veintiocho | Forty-eight—cuarenta y ocho |
| Nine—nueve | Twenty-nine—veintinueve | Forty-nine—cuarenta y nueve |
| Ten—diez | Thirty—treinta | Fifty—cincuenta |
| Eleven—once | Thirty-one—treinta y uno | |
| Twelve—doce | Thirty-two—treinta y dos | |
| Thirteen—trece | Thirty-three—treinta y tres | |
| Fourteen—catorce | Thirty-four—treinta y cuatro | |
| Fifteen—quince | Thirty-five—treinta y cinco | |
| Sixteen—dieciséis | Thirty-six—treinta y seis | |
| Seventeen—diecisiete | Thirty-seven—treinta y siete | |
| Eighteen—dieciocho | Thirty-eight—treinta y ocho | |
| Nineteen—diecinueve | Thirty-nine—treinta y nueve | |
| Twenty—veinte | Forty—cuarenta | |

**FIGURE 8.9.** Numbers from one to fifty/Los números del uno hasta cincuenta.

From *Teaching Literacy in First Grade* by Diane Lapp, James Flood, Kelly Moore, and Maria Nichols. Copyright 2005 by The Guilford Press. Permission to photocopy this figure is granted to purchasers of this book for personal use only (see copyright page for details).

- *Cada niño/Every Child: A Bilingual Songbook for Kids* by Tish Hinojosa. Ages 3–8.
- *Calling the Doves/El canto de las palomas* by Juan Felipe Herrera. Ages 4–8.
- *The Christmas Gift/El regalo de Navidad* by Francisco Jiménez. Ages 4–8.
- *Cuckoo: A Mexican Folktale/Cucu: Un cuento folklórico mexicano* by Lois Ehlert; translated by Gloria de Aragon Andujar. Ages 3–7.
- *Diego* by Jeanette Winter. Ages 6–10.
- *From the Bellybutton of the Moon and Other Summer Poems/Del ombligo de la luna y otros poemas de verano* by Francisco X. Alarcon. Ages 5–9.
- *Gathering the Sun: An Alphabet in Spanish and English* by Alma Flor Ada; translated by Rosa Zubizarreta. Ages 5–10.
- *Hairs/Pelitos* by Sandra Cisneros. Ages 3–7.
- *I Love Saturdays Y domingos* by Alma Flor Ada. Ages 4–8.
- *In My Family/En mi familia* by Carmen Lomas Garza with Harriet Rohmer; edited by David Schecter; translated by Francisco X. Alarcon. Age 5 and older.
- *¡Jump, Frog, Jump!/¡Salta, ranita, salta!* by Robert Kalan.
- *Listen to the Desert/Oye al desierto* by Pat Mora. Ages 4–7.
- *Modestita's Gift: A Christmas Story/El regalo de Modestita: Una historia para la Navidad* by Inez Torres Davis. Ages 6–8.
- *My Very Own Room/Mi propio cuartito* by Amada Irma Perez. Ages 5–8.
- *This House Is Made of Mud/Esta casa está hecha de lodo* by Ken Buchanan. Ages 5–10.
- *The Tortilla Factory/La Tortilleriá* by Gary Paulsen.
- *Tortillas and Lullabies/Tortillas y cancioncitas* by Lynn Reiser; coordinated and translated by Rebecca Hart. Ages 4–8.
- *Tortillitas para mamá: And Other Nursery Rhymes/Spanish and English* by Margot Griego, Betsy L. Bucks, Sharon S. Gilbert, & Laurel H. Kimball. Ages 5–8.
- *Xochitl and the Flowers/Xochitl, la niña de las flores* by Jorge Argueta. Ages 5–10.

**FIGURE 8.10.** Bilingual children's books written in English and Spanish.

## Materials

*Multicultural Literature*

Children need to see themselves in books; they need to see families like their own families, with rituals, games, and routines that represent their culture. Trade books that are written in two languages should be available to your ELL children. Figures 8.10 and 8.11 list examples of books written in English and Spanish that you may want to include in your classroom library. *Brown Bear, Brown Bear, What Do You See?* by Bill Martin Jr. is available through Mantra Lingua Ltd. in Albanian, Arabic, Bengali, Chinese, Farsi, Guarati, Hindi, Kurdish, Somali, Turkish, Vietnamese, and Yoruba. *Goldilocks and the Three Bears* retold by Kate Clynes is available through Mantra Lingua Ltd. in Albanian, Arabic, Bengali, Chinese, Farsi, French, German, Polish, Russian, Spanish, and Turkish.

- *Así vamos a la escuela* by Edith Baer. Ages 5–8.
- *La primera nevada de Clifford* by Norman Bridwell. Ages 4–7.
- *Sonidos y ritmos* by Susana Dultzin Dubín. Ages 5–8.
- *¡Salta, ranita, salta!* by Robert Kalan. Ages 5–7.
- *El nuevo bébe* by Mercer Mayer. Ages 4–7.
- *Yo solito* by Mercer Mayer. Ages 4–7.
- *Cachorritos* by Jan Pfloog. Ages 3–6.
- *El lobo y los siete cabritos* by Roser Capdevila I Valls. Ages 4–6.
- *Ricitos de oro y los tres osos* by Marta Mata. Ages 4–6.

**FIGURE 8.11.** Spanish editions of popular children's books.

### Wordless Picture Books

Wordless picture books have a host of benefits for your ELL students. First, stories can be told in either or both languages; second, wordless picture books help children to gain confidence with the concepts of story because they are not constrained to generate a specific story in their new second language; and third, wordless books help with oral language development—that is, they allow the child to talk freely without worrying about being "right" on every word or idea. The following are excellent wordless books for first graders:

> *Tuesday* by David Wiesner
> *Have You Seen My Duckling?* by Nancy Tafuri
> *Pancakes for Breakfast* by Tomie dePaola

### Familiar Folktales, Fables, and Fairy Tales in Spanish and English

You might want to create class stories, rewritten versions of classics, in the children's native language or in English. The rewritten versions can be illustrated by the children and become permanent entries in your classroom library. Be sure to laminate the stories so that they will last for years. Appendix 8.1 includes two classics, *Goldilocks and the Three Bears* and *Cinderella*, which have been translated into Spanish by Julie Jacobson.

### Grouping for Instruction

The best tip we can offer is to make sure that your ELL students aren't segregated into groups that consist exclusively of ELL children of several languages or into single-language ELL groups, such as a few Vietnamese speakers who are grouped together for instruction without English language models. ELL children need to be with English speakers all day. Although it might seem best to have children segregated by language for some activities like guided reading, this should be done infrequently because it limits the ELL children's chances of advancing in their English skills.

## Language Lessons

ELL children have specific needs in language learning that many native speakers don't have. We include a special lesson here because it deals with the unique needs of ELL children; this lesson focuses on developing syntax. Most native-speaking first-graders have little difficulty with basic syntactic structures like placing adjectives before nouns (pretty dog), but students with a Spanish language background often need some work in this area. In the following lesson, developed by Kevin Jones, ELL students are directly instructed in English syntax through an activity called "Sentence Operation," which has been published in *Teaching Writing* (San Diego: Academic Professional Development, 2004).

Sentence Operation is based on a strategy originally designed by Herrell (2000). This activity helps students understand the grammatical structure of written English. The focus is on the word order of sentences that may differ from the native language English language learners may use at home. This strategy is used to (1) allow students an opportunity to manipulate difficult sentences, helping to reinforce English syntax rules, (2) help students practice English skills they may be having trouble with, and (3) provide an opportunity to dissect hard-to-understand text. The lesson has the following nine steps:

1. Find a sentence in which one of your students has incorrectly placed an adjective. The sentence may be one used in spoken English, a confusing sentence found while reading, or a selected piece of a student's writing.

2. Write the sentence on a long strip of paper. Keep in mind that the sentence will be cut into pieces to show how to order the words correctly in the sentence. Leave enough room between the words so that they can be cut apart.

3. Read the sentence aloud to your students. An example of such a sentence is "My grandpa has a truck green."

4. Cut the strip of paper so that each word fits into a separate pocket of a pocket chart or can be hung from clips on the chalkboard.

| My | grandpa | has | a | truck | green |

5. Arrange the words in the sentence correctly so that the sentence reads "My grandpa has a green truck."

6. Tell the students that this is the correct way the sentence should be ordered in English.

7. Ask the students to explain why the word "green" was moved. If they struggle with this, explain to them that "green" is an adjective. An adjective describes

a noun (or pronoun), and adjectives go before nouns. Mention that this is different from the Spanish language.

**8.** Create more sentences with similar types of syntax errors and "fix" these with your students.

- My brother has a car dirty.
- Our car has a tire flat.
- We live in a house green.
- My dog white is funny.
- I have eyes brown.

**9.** Have the students practice writing the sentences on a sentence strip, allowing time to cut the words apart and manipulate their orders in front of the whole class.

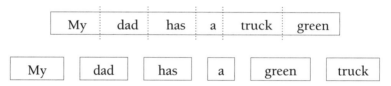

## LOOKING TOWARD THE FUTURE

ELL and AAVE children need time practicing speaking standard. English as well as a great deal of structured, robust instruction. Our classrooms must be places where our ELL children are surrounded with excellent models of English that they can emulate. Our materials must be carefully chosen to introduce them to the best-written works available. They must come to rooms where their abilities are championed and their journey toward English proficiency is a joy for everyone.

**APPENDIX 8.1.** Bilingual Versions of *Goldilocks and the Three Bears* and *Cinderella*

### *Ricitos de Oro/Goldilocks and the Three Bears*

En una ciudad, cerca del bosque, vivía con sus padres una niña a quien todos llamaban Ricitos de Oro.

In a city, near the forest, there lived with her parents a little girl whom everyone called Goldilocks.

Un día, cuando paseaba, descubrió una casita que no había visto antes.

One day, when she was walking, she discovered a little house that she had never seen before.

Ricitos de Oro era niña muy curiosa y pronto olvidó los consejos que su mamá le había dado, como:

Goldilocks was very curious girl and soon forgot the advice her mother had given to her, such as:

"No se debe entrar en una casa a la que no hemos sido invitados," o "Es de muy mala educación espiar a través de la cerradura de las puertas."

"We should never enter a house where we have not been invited," or "It is very bad manners to spy through the locks on doors."

Pero, esto fue exactamente lo que hizo.

But that is exactly what she did.

Primero miró por la ventana y despúes miró por la cerradura.

First she looked through the window, and then she peered through the lock.

No se veía a nadie.

She didn't see anyone.

Entonces empujó despacito la puerta, que no estaba cerrada, y entró de puntitas.

Then she pushed the door open very slowly, and entered tip-toeing.

Se trataba de una casa muy pequeñita.

It was a very small house.

Sobre la pared estaban colgados tres relojes: uno grande, otro mediano, y el tercero más pequeño.

On the wall there were hung three clocks, one big, another medium, and the third very small.

Tac tac, tac tac! sonaba el reloj grande.

Tock tock, tock tock sounded the big clock.

Tic tac, tic tac! sonaba el mediano.

Tick tock, tick tock sounded the medium-sized clock.

Tic tic, tic tic! sonaba el pequeño.

Tick tick, tick tick sounded the small one.

En el comedor, Ricitos de Oro vio sobre la mesa tres platos: uno grande, uno mediano y un pequeñito, en los que alguien había servido una rica sopa, que además tenía un olor delicioso.

In the dining room, Goldilocks saw three bowls on the table: one big one, one medium-sized one, and one little one, into which someone had served a rich soup that had a very delicious smell.

*(continued)*

"Probaré solo un poquito," dijo la pequeña muchacha.

"I will taste just a little bit," said the little girl.

Sin pensarlo dos veces metió la cuchara en el plato más grande.

Without a second thought she put the spoon into the biggest bowl.

"¡Ay! Está muy caliente!"

"Oh! This is too hot!"

Despúes probó la sopa del plato mediano.

Then she tried the soup in the middle-sized bowl.

"¡Uf! ¡Esta sopa está muy fría!"

"Ooo! This is too cold!"

Finalmente metió una cucharita en el plato pequeño.

Finally she put a little spoon in the smallest bowl.

"¡Mmmmm! ¡Esta sopa está muy buena! ¡Tal como a mi me gusta!"

"Mmmm! This is very good! Just as I like it!"

Y Ricitos de Oro comió toda la sopa del plato más pequeño.

And Goldilocks ate all the soup from the smallest bowl.

Una vez satisfecho su apetito, Ricitos de Oro decidió revisar el resto de la casita.

Once her appetite was satisfied, Goldilocks decided to look around the rest of the little house.

¡Qué raro! ¡En esta casa todo lo que veo está de tres en tres!

"How strange! In this house everything I see is in threes."

Tres abrigos, tres sombreros, y también, bien alineadas contra la pared, tres sillas: una grande, una mediana y una pequeña.

Three coats, three hats, and also, very well lined up against the wall, three chairs: one big one, one medium-sized chair, and a little one."

Ricitos de Oro trató de sentarse en la silla grande.

Goldilocks tried to sit in the big chair.

"¡Ah! ¡Está muy alta!"

"Oh! This is too high!"

Entonces se sentó en la mediana.

Then she sat in the medium-sized one.

"¡Tampoco! ¡Está muy dura!"

"Not this one either! It's very hard!"

Finalmente, se sentó en la más pequeña de las tres.

Finally, she sat in the smallest of the three.

"¡Mmm! ¡Muy cómoda! ¡Como a mi me gusta!"

"Mmm! Very comfortable! Just as I like it!"

(*continued*)

Ricitos de Oro empezó a balancearse y . . . de repente, ¡Choque!

Goldilocks began to balance herself and . . . suddenly, Crash!

¡Se rompió la sillita!

The little chair broke!

Afortunadamente, Ricitos de Oro no se lastimó.

Fortunately, Goldilocks did not hurt herself.

Después jugó un poco con las cosas que había dentro de la casa, y dejó un gran desorden por todos lados.

Then she played with a few things that had been inside the house, and left them in a mess everywhere.

Cuando se cansó de jugar, subió por las escaleras y descubrió una habitación en donde habían tres camas: una grande, una mediana, y una pequeña.

When she got tired of playing, she climbed up the stairs and discovered a room where there were three beds: a big bed, a medium-sized one, and a little baby bed.

Como quería descansar un poco trató de subir a la cama grande:

Because she wanted to rest a little, she tried to climb up to the big bed.

"¡Uf! ¡Está muy alta!"

"Ooo! This is too big!"

Luego se tendió en la mediana:

Then she tried the medium-sized bed.

"¡Ay! ¡Qué dura está!"

"Oh! How hard this is!"

Al final, se acostó en la pequeña:

Finally, she lay down on the smallest bed.

"¡Vaya . . . ! ¡Esta sí que es muy cómoda!"

"Wonderful! Oh, this is very comfortable!"

"¡Exactamente como a mi me gusta!"

"Just as I like it!"

Y entonces Ricitos de Oro se quedó completamente dormida.

And Goldilocks fell fast asleep.

Al poco rato regresaron los habitantes de la casa . . . eran tres osos que habían ido a pasear por el bosque antes de la hora de la cena.

A little while later, the three bears, who had gone out for a walk through the forest before eating their dinner, returned home.

"¡Alguien ha entrado en nuestra casa!" dijo Papá Oso con su gruesa voz.

"Someone has come into our house!" said Papa Bear with a very rough voice.

(*continued*)

"¡Alguien ha desordenado todo!" dijo Mamá Osa.

"Someone has messed up everything!" said Mama Bear.

"¡Alguien ha estado jugando con mis juguetes!" dijo el osito casi llorando.

"Someone has been playing with my toys!" said the baby bear, almost crying.

Muy inquietos los tres osos se acercaron a la mesa.

Very anxiously the three bears went over to the table.

"¡Alguien ha probado mi sopa!" dijo Papá Oso.

"Someone has tasted my soup!" said Papa Bear.

"¡Alguien ha probado también mi sopa!" dijo Mamá Osa.

"Someone has eaten my soup too!" said Mother Bear.

"¡Pues alguien se ha comido toda mi sopa y ya no hay más! dijo el osito con su voz de bebé.

"Well, someone has eaten all my soup and it's all gone!" said the baby bear with his little voice.

Muy enojados, los tres osos contemplaron sus sillas.

Very angry, the three bears looked at their chairs.

"¡Alguien se ha sentado en mi silla!" dijo el papá oso.

"Someone has sat in my chair!" said the papa bear.

"¡Alguien se ha sentado también en mi silla!" dijo la mamá osa.

"Someone has sat in my chair!" said the mother bear.

"¡Pues alguien se ha sentado en mi silla y la ha roto!" dijo el pequeño osito, esta vez llorando de su tristeza.

"Well, someone has sat in my chair and has broken it!" said the little baby bear, this time crying from his sorrow.

Verdaderamente asqueados, los tres osos subieron las escaleras y entraron a su alcoba.

Truly disgusted, the three bears climbed the stairs and entered their bedroom.

¡Alguien se ha acostado en mi cama!" dijo el papá oso.

"Someone has lain down in my bed!" said the papa bear.

¡Alguien se ha acostado en mi cama!" dijo la mamá osa.

"Someone has lain down in my bed!" said the mama bear.

Cuando el osito descubrió el cabello lindo de Ricitos de Oro encima de su cama, el dijo llorando, "¡Pues alguien se ha acostado en mi cama y allí está!"

When the little bear discovered the lovely hair of Goldilocks on top of his bed, he said, sobbing, "Well, someone has lain in my bed, and there she is!"

Ricitos de Oro oyó entre sueños la voz de papá oso, pero creyó que había sido un trueno.

Goldilocks heard in her dreams the voice of the papa bear, but she thought it was thunder.

Después oyó la voz de mamá osa, pero pensó que había sido el viento.

Then she heard the voice of the mama bear, but she thought it was the wind.

(*continued*)

Sin embargo, la voz aguda del osito le atravesó los oídos . . . y ésa sí que la despertó.

However, she heard the sharp voice of the little bear and that is what woke her up.

Cuando vio a los tres osos junto a ella, salió de la cama de un brincó, corrió hacia la ventana . . . y saltó!

When she saw the three bears next to her, she got out of the bed and in one jump, she ran toward the window, and . . . she jumped!

Por suerte, no estaba muy alto.

Luckily, it wasn't very high.

Muy sorprendidos, los tres osos se quedaron en la ventana, viendo a Ricitos de Oro que corría, corría, y corría . . . mirando hacia atrás por si alguien la seguía.

Very surprised, the three bears stayed by the window, watching Goldilocks, who was running, running, and running . . . watching behind her for anyone who was following.

Pero nadie la perseguía.

But no one was following.

Ricitos de Oro llego a su casa con su mamá, y nunca, nunca más regreso a esa parte del bosque.

Goldilocks arrived at her house with her mother, and never, ever returned to that part of the forest again.

¿Y qué pasó con los osos?

And what happened with the three bears?

Pues bien, muy enojados y refunfuñando tuvieron que arreglar todos los destrozos que Ricitos de Oro había hecho en su casa.

Well, angrily and reluctantly, they had to fix up all the disasters that Goldilocks had created in their house.

## *Cenicienta/Cinderella*

En un país muy lejano vivía un caballero viudo con su bella y bondadosa hija.

In a far away country there lived a gentleman with his beautiful and kind daughter.

El padre contrajo matrimonio con una huraña viuda que tenia dos hijas, y luego murió poco despúes.

The father married an unsociable widow who had two daughters, and then died shortly afterward.

Quedó la huérfana a merced de su madrastra y hermanas.

The orphan was left to the mercy of her stepmother and stepsisters.

Era muy infeliz porque la maltrataban, y le daban las tareas más pesadas y sucias.

She was very unhappy because they mistreated her, and they gave her the most difficult and dirtiest jobs.

La pobre niña iba siempre llena de ceniza.

The poor girl always went around in ashes.

*(continued)*

"¡Te llamaremos Cenicienta!"

"We shall call you Cinderella!"

Cierto día el emisario del rey les llevó una invitación.

One day, the emissary of the king brought them an invitation.

"Es para un baile de palacio!"

"It's for a dance at the palace!"

"Y el príncipe escogerá su esposa!"

"And the prince will choose his wife!"

"¡Seré yo, seré yo!""

"It will be me, it will be me!"

Así decían las dos hermanastras.

So said the two stepsisters.

El día del baile Cenicienta tuvo más trabajo que nunca.

The day of the dance, Cinderella had to do more work than ever.

"¡Plánchame el traje . . . !"

"Iron my outfit!"

"Péiname bien . . . !"

"Comb my hair beautifully!"

Cenicienta no paraba.

Cinderella never stopped.

Cuando la madrastra y sus hijas estuvieron arreglas, Cenicienta les dijo, "¡Espérenme, yo también iré con ustedes!

When the stepmother and her daughters were ready, Cinderella said to them, "Wait for me, I also will go with you!"

"¿Tú con nosotras?"

"You go with us?"

"¡Tú a trabajar!"

"You go to work!"

Y le rompieron el precioso vestido que le habían hecho para el baile sus amigos del bosque.

And they ripped the beautiful dress that her friends of the forest had made her for the dance.

La pobre niña quedó muy triste, llorando con desconsuelo.

The poor girl was very sad, crying without consolation.

Pero entonces se le apareció de repente su hada madrina.

But then her fairy godmother suddenly appeared to her.

"No te aflijas, irás al palacio!" le dijo.

"Don't worry, you will go to the palace," she said.

(*continued*)

¡Ante el asombro de la niña, el hada transformó una calabaza en carroza, los ratoncitos en caballos!

To the amazement of the girl, the fairy transformed a pumpkin into a carriage, and little mice into horses!

Y tocando a Cenicienta con su varita, transformó su vestido en el más hermoso en que nadie nunca pudo soñar.

And touching Cinderella with her wand, she transformed her dress into the most beautiful one anyone could dream of.

"¡Vete, pero recuerda, a las doce quedará roto el encanto!"

"Go, but remember, at twelve o'clock the spell will be broken!"

Cuando Cenicienta llegó al palacio, todos quedaron admirados de su belleza.

When Cinderella arrived at the palace, everyone admired her beauty.

"¿Quién será esta hermosa desconocida? ¡Padre, qué linda es!" comentó el príncipe.

"Who might that beautiful stranger be? Father, how pretty she is!" commented the prince.

Y con gran envidia de todas las damas de la corte, el príncipe empezó a bailar con ella, no dejándola ni un solo instante.

And with great envy of all the ladies of the court, the prince began to dance with her, never leaving her for an instant.

Pero de pronto . . . Ding dong, ding dong!

But suddenly . . . Ding dong, ding dong!

"¡Ah, son las doce, debo marchar! Lo siento pero tengo que salir!"

"Oh, it is twelve o'clock, I should go. I'm sorry, but I have to leave!"

Y ante la extrañeza del príncipe, Cenicienta huyó corriendo del palacio,

And to the shock of the prince, Cinderella ran away from the palace.

Pero salió con tanta prisa, que perdió su zapatito cristal que recogió el príncipe.

But she left in such a hurry that she lost her crystal slipper, which the prince picked up.

El príncipe quedo tan prendado de Cenicienta, que decidió que se casaría con ella, y mandó publicar un bando:

The prince was left so in love with Cinderella that he decided that he would marry her and commanded an announcement to be published:

"¡El príncipe se casará con la dama que pueda calzar el zapatito que encontró en la escalinata!"

"The prince will marry the lady who can fit into the slipper he found on the staircase!"

Cuando los emisarios del palacio llegaron a la casa de Cenicienta para probar el zapatito a sus dos hermanastras, por más que éstas quisieron ponérselo, no pudieron esforzar su pie dentro del zapatito.

When the emissaries of the palace arrived at Cinderella's house to try the shoe on her two stepsisters, as much as they tried they couldn't fit their feet inside the shoe.

¡Ay, ay, qué dolor!

Oh, oh, how painful!

(*continued*)

Sin embargo, en cuanto probaron el zapato con Cenicienta, ante el asombro de todos, el zapatito se ajustó a su pie como un guante.

However, when they tried the shoe on Cinderella, to the amazement of everyone, the slipper fit like a glove.

¡Qué alegría llenó el príncipe!

What happiness filled the prince!

En castigo por sus malas acciones, la madrastra de Cenicienta y sus hijas fueron expulsadas del reino.

As punishment for their bad actions, Cinderella's stepmother and her daughters were expelled from the kingdom.

No olvidó Cenicienta a sus amigos los ratones y los otros animales del bosque y los invitó a vivir en el palacio con ella por el resto de sus días donde pudieron hartarse de pasteles y queso.

Cinderella did not forget her friends the mice and the other animals of the forest and invited them to live with her in the palace for the rest of their days, where they could fill themselves with pastries and cheese.

Cenicienta y el príncipe se casaron y vivían contentísimos por el resto de sus días.

Cinderella married the prince, and they lived happy for the rest of their days.

---

All translations by Dr. Julie Jacobson. Used with permission.

## CHAPTER 9

# HOW DOES THE YEAR CONTINUE?

So you have survived the first day, the first week, the first month! It took planning, resourcefulness, and energy, but you did it. You're feeling quite pleased with yourself, and then you glance at the calendar and realize you have nine months still to go.

## ASSESS, PLAN, TEACH, REFLECT

Careful, thoughtful planning has carried you through the start of the year. Now, a continuous cycle of *assess*, *plan*, *teach*, and *reflect* is what will support long-term success in your classroom. The best news is that you do not have to engage in this cycle in isolation. Many districts and school sites have built-in structures that allow for grade-level teams to meet and work through the cycle together. Even if you are not given structured time for this purpose, teaming up with at least one other grade-level colleague can make the work more enjoyable as well as more effective.

A discussion of the following questions can help you to begin the cycle of assessing, planning, teaching, and reflecting:

➢ "What information do I use to help me plan?"
➢ "What reading instruction do the standards call for?"
➢ "What about comprehension strategies?"
➢ "What does a generic, yearlong plan look like?"
➢ "What is a unit of study?"
➢ "How does a workshop work?"
➢ "How do I develop a unit of study?"

## Assess

Continuous assessment of each child's growth occurs during each school day. As suggested in Chapters 4 and 5, you will need to continually identify factors that contribute to and inhibit each child's success. This information is what will help you to design "the next steps" in the child's literacy learning.

## Plan

As we discuss the planning phase of this cycle, we focus on reading instruction and, more specifically, on planning units of study for the readers' workshop. To plan effectively for the long term, you must work to balance a number of sources of information. The most prominent of these sources are:

> ➢ *The assessed needs of your students.* As discussed in Chapter 5, assessing is a continuous process of understanding where each child is in his or her development, and what the child's next steps are.

> ➢ *National and/or state and/or district grade-level standards.* You will need information from your school site as to which standards you are to refer to in your planning.

> ➢ *A vision of reading proficiency.* We all agree that literal-level comprehension is not enough. But do you have a clear sense of what constitutes a proficient first-grade reader? As you develop your understanding of reading proficiency, consider readers who are able to:

- Read with an active mind versus a passive mind.
- Embrace challenges.
- Develop their own points of view.
- Cite evidence.
- Consider different perspectives.
- Be flexible.
- Read fluently.
- Read critically.
- Communicate their thinking.
- Use what they read to inform their lives.

> ➢ *The demands of grade-level texts.* Begin to read grade-level texts carefully and consider what the reader needs to be able to navigate and ways the reader needs to think to make meaning. Does the reader need to recognize and compare information in a compare/contrast structure? Does the reader need to understand a new word through the context of the sentence? Does the next

sentence indirectly define the new word? Does the reader need to infer a character's true feelings from what he or she said to another character?

➢ *Knowledge of reading process.* As children embark on the journey from emergent reading to fluency, each progresses in his or her unique way (Clay, 1998). As discussed in Chapter 2, there are common behaviors that most readers exhibit as they progress. Knowing these behaviors can support you in planning for your readers. Using a reading continuum, such as the First Steps continuum, can guide your understanding of the reading behaviors for which your children may need instruction and support.

How does a new teacher, or any teacher for that matter, not only begin to learn all of this, but strike the right balance while designing curriculum? There is no easy answer. Even if you have the standards at hand and all of your assessments compiled and organized, knowing where to begin with these two sources alone can be daunting. Add the other sources of information, and it seems impossible.

You will need to develop familiarity with these sources of information over time as you immerse yourself in grade-level text, spend time watching the range of readers you typically work with, and come to understand what can be achieved in terms of proficiency.

In this chapter, we get you started with a *generic* yearlong plan. We emphasize the term *generic* on purpose. It is impossible for us to design your year, as we have never met your students. But we can give you a starting place. It's always easier to revise something that's already started than to begin from scratch. As you put the assess-plan-teach-reflect cycle in place, revise is exactly what you will need to do.

## A Note of Caution

When working with standards, it is important to look at the way individual standards cluster to form broad, overarching goals for the year. Looking at individual standards in isolation leads to the teaching of discrete skills void of a larger purpose. For example, the New Standards Reading Standard 2 for first grade suggests that children should be able to describe causes and effects of specific events. This objective could be dealt with after their reading by asking children to address right-answer types of questions on a worksheet. However, if we read through all of the New Standards for reading comprehension, we realize that the children should be developing a sense of story elements, such as characters, and themes in their reading. We can then look at cause-and-effect as a tool for better understanding the characters and theme as we integrate this into their conversations, writing, and reading work.

For example, when Wemberly is worried, in *Wemberly Worried* by Kevin Henkes, we can discuss the idea that fear of the unknown is causing this worry, which better helps us to understand both Wemberly and ourselves. We can then use the text-based discussion as a springboard to investigate fear as a theme in literature. As we do so we can also address the strategy of cause-and-effect, as it appears in the text being studied. The standards used in guiding our instruction are now integrated and more meaningful in the literacy development of our students.

## HOW IS READING INSTRUCTION ADDRESSED IN THE STANDARDS?

As discussed throughout this text, reading instruction must always engage the reader in meaning making. To provide such instruction, we must teach children both strategies for problem solving at the word level, and strategies for problem solving at the meaning level, commonly referred to as strategies for deepening comprehension.

Much of the work required by the New Standards Reading Standard 1, the print–sound code, involves supporting children in problem solving at the word level. This work will need the heavy support and demonstration offered in shared reading and follow-up opportunities for children to take on the word work themselves in small-group instruction, including small-group shared reading and guided reading. Interactive writing, both whole-group and small-group, also helps children to solidify concepts related to the print–sound code and problem solving strategies. The word study block, with phonemic awareness, phonics, and spelling components, support this standard as well. This work is discussed in Chapter 2.

The New Standards Reading Standard 2, *getting the meaning,* encompasses a range of abilities children need to develop as readers. The first three abilities addressed in this standard are accuracy, fluency, and self-monitoring and self-correcting. Children need to read grade-level text with minimal errors, sounding

fluent, and recognizing and correcting many of their own errors. Again, this is the work of shared reading and small-group instruction (Chapters 2 and 6).

Within a readers' workshop instructional plan we focus on the last bulleted ability in Reading Standard 2, comprehension.

The abilities spelled out under the heading "Comprehension" give only a general sense of what is to be taught.

➤ In children's independent reading, they need to develop the ability to:
- Retell a story
- Summarize
- Discuss new information learned from reading
- Answer comprehension questions

➤ When more complex text is read to them, children should develop the ability to:
- Extend the story
- Make reasonable predictions with supporting evidence
- Discuss character motive

Consider these instructional goals of Standard 2 in relation to some of the other sources of information that will inform our planning for comprehension instruction.

Figure 9.1 gives the work to be done in relation to Standard 2 a little more form and depth. Embedded in the work are a variety of comprehension strategies. Although not all of these are specifically identified in the standards, the work laid out will require strategy instruction.

## WHAT ABOUT COMPREHENSION STRATEGIES?

Utilizing the research of Pearson and Gallagher (1983), Susan Zimmermann and Ellin Keene (1997) outline the most prevalent strategies for deepening comprehension used by readers in their book, *Mosaic of Thought*. These research-based strategies include:

➤ *Making connections*: Using what you know (schema) from your life, the world, or other texts you have read to make sense of new information.

➤ *Predicting*: Monitoring as you read for the purpose of anticipating what might reasonably happen next.

| Ability required by Standard 2 | A few of the assumed abilities | Vision of reading proficiency | Grade-level text |
|---|---|---|---|
| Retell | Literal-level comprehension as a baseline to build on | • Have purpose for retell, such as persuading someone to read or warning him or her away from the text | |
| Summarize | Some sense of important versus less important details | • Understanding of the way ideas in a book are linked<br>• Using more important details to give big idea | Even simplest books have an organizing idea |
| Discuss new information | Pull literal information out of text | • Flexible use of schema—knowing when to hold onto what you think you know, and when to let it go<br>• Ability to make sense of factual information<br>• Discuss central question around which information is being collected | • Nonfiction has range of high-interest topics that may be unfamiliar<br>• Texts have a variety of structures that organize new information |
| Answer comprehension questions | Literal-level comprehension as a baseline to build on | • Using a variety of comprehension strategies to move beyond a literal understanding<br>• Understanding of some structures | • Fiction text generally presents situations children can relate to<br>• Nonfiction has range of high-interest topics |
| Extend the story | Literal-level comprehension as a baseline to build on | • Develop strong enough understanding to anticipate a reasonable "what might happen next?" scenario<br>• Ability to make inferences | |
| Make reasonable predictions | Ability to connect to text | • Use schema and textual clues to think ahead<br>• Explain thinking to others | Engaging, action-based text propels the reader to respond as a natural response |
| Discuss character motive | • Understanding of main character<br>• Ability to connect to character<br>• Ability to question character<br>• Ability to draw inferences<br>• Understand character's relationship with other characters, setting | • Use other texts to propel thinking | Independent reads may not have characters developed enough for this work |

**FIGURE 9.1.** Using standards to inform assessment and instruction.

➤ *Determining importance*: Making decisions as you read that enable you to focus on the most important ideas.

➤ *Questioning*: Monitoring real wonder and asking sincere questions about the characters, author, and facts as you read.

➤ *Creating sensory images*: Creating visual, auditory, or other sensory images for yourself as you read.

➤ *Inferential thinking*: Mixing what you know with text-based information to predict, think critically, or use other means of thinking beyond the text.

➤ *Synthesizing*: Holding onto important details and forming them into your own clear, comprehensible thoughts about the text.

➤ *Using a variety of fix-up strategies*: Recognizing when meaning has broken down, and taking steps to rebuild meaning, such as rereading, reading on, thinking about new words using context, and so forth.

Many, if not all, of these strategies are not new to children. Most children are able to watch a TV show and say, "Oh-oh, I bet he's going to. . . . " Or they are able to think about a best friend, and gauge his or her reaction to a particular situation. This is predicting.

A child hearing a certain tone in their mother's voice when she calls them will know instantly that they are in trouble. This is inferential thinking. Or they can use what they know about Disneyland to anticipate what a day at Magic Mountain might be like. This is using schema. These are not just strategies for reading; they are strategies for thinking. However, it's not always obvious to children that these ways of thinking can support their efforts to make meaning when reading. We need to model using these strategies for the purpose of meaning making for children. Preferably, they should be modeled in orchestration to avoid giving the children the false impression that readers can make rich meaning while using single strategies in isolation. *Orchestration* refers to a reader's ability to use a variety of strategies at any given time. Often, they are so intertangled that separating a thought that arose from an individual strategy is very difficult.

The heavy support offered by a teacher in a read-aloud makes it the approach of choice for modeling a range of strategies. In a read-aloud, the teacher reads a carefully selected text at a more complex level than the children are able to undertake independently. As the text is read, the teacher pauses in key places, allowing conversations to develop for the purpose of building strong meaning. Many of these pauses are preceded by a modeling of the teacher's own use of these strategies for meaning making. This modeling of thinking is known as a "think-aloud."

A think-aloud is a teaching opportunity, in which the reader disengages from the flow of the text, pauses, and actually thinks out loud for the benefit of those listening. Consider the following think-aloud embedded in a read-aloud with a focus on understanding characters. The teacher in this scenario is reading *Wemberly Worried* by Kevin Henkes.

Teacher: (*reading*)

> "You worry too much," said her mother.
> "When you worry, I worry," said her father.
> "Worry, worry, worry," said her Grandmother.
> "Too much worry."

(*Puts book down, gazes up to indicate she is no longer reading.*) As I read this part, I'm wondering why Wemberly worries so much. I get like that sometimes when I don't feel safe or secure, or when I'm trying something new, but I'm not worried *all* the time. And as I look at the pictures (*flips back to review pages already read*), I can see she does look worried *all* the time. Why would this be? As readers, when we wonder or have a question about our character, we need to stop and think.

This think-aloud does two things to support the children's meaning-making ability. First, it scaffolds an opportunity to think about this text in ways that will build stronger comprehension (in this case, a combination of questioning and using schema). And by adding "As readers . . . " at the end of the snippet of thought, it helps children to understand that this way of thinking is used anytime we read, which is generative teaching.

Once you think aloud, you will want to invite the children into the conversation. "Why would Wemberly be so worried *all* the time?" you may ask. Trust your students to come up with some amazing possibilities.

The following is a list of books we have used successfully to model a wealth of strategic thinking for first graders. You can gradually add your own favorites to the list.

- *Pumpkin Jack* by Will Hubbell
- *Barn Dance!* by Bill Martin Jr. and John Archambautt
- *Sarah's Sleepover* by Bobbie Rodriguez
- *The Leaving Morning* by Angela Johnson
- *Do Like Kyla* by Angela Johnson
- The *Poppleton* series by Cynthia Ryland
- The *Franklin* series by Paulette Bourgeois
- *Julius, the Baby of the World* by Kevin Henkes
- *Chrysanthemum* by Kevin Henkes
- *Wemberly Worried* by Kevin Henkes

➤ Other titles by Kevin Henkes

➤ *Big Bear, Little Bear* series by Martin Waddell

➤ *Olivia* by Ian Falconer

➤ *At the Edge of the Forest* by Jonathan London

➤ *A Chair for My Mother* by Vera B. Williams

➤ *Pet Show!* by Ezra Jack Keats

➤ *The Very Best of Friends* by Margaret Wild

Ideally, we want children to understand that readers use this rich mix of comprehension strategies at all times, and we want to embed our strategy instruction into strong content, such as in a study of character. We consider embedded strategies in the following plan.

The end goal for strategy instruction is for strategic reading to be so automatic that it becomes invisible to the reader. This is the reason we have trouble envisioning strategy use and instruction; for us, as fluent readers, the process is invisible. If you want to get a sense of what it feels like to consciously use comprehension strategies, find a piece of text that is challenging for you—an unfamiliar genre, an insurance form, the kinds of things you avoid reading. Then pay close attention to what you are doing in your head to try to make meaning. You should be doing, or trying to do, exactly what you will be modeling for your children.

## WHAT DOES A GENERIC, YEARLONG PLAN INCLUDE?

So, what might a year of study that combines standards as outlined in the New Standards, embedded strategy work, visions of proficiency, and an understanding of grade-level text look like? The progression of instruction depicted in Figure 9.2 is not intended to be used as is. Rather, it is an example of the way a year *might* flow and, more important, how standards are addressed again and again in a variety of contexts and increasingly complex ways.

The plan is divided into units of study, which are discussed in the following section. Within each possible unit, a range of standard work is included, most likely more than is indicated by the bulleted items. Working with standards is not only teaching, testing, and checking off, but a continuous process of revisiting as well.

Strategies the children will need to use are also indicated. Remember, strategy work is an orchestration, with readers drawing on a mix of strategies at any given time. However, certain ways of thinking may necessitate heavier reliance on some strategies. Considering this may help you with students who are struggling.

| Units of study: Readers' workshop | A few of the embedded standards | Units of study: Writers' workshop | A few of the embedded standards |
|---|---|---|---|
| Creating a community of readers and a sense of self as a reader | Standard 3:<br>• Read 4 or more books every day<br>• Discuss at least one | Creating a community of writers and a sense of self as a writer | Standard 1:<br>• Write daily<br>• Generate topics<br>• Reread<br>• Solicit responses |
| Matching ideas to text | Standard 2:<br>• Retell the story<br>• Summarize<br>Standard 3:<br>• Reread favorites | Writing from the power of our lives | Standard 1:<br>• Generate topics<br>• Reread<br>• Solicit responses<br>Standard 2:<br>• Plan writing<br>• Develop narratives with sequenced events |
| Using structures and features to support meaning making in nonfiction (connecting, schema) | Standard 2:<br>• Make predictions<br>Standard 3:<br>• Cite evidence | Author's craft: ways with words | Standard 1:<br>• Generate topics<br>• Reread<br>• Solicit responses<br>Standard 2:<br>• Plan writing<br>• Growing awareness of author's craft<br>Standard 3:<br>• Style and syntax |
| Considering big ideas in nonfiction reading (schema, inferential thinking, questioning, determining importance, synthesis) | Standard 2:<br>• Retell the story<br>• Summarize<br>• Describe new information<br>Standard 3:<br>• Understand new words in context | Nonfiction: writing what we know about the world | Standard 1:<br>• Generate topics<br>• Reread<br>• Solicit responses<br>Standard 2:<br>• Plan writing<br>• Incorporate features<br>• Give instructions<br>• Sequence |
| Thinking about characters (inferential thinking, schema, questioning, using sensory images) | Standard 2:<br>• Retell the story<br>• Make predictions<br>• Use story elements<br>• Talk about the motives of characters<br>• Describe cause and effect<br>Standard 3:<br>• Cite evidence<br>• Question others<br>• Defend interpretation | Informing others: reports or informational writing | Standard 1:<br>• Generate topics<br>• Reread<br>• Solicit responses<br>Standard 2:<br>• Plan writing<br>• Incorporate features<br>• Gather information<br>• Determine relevance<br>• Develop points, write with purpose<br><br>(continued) |

**FIGURE 9.2.** A possible year of readers' and writers' workshop in grade 1.

| Units of study: Readers' workshop | A few of the embedded standards | Units of study: Writers' workshop | A few of the embedded standards |
|---|---|---|---|
| Combining characters with other elements of fiction (story elements) to deepen comprehension (questioning, inferential thinking) | Standard 2:<br>• Retell the story<br>• Make predictions<br>• Use story elements<br>• Talk about the motives of characters<br>• Describe cause and effect<br>Standard 3:<br>• Compare books by the same author<br>• Cite evidence<br>• Question others<br>• Defend interpretation | Author's craft: structures | Standard 1:<br>• Generate topics<br>• Reread<br>• Solicit responses<br>Standard 2:<br>• Plan writing<br>• Demonstrate growing awareness of author's craft |
| Understanding big ideas in fiction (theme) (inferential thinking, determining importance, synthesis) | Standard 2:<br>• Retell the story effect<br>Standard 3:<br>• Compare books by the same author<br>• Talk about several books on the same theme<br>• Cite evidence<br>• Question others<br>• Defend interpretation<br>• Make predictions<br>• Use story elements<br>• Talk about the motives of characters<br>• Describe cause and effect | Incorporating story elements | Standard 1:<br>• Generate topics<br>• Reread<br>• Solicit responses<br>Standard 2:<br>• Plan writing<br>• Develop narratives with sequenced events<br>• Demonstrate growing awareness of author's craft<br>• Imitate narrative elements<br>• Include inner thoughts |
| Using big ideas and structure to determine author's purpose in nonfiction | Reading Standard 2:<br>• Summarize<br>• Discuss new information<br>Reading Standard 3:<br>• Compare books<br>• Refer explicitly to parts of the text<br>• Attempt to explain interpretation | Memoir | Standard 1:<br>• Generate topics<br>• Reread<br>• Solicit responses<br>Standard 2:<br>• Plan writing<br>• Develop narratives with sequenced events<br>• Demonstrate growing awareness of author's craft<br>• Imitate narrative elements<br>• Include inner thoughts |

**FIGURE 9.2.** *(continued)*

What this generic year left out is your children's assessed needs and your own state and/or district standards. Only you can add these sources of information to the plan, which will have to be revised when they are added. As you consider this possible instructional flow, be sure to weigh your district standards and expectations and, most important, the needs of your students.

Although the discussion in this chapter focuses on reading, a year of possible writing studies is included as well.

Notice that some studies in writing are based on what children study as readers. These studies do not progress side by side. Rather, writing lags behind reading, giving children a chance to immerse in the work as readers before they produce it as writers. The work in these units is rigorous, incorporating standards for independent reading and being read to. Again, you will have to assess and revise if this plan does not match your children's abilities. But do not lose sight of your vision of grade-level proficiency.

Once you plan your year, you must consider the plan flexibly. The accumulation of day-to-day assessments may cause you to reconsider the length of any one unit of study, add a new study, see the need to explore certain comprehension strategies in more depth, or make other adjustments.

## WHAT IS A UNIT OF STUDY?

An efficient and effective means of scaffolding instruction for children as well as developing an understanding of a year's worth of comprehension work, can be accomplished through planning units of study. The continuing goal throughout your units of study is to enable children to develop as independent readers.

A unit of study can be viewed as a group of learners exploring the power of a certain aspect of thinking about their reading or writing together. Essentially, it is "some big thing you and your class are digging into over time" (Nia, 1999).

A unit of study is typically a 4- to 6-week evolving study of a way of thinking about reading or communicating through writing. As described in the next section and in Chapters 2 and 3, a workshop model is the structure used as a daily plan to teach and immerse children in study.

Does this seem fairly complicated? Take a moment to review.

➢ First, a variety of sources of information are used to make decisions about the curriculum of the readers' workshop for the year.

➢ Then the curriculum is broken down into units of study.

The readers' workshop gives you and the children a structure for transferring the content of each study to the children's independent reading.

# HOW DOES A CLASSROOM WORKSHOP WORK?

As described in Chapter 2, the concept of *Workshop* is based on a constructivist model of learning. In *Methods That Matter*, Daniels and Bizar (1998) refer to workshop classrooms as "working laboratories or studios, where genuine knowledge is created, real products are made, and authentic inquiry pursued." Daniels and Bizar go on to say: "The workshop model is simple and powerful. It derives from the insight that children learn by doing, and that in the past schools have simply failed to provide enough time for doing math, science, reading, writing, art, music and history."

This tells us that we need to create workshop environments that allow children social opportunities. Although some reading time may be silent, the children also need to be engaged in conversations that invite them to develop their own understandings of what they read. During a workshop, the children need to live as all literate people do, making choices about reading, reading for a purpose, and transferring knowledge from reading to their own lives. Workshop should be an enjoyable time that the children look forward to each day.

A workshop has a predictable daily structure (Lapp & Flood, 1974; Calkins, 2001). It moves from a mini-lesson (often with a shared reading component), to independent reading with conferring, time for partner work and reflection, and a purposeful teacher-led sharing that furthers the children's understanding of the work they are taking on.

## The Mini-Lesson

The readers' workshop itself begins with a mini-lesson. A mini-lesson is a short (10–15 minute) lesson that enables children to take on the reading work. Mini-lessons may be procedural (ways of handling supplies, choosing books, finding a reading spot) or instructional (strategies for reading).

The mini-lesson is divided into the following five phases (Calkins, 2001).

1. *Connect.* The teacher calls the children together on the rug, shares what he or she notices about them as readers, and tells them that he or she is going to teach strategies for growing stronger as readers. This phase may sound like this:

"As I've been conferring with you, I've noticed that many of you are able to retell information that you have learned from your nonfiction reading. Our next step as readers is to make sense of this information. Readers ask themselves, 'What exactly does this mean?' "

2. *Teach.* The teacher shows the children what he or she would like them to try. This teaching may be procedural ("Here's how we find a smart spot to read"), or it may be instructional. Generally, with instructional mini-lessons, a piece of

shared text that allows you to model and release responsibility for the work is used.

In the preceding scenario, a nonfiction book with several facts would be used. This should be a text the children have read previously so they are not trying to problem solve at the word level while they focus on comprehension strategies. (Remember, shared reading is still strong support, in this case word-solving support and some comprehension support.)

The teacher models thinking about the first fact.

"One way readers make sense of new facts is to use their schema—what they already know. 'Penguins jump 6 feet in the air.' Hmm—I'm 5 feet tall. If penguins can jump 6 feet—they can jump over my head! I used what I know to make sense of a new fact."

3. *Active involvement.* The teacher keeps the children on the carpet and has them try out what they are being asked to do. This is an assessment opportunity for the teacher, and an opportunity for the children to try the work with support.

"Now, it's your turn. Let's read this new fact. Think for a minute. Then, turn to your partner and talk. How can you use what you already know to make sense of it?"

4. *Link.* The teacher shares expectations with the children and gives hints about how or when ("Everyone must . . . " or "If this works for you in your reading today . . . " or " If you are confused, you might . . . ") to use this teaching. The link sends the children off to their independent reading.

"You will come to new facts while you are reading today. See if you can use what you already know to make sense of them."

5. *Follow-up.* This phase of the mini-lesson generally comes after independent reading. This is a purposeful sharing used by the teacher to highlight the way one reader used the new way of thinking about reading (or writing) explored in the teach phase. Generally, the decision about whose work to share is made while conferring with the readers. The teacher may discover a reader whose work is strong and can be highlighted as is, or a reader whose work can be improved by the teacher, then both the process and the end result can be shared. Either way, this is another opportunity for readers to see how this new way of thinking strengthens reading.

"Readers, as Giovanni was reading today, he read that sloths are the slowest animals in the rainforest. He knows that there are also big snakes in the rainforest, and he has seen them in the zoo. They move pretty slowly. So he knows that if the sloth is the slowest, it moves even more slowly than these snakes."

### Conferring

It is important to recognize that a strong conference is not a list of questions (an interrogation), but rather a conversation (Anderson, 2000). During conferring time, the teacher sits next to a child and talks with the child about his or her reading. You need to be prepared to ask open-ended questions that allow you to assess how well the child comprehends what he or she reads. With first graders, you may want to have them read a small amount of text to assess reading process as well. As you talk with each child, you will want to get a sense of how the ideas presented in the mini-lesson have been learned. This is for the purpose of assessing each individual reader and for gauging needs among readers that will support you in planning the next day's mini-lesson. Will you need to reteach? Teach the same mini-lesson, but with more complex text? Rethink some aspect of the mini-lesson that the children misunderstood? Think through a complexity in the work that you had not anticipated? It is this assessing, along with your reflection at the end of each day (remember the cycle of assess, plan, teach, reflect?), that determines your curriculum for the year. This is where partnering with a grade-level colleague can be a great help.

### Small-Group Instruction

Once you have finished conferring and the children have been invited to work at related center activities (as discussed in Chapter 6), you can begin to work with children who have similar needs in small guided-instruction groups.

## HOW DO YOU DEVELOP A UNIT OF STUDY?

A unit of study can be developed for any number of subjects, such as an understanding of characters. How do you know when your students are ready to study characters? The answer to this question depends on the children—that is, when they are ready to read texts that enable them to do some strong work with characters.

As children develop as readers, there is a natural transition in the types of texts they are reading. Texts created for emergent and early readers in instructional situations are left behind during independent reading as children become able to access trade books. Texts such as *Rookie Readers*, *Hello Readers*, and books for early readers by authors such as Harriet Ziefert, Rosemary Wells, and Donald Crews, become closer to a "just-right read." The *Little Bear* books by Frank Asche, *Little Critter* books by Mercer Mayer, and the *Biscuit* books by Alyssa Satin Capucilli may become favorite series.

As the children make the transition to more challenging, real-world text, slowing down their reading to think about characters will be crucial to understanding what they read. A unit of study on character development should take place as this transition is occurring, as it will enable stronger comprehension. In the possible flow of a year, this character study may be placed at approximately the midyear mark. But in actuality, it is your readers' needs that will dictate when this study occurs. When planning a unit of study, a helpful approach is to begin by envisioning what a rigorous but realistic end result of the study would be. Ask yourself, "What texts should my children be reading at the end of the year? What should their conversations about these texts sound like?"

By the end of a study on character development, the children should be able to talk about what their character is like and cite evidence for their thinking. They should consider causes for their character being this way (motive) and recognize whether their character changes and why. In planning for this end result, we need to consider how a reader figures these things out and how we would teach our readers to do this. One of the best ways to determine these things is to take on the work yourself with an adult-level text. If you can find a text that's slightly challenging (an author's style that's uncomfortable for you, a less familiar genre such as biography, etc.), your own strategy work will become more visible to you. Or pick up one of the children's picture books, and try it. As you read, ask yourself these questions:

➤ "What is my character like?"

➤ "Why is my character this way?"

➤ "How do I know?"

➤ "Did my character change during the course of my reading?"

➤ "What might have caused this change?"

➤ "How did I know a change had occurred?"

As you read, you should become aware of yourself doing much of what is in Figure 9.3. This work, planned in a logical progression, becomes the unit of study about characters.

This is easily 4–6 weeks' worth of work. You may or may not need to begin with identifying the main character, depending on your children. If the children are more sophisticated readers, they may be reading lengthier texts in which characters develop slowly, and you may need to add work on forming a theory about a character and tracking it over a longer read. There may be more characters, with more of them well developed, so you may need to consider interactions between characters. Again, assessment always drives your planning.

Consider the strategy work embedded in this study. Children will have to use connections, questions, predictions, and inferential thinking and will have to determine importance and summarize. Sensory images will be used as they imag-

| Focus point | How readers do this |
|---|---|
| Determining main character(s) | Readers notice:<br>• If a character's name is in the title<br>• If a character's picture is on the cover<br>• If a character seems to be on most pages<br>• If the text seems to be mostly about that character |
| Thinking about what a character is like | Readers think about:<br>• What the character does<br>• What the character says<br>• What the character thinks<br>• What other characters say or think about this character<br>• How other characters behave with this character |
| Noticing change or surprise | Readers think about:<br>• Times when their character does, says, or thinks something different than previously<br>• Whether the character is this way just once, or if this different way of being is permanent |
| Thinking about the cause of change or surprise | Readers think about:<br>• How the character interacts with other characters<br>• How the setting might affect the character |

**FIGURE 9.3.** Character study.

ine the tone of voice when a character speaks. You will need to watch for children who seem to be having difficulty with any of these strategies, as this may get in the way of developing an understanding of their characters.

The standards also call for students to develop the ability to cite evidence for their thinking about characters. This evidence will be found in the text, in the pictures, and in the reader's schema, so you will need to model using all three.

Not mentioned in our yearlong plan is work that needs to be integrated through every study. In reading, this work includes:

➤ *Learning to value rereading.* We don't want to create an environment where children rush through piles of books without taking time to draw all they can from each book. We need to teach children to linger with great reads, reread parts that matter or from which they can learn more, and return to texts when they realize they can make more of the information because of new knowledge.

➤ *Developing strong talk.* Children need to communicate their ideas with clarity and purpose. We need to build conversations around ideas in reading

in whole-group and small-group instruction so that talking smartly about reading transfers to independent reading.

➤ *Developing reading partnerships.* Partnerships are a means for developing this talk about reading. We need to work to transfer ways of talking about reading from whole-group to small-group to independent practice and help children to see the value of this talk.

➤ *Reading between texts.* Readers move between texts to gain more information to support their thinking, compare ideas and information, and look at the ways different authors address similar ideas or themes.

This embedded work also addresses the standards in a variety of ways.

## Teach

### Modeling with Read-Aloud

During a read-aloud, the teacher reads a text at a level above that which the children are able to access themselves. For a character study, the texts chosen for the initial modeling would need to have well-developed characters. Eventually, you can introduce texts with characters who change, at first for obvious reasons, and then for reasons that are less obvious.

Think-alouds can be used at first to model the thinking work for the children. The read-aloud must be planned with stopping places for children to develop their thinking through talk. Eventually, the children will begin to take over more of the talk. This is your cue that the children are ready to take on this aspect of the work independently, and you begin to model the next step in read-aloud.

### Shared Reading

Shared reading is used to transfer the work to the children's independent reading. The shared work is included in the mini-lesson. The shared text may be a short text, poem about a character, or excerpt from a longer text. The work begins with teacher modeling, but then the teacher re-  leases responsibility to the students for the attempt phases of the mini-lesson.

### Independent Reading

During independent reading, children select texts in their just-right range that allow them to take on the work at hand. For this study, the children will need to have fiction text with rich characters.

### Conferring

Conferring is both a chance to assess and a chance to teach. As you talk with a reader and gather information about his or her process, you will choose one point to teach to. The teaching is quick, and you ask the reader to take on the work immediately. At times, you may check back with the reader later in the workshop, or the next day, to discuss his or her success or offer more support.

### Small-Group Instruction

It is during small-group instruction that you are able to work with children who have similar needs. The number of children in the group will depend on the number of children who need explicit instruction.

### Reflect

As you plan the rest of the year, you do so knowing that continued assessments may change the plan at any point. Reflection gives you an opportunity to assess your own planning and teaching, and the children's growth as readers.

Your sense of the work, plus your assessment records, are your tools for reflection. Assessment records should include:

➤ Conferring notes

➤ Notes from other instructional opportunities, such as guided and shared reading

➤ Formal reading assessments, such as running records with analysis

➤ Notes from individual lessons

The children's growth as readers is directly related to your planning and instruction. If you are not seeing what you hope to see, then it's time to rethink long-term plans.
Questions to ponder:

➢ "Is this content meeting the needs of my children right now?"

➢ "Am I offering enough time or too much time for each study?"

➢ "Am I modeling the work enough?"

➢ "Is my teaching explicit?"

➢ "Do I offer an opportunity for the children to try the work with support before moving it to independent practice?"

➢ "Do my children have the right texts for the work at the right levels?"

Even when things seem to be going well, reflection is a key to growing professionally. To grow stronger in our practice, we must always ask ourselves, "How could I have taught that better?"

# WHEN SHOULD YOU START PLANNING FOR NEXT YEAR?

As teachers, we have all planned many, many years of instruction. Rarely do we wait for one year to be over before we begin to plan the next. Rather, take notes all year long with the intent of making planning that much easier. To help yourself with this work, push yourself to keep the following reflection questions about the sources of information for long-term planning at hand, and jot notes whenever possible.

➢ *Assessed needs.* (This is the hardest source to prethink, as individuals in your class will vary year to year).

■ "What trends do I notice in ability to comprehend text beyond the literal?"

■ "What trends do I notice in ability to problem solve at the word level?"

➢ *Standards.*

■ "Which standard(s) had the children accomplished before our year began?"

■ "Which standard(s) could not be addressed without teaching some prerequisite knowledge the students did not have in place?"

■ "Which standard(s) was I able to push beyond grade level?"

➤ *Vision of proficiency.*

- ■ "What type of text do I (and my district and the standards) expect my students to be reading?"
- ■ "What should the student's talk about this text sound like?"
- ■ "How much of the talk should be independent, coming from the student without any adult questioning or other prompting?"

➤ *Grade-level texts.*

- ■ "What content do grade-level texts seem to deal with?"
- ■ "What do I notice about the language (word complexity and semantic structures) in grade-level texts?"
- ■ "What features do my students need to navigate in grade-level texts?"
- ■ "What structures do the grade-level texts present?"

If you are able to develop answers to these questions over the course of your first year, you will have some data to inform your planning for next year. Unfortunately, it does not get easier every year, it just becomes more familiar.

# CHAPTER 10

# YOU CAN'T DO THIS ALONE
## The Home–School Connection

Children's literacy development begins in their homes. "For the first five years a child's language growth is entirely dependent on what people say to him—on how much they speak to him, about what things, in what dialect or language, and in what manner, whether gentle and explaining or peremptory and imperative" (Clay, 1991, p. 70). Unfortunately, because of differences in social class and educational background, not all children are recipients of supportive early literacy experiences (Hart & Risley, 1995).

These differences are all too well illustrated by Rosow (1992) who tells the story of Irma, a third-generation housing project child who was born into an environment where illiteracy is passed from one generation to the next. There were no models of school-related literacy in Irma's home, because the adults in the family did not know how to read and may not have realized the value of reading, or because they believed that literacy development was a function of the school experience (Lapp, Fisher, Flood, & Moore, 2003). In Irma's home books were nonexistent, or when they were sent home they were lost. Notes from teachers, even those pinned to Irma's clothes, went unsigned because her mother could not read them. Irma's situation was not unique; not all children learn the functions of literacy in their family settings (Cairney, 1997).

We believe that as a teacher you may meet many Irmas and that you have the power to make the ending to stories like Irma's, which depict the ravages of illiteracy, have a positive ending in regard to literacy. This can be accomplished if you provide appropriate school literacy instruction that enables the development of the literacy foundation that other children receive at home dur-

ing the first 5 years of their lives. Irma's lack of these experiences does not suggest that she would be unable to learn to read and write; rather, it simply means that she had had early experiences that were not closely related to literacy. We believe that you have a chance to make a difference for every child, with or without the support of his or her home. Certainly, it is easier to do so with the preschool and continuing involvement of the family, but you cannot use parental lack of involvement as a signal that they don't care or as an excuse for your not supporting their children. You are the common denominator for all of your students. You *can* and *must* make a difference.

## MAKING CONNECTIONS

It won't take long for you to meet most of the parents of your students. Most parents will bring their child on the first day of first grade, and many will have difficulty leaving. This alerts you to their feelings; they are entrusting you with their most precious jewel—their child. Because your time and attention must be centered on your students, especially on the first day, you may want to send a letter the parents will receive prior to the first day of school, telling them how excited you are to teach their child, introducing them to the initial class routines, and inviting them to be part of your classroom community and to share their insights about their child. (Figures 10.1–10.3 are examples.)

In addition to, or instead of, sending this letter and enclosures, you can put an easel outside your classroom door on the first day of school. Use a large, friendly decorated poster board with a message that greets families and students, makes them aware of morning procedures and where to put backpacks and lunch boxes, and politely asks parents to say goodbye at the door, rather than inside (see example in Figure 10.4). This will eliminate drawn out and disruptive farewells. The survey and schedule, as shown in Figures 10.2 and 10.3, can be given to parents on the first day as you greet them and their child. You may need to mail a few to parents who did not escort their child to school.

Get to know each child's parents or family contact person quickly, because by getting to know the families, you know the children. It is the family that teaches the "habits, traditions, and ways of life" (Gibson, 1999, p. 19). Teachers and parents who work well together are very fortunate, because they can depend on one another as they take on the arduous and rewarding task of developing a child's literacy. Their collaboration in the process of literacy

Date: _____

Dear Family Members of _____,

Soon you and your child will become members of the classroom community in Room _____. I am looking forward to having the pleasure of getting to know you and of being [child's] teacher. Although sending [child] to first grade is a landmark in [his or her] life, it may be difficult for you because it signals a passing of the early years when most of her day was probably spent at home with you. Realizing this, I will take extra good care of [child]. I hope you will share your insights about [child] with me. The more I know about [him or her], the better able I will be to make [his or her] instruction very personal. I've included a survey that I hope you can return on your first visit to our classroom. The information you provide helps me to better understand and teach [child]. On the first day of school, Room _____ will be a very busy place and I will need to focus my time on the children and getting our routines established. Because I won't have time to share detailed information with you if you bring [child] to class, I'll be sending you updates about the activities in Room _____ frequently throughout the year. Open house conferences, which are scheduled for [date], is another good time for us to get acquainted. I will be available for additional conferences by appointment after school. I've also included information regarding our classroom schedule. Please do not hesitate to call me at [number].

I look forward to this school year with you and [child].

Best regards,

[Teacher]

**FIGURE 10.1.** Sample letter 1 to be sent to parents before the first day of school.

From *Teaching Literacy in First Grade* by Diane Lapp, James Flood, Kelly Moore, and Maria Nichols. Copyright 2005 by The Guilford Press. Permission to photocopy this figure is granted to purchasers of this book for personal use only (see copyright page for details).

Dear Parents,

In order to get to know your child, I would like to gather some information from you. Please take a moment to complete the survey and bring it with you on your first visit to our classroom. Please share any additional information that you think will help your child to have a successful school year.

1. What are your child's general feelings about school?

2. How does your child respond when reading or being read to?

3. How well does your child work and play with other children?

4. What social skills would you like to see your child develop this year?

5. In what ways can I make this a successful year for your child?

6. How much time can you spend helping your child with homework each evening?

Thanks for your responses. Having communication with you will help your child have a more successful year. What are the best ways for me to contact you?

Home phone: _____

Work phone: _____

E-mail: _____

The best times to be reached are _____

Please feel free to contact me at:

School phone: _____

E-mail: _____

Best regards,

[Teacher]

**FIGURE 10.2.** Sample survey 1: Getting to know your child (to accompany letter 1).

From *Teaching Literacy in First Grade* by Diane Lapp, James Flood, Kelly Moore, and Maria Nichols. Copyright 2005 by The Guilford Press. Permission to photocopy this figure is granted to purchasers of this book for personal use only (see copyright page for details).

Dear Parents,

The following information will help you with school and classroom routines.

1. School begins each day at **7:45**. The children may line up each morning in front of the classroom.
2. Instruction will begin promptly at **7:50**. While I recognize that situations arise from time to time that can cause you to be late, children who are late on a continual basis will miss out on valuable instructional time.

A schedule of our day includes:

        7:50–8:00 Opening(attendance, pledge, etc.)
        8:00–8:20 Word Study
        8:20–9:30 Readers' Workshop
        8:20–8:45 Read-Aloud or Shared Reading
        8:45–9:00 Modeled Mini-Lesson
        9:00–9:25 Independent Reading
        9:25–9:30 Sharing
        9:30–10:15 Guided Reading/Literacy Centers
        10:20–10:35 Recess
        10:40–11:50 Math
        11:55–12:30 Lunch
        12:40–1:15 Social Studies/Science or P.E./Art
        1:15–2:00 Writers' Workshop
        2:00–2:10 Cleanup/Dismiss
    Music: Mon. 1:15–2:10, Computers & Library: Wed. 9:00–10:00

3. Your child will be coming home today with a new "Home to School and Back Again!" folder. Please check inside for the Sept. book order form, and other important notices. Your assistance in helping your child to remember to bring this folder to school **every day** will be appreciated. [See letter 2.]
4. Our lunch is scheduled for 11:55–12:30. Please check with the office to make sure your child's lunch account has funds if he or she is to buy lunch. Please complete the free lunch card if your child qualifies.
5. Dismissal is at **2:10** Mon., Tues., Thurs., and Fri., and at **11:50** on Wed. The children will be dismissed right from the classroom.

Please mark your calendars for **Back-to-School Night** on **Wed., Sept. 25**. We will discuss reading, writing, mathematics, and science/social studies. We will also go over homework expectations, and include examples of how to have conversations about reading, because that will be a major component of the homework. Homework will begin the following Monday (Sept. 30). Information including due dates will be coming home soon!

Until then, please feel free to contact me with any questions or concerns. We look forward to seeing you on the 25th!

Best regards,

[Teacher]

**FIGURE 10.3.** Sample attachment 1: School schedule (to accompany letter 1).

From *Teaching Literacy in First Grade* by Diane Lapp, James Flood, Kelly Moore, and Maria Nichols. Copyright 2005 by The Guilford Press. Permission to photocopy this figure is granted to purchasers of this book for personal use only (see copyright page for details).

> GOOD MORNING and WELCOME TO FIRST GRADE
>
> We are going to have FUN today.
>
> Please put your lunch in the basket and hang your backpack on a hook.
>
> Parents, THANKS for saying goodbye at the door. We'll see you at 2:10.

**FIGURE 10.4.** Sample poster: Hello to parents and children.

From *Teaching Literacy in First Grade* by Diane Lapp, James Flood, Kelly Moore, and Maria Nichols. Copyright 2005 by The Guilford Press. Permission to photocopy this figure is granted to purchasers of this book for personal use only (see copyright page for details).

learning lightens the burden for each, and both children and parents are fulfilled when the task is successfully completed. Their partnership, collaboration, and mutual trust and respect produce a relationship that has been well documented as a necessary ingredient in ensuring a child's success in school (Flood, 1975; Goodman, 1986; Heath, 1983; Morrow, 1993; Yaden & Paratore, 2003).

Realizing the significant influence of the family should encourage you to keep *all* parents involved in some way, because "what parents do to help their children is more important to academic success than how well off the family is" (U.S. Department of Education, 1986). Including parents will at times seem difficult, because there may be some who want to be unduly involved or some who are reluctant or nonparticipatory. These missed connections, however well intentioned the teachers and parents, require careful analysis to determine the roots of the difficulties. Such problems may stem from myriad sources, ranging from primal biases of one party toward the other, gaps in teachers' and parents' knowledge about literacy, to ineptness on the part of one or the other—the parent or the teacher.

In a recent study, Lapp et al. (2003) surveyed parents about their role in their child's early literacy development and found significant differences between the perceptions of parents who were poor and of those who were very poor when they were.

Findings suggested that not every parent is aware that children who learn the functional uses of literacy through daily family life experiences are well on their way to succeeding in literacy. They also suggested that many families may have a very positive attitude about school and learning, but not the skills, knowledge, or means to develop their children's early literacy awareness. These insights have been supported by the

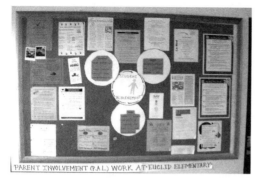

PARENT INVOLVEMENT (P.A.L.) WORK AT EUCLID ELEMENTARY

work of others (Neuman & Celano, 2001; Purcell-Gates, 2000; Taylor, 1997; Taylor & Dorsey-Gaines, 1988).

Rather than criticizing the family, we encourage you to reexamine your assumptions and to stay connected through letters, calls, and even visits. The following section offers a few ideas that will help you to be the "great communicator," whose classroom door is always open.

## SEND LETTERS, LETTERS, AND MORE LETTERS

After you send or deliver the first letter to your students' families, it is important to send letters on a regular basis that explain your classroom policies, practices, instruction, and ways in which parents can stay connected. Ideas for routines, procedures, and rules are discussed in Chapter 4; your classroom practices must be shared with parents. You may send home the letter presented in Figure 10.5 to let parents know of your classroom routines.

## GRADING AND HOMEWORK

It's understandable if you haven't completely finalized your grading and homework practices, because homework has been a controversial issue throughout the history of education. Proponents suggest that homework provides practice in skills that require a great deal of time to master. They also suggest that homework builds positive attitudes toward learning while creating a mindset in the student that learning is an "ongoing process." Opponents argue that many of the assignments are "busywork" that do not particularly improve prerequisite skills, and that homework can become so burdensome that it has the negative effect of alienating children from learning. They argue that homework frequently intrudes into family life and creates disharmony in the home among all members of the family, especially between parent and child in homes not conducive to doing homework because of large numbers of people living in small environments. Some families simply do not have the monetary resources to provide a quiet place for a child to perform the tasks nor the knowledge or language needed to help with the homework.

We encourage you to be realistic about *how much time* is needed to complete your homework assignments. Be careful not to require homework that necessitates significant amounts of *money* and *resources*, which may not be available in the

Date: _____

Dear Parents,

As I hope you read in our opening letter, homework will not begin until we have met for Back-to-School Night, which is scheduled for Wednesday, Sept. 26, 5:30–6:30.

Until then, I want to keep you up to date with our classroom activities so you are able to support your child at home.

*Community and Learning*

We are setting the tone for working together throughout the year. We have been talking about taking responsibility for our own learning and learning classroom manners. The chart we have created together hangs in our classroom. We designed it so that we can remind ourselves of how we can **GET SMARTER**. Please ask your child about our classroom promise to each other!

Here's what the children are learning this year:

*Spelling*

We are learning to spell words that support our reading and writing.

*Writing*

Powerful writing comes from our own lives. We are writing about real events and people. We are working on getting at the "heart" of a story—why was this important enough to put on paper?

*Mathematics*

We are exploring mathematics manipulatives, getting used to them so we will be able to use them as math tools rather than toys when the time comes. As the children explore and count the manipulatives like blocks, I have been assessing to inform instruction.

*Reading*

We are discussing the importance of talking about books. We talk as we read when we read together, and after we read when we read alone. Talking helps us to understand and deepen our own ideas. As you read with your child, make sure to stimulate great conversation. I'll be sending you more ideas about this in my next letter.

Thank you, and hope to see you at Back-to-School Night!

[Teacher]

**FIGURE 10.5.** Sample letter 2: Classroom routines (to accompany "Being Smarter" chart—Figure 4.1 in Chapter 4).

From *Teaching Literacy in First Grade* by Diane Lapp, James Flood, Kelly Moore, and Maria Nichols. Copyright 2005 by The Guilford Press. Permission to photocopy this figure is granted to purchasers of this book for personal use only (see copyright page for details).

homes of your students (e.g., access to the Internet, to reference books at home (encyclopedias, dictionaries, almanacs, magazines), to computers, e-mail, art supplies, and photographs. Be thoughtful by making assignments that consist of personal reading of books that are sent home from school. Try to design homework that can be *completed independently* by the child. Do not make the completion of homework count for more than 10% of the child's total grade in any subject. Too often children receive failing grades because of uncompleted homework assignments. Assess the potential of completing homework in each child's home before making any blanket decisions.

Independent reading is a very appropriate homework assignment. There is overwhelming evidence that good readers read more than poor readers and that frequent, wide independent reading improves comprehension and other literacy skills (Cunningham & Stanovich, 1997). When you establish the habit of reading at home (i.e., homework), you are inculcating a skill that your students will be able to use for the rest of their lives. Accountability for this type of homework can include class book talks in which children tell about books they have read. Remember that reading in first grade includes enjoying a wordless picture book. The format for grading and the relationship to a set of standards may be dictated by the district, but the criteria you use will probably be your own.

Be precise and clear in assigning homework or grades so that children and parents are not unclear about what has been assigned, what they are to do, or how it will be assessed. For example, hold up an example of a book at the independent reading level of most of the class and say, "For homework read one of your independent readers. Think about it. Be ready to talk about it tomorrow." Or give each child a piece of construction paper folded into four sections and say, "Tonight, after you watch your favorite TV program, draw a picture in each section that tells what the show was about. Tomorrow we will share these to see who likes the same or different shows."

Figures 10.6–10.9 are examples that illustrate how you will convey this information to the parents of your students.

## PARENT PARTICIPATION

Send home a monthly schedule with specific time slots that invites each family to select one time slot. After each has selected, those wishing additional visits may take other leftover time slots. This process helps you to plan for when parents will be visiting the room. Although not all parents will

Date: _____

Dear Parents,

Today your child received a homework folder with a homework assignment sheet. From now on, homework folders will be sent home on Mondays and need to be returned to school on Fridays, with a parent signature [Figure 10.7]. Students will be required to read at least 20 minutes each night. When reading, students may read silently, read aloud to an adult, or read together with an adult [Figure 10.8]. Please record the number of minutes your child has read each night on the homework sheet. Students should be reading every night (weekends, too!). Children need lots of practice to grow as readers. Making sure your child reads nightly is very important. Children should assume responsibility for their homework. A survey is also included that I hope you will encourage your child to complete [Figure 10.9].

Math homework will be given daily. For this reason, students should keep their homework folders in their backpacks. Math assignments should be kept in the homework folder, to be turned in on Friday. Please check off each night your child completes his or her math work.

A spelling list and spelling activity will be attached to the homework assignment sheet. Students should write spelling words and complete the activity in the spelling journal. The spelling journal can be kept in the homework folder and used each week. Also, please sign and feel free to include any questions or comments on the homework sheet, as I will read them weekly.

Behavior Reports: On Fridays, I will record students' work habits and respectful choices (behavior) for the week. I will send behavior reports home every Friday. Please expect this sheet from your child and discuss the behavior noted. Thank you for your support!

Sincerely,

[Teacher]

**FIGURE 10.6.** Sample letter 3: Homework procedures.

From *Teaching Literacy in First Grade* by Diane Lapp, James Flood, Kelly Moore, and Maria Nichols. Copyright 2005 by The Guilford Press. Permission to photocopy this figure is granted to purchasers of this book for personal use only (see copyright page for details).

# Homework Report

## Week of _____

The homework folder must be returned to school on Friday with a parent's signature.

**Reading**:

Number of minutes read:    Mon.____ Tues.____ Wed.____ Thurs.____

Title of one book read: _____

Author: _____

**Math**:

Math work and activities will be sent home daily. Complete and keep in the homework folder to turn in on Friday.

Check if completed:          Mon.____ Tues.____ Wed.____ Thurs.____

**Spelling** :

Lesson #_____

Complete the spelling activity in your spelling journal. Test on Friday!

**Reminders**:

Student's Name: _____

Parent's Signature: _____

**Questions/Comments:**

**FIGURE 10.7.** Sample attachment 2: Homework report (to accompany letter 3).

From *Teaching Literacy in First Grade* by Diane Lapp, James Flood, Kelly Moore, and Maria Nichols. Copyright 2005 by The Guilford Press. Permission to photocopy this figure is granted to purchasers of this book for personal use only (see copyright page for details).

# Weekly Behavior Report

Student's Name: _____     Date: _____

## Work Habits:

Very Engaged            Engaged            Most of the Time            Off-Task

## Respectful Choices:

Very Respectful            Respectful Most of the Time            Improvement Needed

Comments:

**FIGURE 10.8.** Sample attachment 3: Weekly behavior report (to accompany sample letter 3).

From *Teaching Literacy in First Grade* by Diane Lapp, James Flood, Kelly Moore, and Maria Nichols. Copyright 2005 by The Guilford Press. Permission to photocopy this figure is granted to purchasers of this book for personal use only (see copyright page for details).

## Reading: How Am I Doing?

Readers become better readers by reading! Read for at least 20 minutes each day. Fill out this log before turning in your homework folder.

**I read on:**

Monday ____    Tuesday ____    Wednesday ____

Thursday ____    Friday ____

I plan to read over the weekend ____

**Different ways to read**

I read out loud to someone. ____

Someone read out loud to me. ____

I read by myself. ____

**This week, I read . . .**

A picture book ____    A chapter book ____

A magazine ____    A newspaper ____

A poem ____    Directions ____

Something else ____ (What was it? _____ )

**I talked about my reading to . . .**

Share ideas ____

Grow ideas ____

Get help when I (or someone else) was confused ____

**FIGURE 10.9.** Sample attachment 4: Child's personal survey (to accompany sample letter 3).

From *Teaching Literacy in First Grade* by Diane Lapp, James Flood, Kelly Moore, and Maria Nichols. Copyright 2005 by The Guilford Press. Permission to photocopy this figure is granted to purchasers of this book for personal use only (see copyright page for details).

be able or willing to visit the classroom, it's necessary that they realize how important their participation is to their child's learning. You may need to teach parents the difference between supporting learning and doing the work for the child. Invite parents who can't come in on a regular basis to sign up to help the class by preparing something at home to be used in class. Send home projects with directions, such as making paper animal puppets the children can use in retelling a story. Parents can also be invited to sign up to be "special event" helpers (field trips, baking cookies/healthy treats for celebrations or Friday afternoon relax day, etc.) Other parents who are unable to provide time may be quite willing to provide supplies. You may include a wish list, like that in Figure 10.11, to accommodate these parents. The message you want to convey to families is that everyone's participation is welcome. Figures 10.10–10.12 provide ideas for involving all parents in their child's literacy at home and at school.

## STAY CONNECTED

The early connections you make with family members must be maintained by keeping them up-to-date about *all* that is occurring in your classroom. Additional communication may include information about the ongoing work in each major curricular area; upcoming classroom events; upcoming school-wide events; dates of vacations, field trips, classroom performances, etc.; and supplies needed. A message written by the children would also be appreciated by the parents. Figures 10.13–10.15 present examples of how to update parents and maintain this relationship.

So very much about a child's success depends on the support of the family and the interactions that occur within the home. Your suggestions will be heard by parents if you stay connected. Most parents care and want to do their best. They often need a model to know how to do it. The poem "Which Parent Will I Be?" (see Figure 10.16) is one you'll want to share as you continue to establish a community with your students and their families.

## Volunteer Sign-Up Sheet

If you are interested in volunteering in our classroom, please list your name, phone number, and the way you'd like to help.

We need parents to:
be a "room mom or dad," chaperone field trips, help plan or donate for holiday celebrations, help organize a class craft or project, staple papers, cut things out, design our yearbook page, be a "guest reader" for the class, send treats for Friday afternoons, etc.

| Name | Phone number | Way you'd like to help |
| --- | --- | --- |
| _____ | _____ | _____ |
| _____ | _____ | _____ |
| _____ | _____ | _____ |
| _____ | _____ | _____ |
| _____ | _____ | _____ |
| _____ | _____ | _____ |
| _____ | _____ | _____ |
| _____ | _____ | _____ |
| _____ | _____ | _____ |
| _____ | _____ | _____ |
| _____ | _____ | _____ |
| _____ | _____ | _____ |
| _____ | _____ | _____ |
| _____ | _____ | _____ |
| _____ | _____ | _____ |
| _____ | _____ | _____ |
| _____ | _____ | _____ |
| _____ | _____ | _____ |
| _____ | _____ | _____ |
| _____ | _____ | _____ |
| _____ | _____ | _____ |
| _____ | _____ | _____ |
| _____ | _____ | _____ |

**FIGURE 10.10.** Sample attachment 5: Volunteer sign-up sheet.

From *Teaching Literacy in First Grade* by Diane Lapp, James Flood, Kelly Moore, and Maria Nichols. Copyright 2005 by The Guilford Press. Permission to photocopy this figure is granted to purchasers of this book for personal use only (see copyright page for details).

# Room 8 Wish List 2005–2006

Throughout the year, a number of classroom supplies are needed. Donations from parents are always appreciated. The following is a list of things our class can use. Thanks in advance far your contributions!

Sincerely,

[Teacher]

35mm film or disposable cameras

Zip-lock bags (gallon, quart, sandwich, or snack size)

Electric pencil sharpener

Electric stapler

Small paper cutter

Facial tissues

Napkins

Paper towels

Liquid hand soap

No. 2 pencils

Printer ink cartridges—HP 23 (color) and HP 45 (black)

Colored copy paper

Large-size glue sticks

Colored pencils

Colored markers

Old magazines

Jump ropes

Frisbees

Rubber playground balls

Friday treats*

*Boxed juices, fruit, cookies, or crackers for the class can be sent to school on Friday. Plan for 20 students if treats are sent. Thanks.

**FIGURE 10.11.** Sample attachment 6: Wish list.

From *Teaching Literacy in First Grade* by Diane Lapp, James Flood, Kelly Moore, and Maria Nichols. Copyright 2005 by The Guilford Press. Permission to photocopy this figure is granted to purchasers of this book for personal use only (see copyright page for details).

## How Parents Can Help

The following list includes ways you can help your children learn:

- Read to your child.
- Play games and talk with your child.
- Help your child get a library card from the public library nearest you. Encourage your child to go to the library as often as possible. (Go with your child, find your own book, and read.)
- Go to the library with your child. Help him or her pick out interesting books to read.
- Find out about activities for children that take place at your library and participate when possible.
- Subscribe to a children's magazine (in the child's name).
- Bring books for your child to read in the car while he or she joins you to run errands.
- Look up words in the dictionary or encyclopedia with your child.
- Talk to your child about subjects that are interesting to him or her.
- Listen to your child for 10–15 minutes after school or at dinnertime.
- Set aside a special "reading time." Let your child know that you look forward to and enjoy your time together.
- Give your child his or her own place to keep books.
- Write special notes to your child. Slip them into his or her lunch or backpack for a neat surprise.
- Help your child write letters and notes.
- Encourage your child to keep a scrapbook about a subject that interests him or her: stamps, dogs, birds, trucks, etc., or to develop a collection of his or her own.
- Limit your child's television watching—select certain shows to watch. Turn the television set on for a show and turn it off immediately after the show is over.
- Read and discuss your child's schoolwork with him or her.
- Give encouragement.
- Provide materials such as crayons, art paper, and paint for creative projects.
- Give your child a calendar so he or she can write about special events and mark off each day. This is a great way to help your child learn the values of time and planning.
- Help your child make a telephone directory with the names and phone numbers of his or her friends (a practical skill).
- Ask your child to add a sentence or two to letters you write to faraway relatives. (A young child can dictate a sentence to you to write.)
- Give your child specific duties to perform on a regular basis at home, without an allowance.
- Let your child help you prepare dinner. Talk with your child.
- Encourage your child to show his or her schoolwork to your friends and family members.
- When traveling, read road signs with your child. Discuss what they mean. Make a game of it. Use an atlas and teach your child to be a mapper or guide.
- Show your child how to use a yardstick, ruler, and tape measure for measuring objects around the house. Many children cannot read a ruler confidently.
- Provide counting experiences for your child (counting change, stairs in your house, etc.).
- Show your child how to tell time on various types of watches. Many children rely solely on digital watches and have difficulty telling time with a traditional clock face.
- Give your child a special place (box, dishpan, etc.) to keep items he or she must take to school each morning. (This ends last-minute searching for library books, papers, bike keys, etc., which can cause your child to be late for school.)

**FIGURE 10.12.** Sample attachment 7: Parents help by helping their child.

From *Teaching Literacy in First Grade* by Diane Lapp, James Flood, Kelly Moore, and Maria Nichols. Copyright 2005 by The Guilford Press. Permission to photocopy this figure is granted to purchasers of this book for personal use only (see copyright page for details).

Date: _____

Dear Parent,

Thank you for all of the wonderful support you are providing to the children and me. I want to give you an update on what we've been doing and where we're headed.

## Folders

Each child's personal folder is an important learning tool because it helps him or her to organize papers, homework, book orders, etc. Our new spelling envelopes will be housed in the folders as well. If your child has lost his or her folder, you will need to replace it with a similar folder. Please make sure that the folder has two pockets, not binder rings. Folders do need to come to school every day!

## Reading

During the next 5 weeks, we will be immersed in a study of nonfiction. To help your child to progress in this study, please be sure to include plenty of nonfiction reading in your reading time at home. This can include information books, how-to books, newspapers, magazines, recipes, etc. I've attached a list of books as examples.

In shared reading (reading together), we will be learning the features of nonfiction and studying the ways they can help us to read and learn from nonfiction books. Features of nonfiction include photographs, captions, diagrams with labeling, charts, maps, bold and italic text, sound spelling, table of contents, headings, index, glossary—anything that helps the reader gain information easily.

As you read nonfiction texts at home, please look for these features and discuss them. In your discussion, talk about how the features helped you to read and learn!

During read-aloud, and then in independent reading, we will be discussing the use of schema in nonfiction reading. Schema is what we already know (or think we know) about a topic. Good nonfiction readers think about what they already know and use this as a base for learning more. Sometimes we are able to build on what we already know as we read, other times we have to change our thinking (our idea may have been wrong!).

As we read and study nonfiction, we will also be improving our base of scientific knowledge. You may hear your child sharing exciting information on space, sea life, the desert, etc.

Our homework packet will include a copy of the chart we will be using in the classroom for this work so the children will be able to practice working on schema with books they are reading at home.

*(continued)*

**FIGURE 10.13.** Sample letter 4: Room 8 news.

From *Teaching Literacy in First Grade* by Diane Lapp, James Flood, Kelly Moore, and Maria Nichols. Copyright 2005 by The Guilford Press. Permission to photocopy this figure is granted to purchasers of this book for personal use only (see copyright page for details).

We have studied our conversation about nonfiction reading and found that it includes sharing what we know (our schema), building on each other's thinking, making sense of new information, sharing sources of information, and asking questions. Good nonfiction readers ask a lot of questions—this means they are really thinking while they read! Don't think that you have to answer all of your child's questions. Questions are the beginning of research. Help your child to find resources (other books, the Internet) to learn more on his or her own.

*Writing*

To start, we will be working on lengthening our pieces using a craft technique called Zooming In. This technique helps us to lengthen a piece by thinking about a moment, feeling, or place and really describing it well.

Once pieces begin to increase in length, we will begin to study different authors' use of beautiful words and use them to improve our own writing.

*Spelling*

We are adding to our spelling program by adding a sight word component. Each first grader will have a list of words he or she should be able to spell by the end of the year. The list will be in an envelope, which is to be kept in your child's folder. This way, your child has the list to study at home and to use as a resource during writers' workshop. Please spend some time every night helping your child to study the words, using the directions on the cover of the envelope. I've attached it so that it won't get lost. Included will also be a page for words your child wants to learn to spell.

Your child should try, twice, on his or her own, to spell the word and then find it in print to check and make sure it is correct.

*Other Change in Homework*

Our current handwriting page will soon be replaced with a practice page for capitalization, punctuation, sight word spelling, and handwriting. Directions will accompany the new page.

*Math*

In math, we are beginning our work on place value. We will be studying the tens and ones places and numbers to 100. For parents interested in extra practice, many good books are available commercially and are generally not very expensive. Try Target, Wal-Mart, or a similar store.

Again, thank you for all of your support. I'll keep you posted about activities in Room 8.

[Teacher]

**FIGURE 10.13.** (*continued*)

## Nonfiction Books for First Grade

- *Seeds Get Around* by Nancy White—This nonfiction text shows students how books often use photographs as illustrations in explaining how seeds travel by land, air, and water.

- *The Story of the Statue of Liberty* by Betsy and Giulio Maestro—This book tells the story of how the Statue of Liberty was built, rebuilt, and is maintained. The back of the book has interesting facts, dates, and lists of people who helped in the construction and reconstruction.

- *You Are What You Eat* by Melvin Berger—Need to teach your first grader how to use a table of contents? Use this text as your student learns what helps us grow, what food gives us, the food pyramid, and why we need food.

- *See, Hear, Touch, Taste, Smell* by Melvin Berger—First graders will enjoy learning about their five senses while also learning how diagrams and labels are a part of texts that aren't fiction.

- *Life in the Sea* by Melvin Berger—This is a great text to teach students how captions can be a part of nonfiction. Students will enjoy the vibrant photos of creatures in the sea.

- *The Human Body* by Melvin Berger—"Your Senses," "Growing and Change," and "Being Healthy" are some of the chapters in this nonfiction text.

- *The World of Ants* by Melvin Berger—Diagram labels are another feature of texts that aren't stories. Introduce this text to your child as he or she learns all about ants.

- *Spiders Are Special Animals* by Fred and Jeanne Biddulph—Your first grader can learn how to use an index as he or she explores this nonfiction text about spiders.

- *Where Do the Animals Live?* by Melvin Berger—This nonfiction text is very useful in introducing features such as a table of contents and an index. Your child will be awed by the fascinating photos in this book as well.

- *Bread, Bread, Bread* by Ann Morris—The most interesting text feature of this book comes at the end. The author provides a list of countries and how each country makes bread, where it is sold, and how it is eaten.

**FIGURE 10.14.** Sample attachment 8: Examples of nonfiction for first graders (to accompany letter 4).

From *Teaching Literacy in First Grade* by Diane Lapp, James Flood, Kelly Moore, and Maria Nichols. Copyright 2005 by The Guilford Press. Permission to photocopy this figure is granted to purchasers of this book for personal use only (see copyright page for details).

# Instant Words

These are the 100 most common words in English, ranked in order of frequency. The first 25 make up about a third of all printed material. The 100 make up about half of all written material. Is it any wonder that all students must learn to recognize these words instantly and to spell them correctly too?

| Words 1–25 | Words 26–50 | Words 51–15 | Words 75–100 |
|---|---|---|---|
| the | or | will | number |
| of | one | up | no |
| and | had | other | way |
| a | by | about | could |
| to | word | out | people |
| in | but | many | my |
| is | not | then | than |
| you | what | than | first |
| that | all | these | water |
| it | were | so | been |
| he | we | some | can |
| was | when | her | who |
| for | your | would | oil |
| on | can | make | its |
| are | said | like | now |
| as | there | him | find |
| with | use | into | long |
| his | an | time | down |
| they | each | has | day |
| I | which | look | did |
| at | she | two | get |
| be | do | more | come |
| this | how | write | made |
| have | their | go | may |
| from | if | see | part |

Common suffixes: -s, -ing, -ed, -er, -ly, -est

Source: Words from Fry, E. B., Lee, J. E., & Fountoukidis, D. L.(2000). *The reading teacher's book of lists* (4th ed.). Columbus, OH: Prentice-Hall.

**FIGURE 10.15.** Sample attachment 9: First-grade word list (to accompany letter 4).

From *Teaching Literacy in First Grade* by Diane Lapp, James Flood, Kelly Moore, and Maria Nichols. Copyright 2005 by The Guilford Press. Permission to photocopy this figure is granted to purchasers of this book for personal use only (see copyright page for details).

Dear Parents,

This is a wonderful poem that emphasizes the importance of your role in your child's life. Thank you for being such an important part of the learning community in Room 8.

## Which Parent Will I Be?

"I got two A's," the small boy cried.
His voice was filled with glee.
His father very bluntly asked,
"Why didn't you get three?"
"Mom, I've got the dishes done,"
the girl called from the door.
Her mother very calmly said,
"Did you sweep the floor?"
"I've mowed the grass," the tall boy said,
"and put the mower away."
His father asked him, with a shrug,
"Can you clean off the clay?"

The children in the house next door
seem happy and content.
The same thing happened over there,
and this is how it went.

"I got two A's," the small boy cried.
His voice was filled with glee.
His father proudly said, "That's great;
I'm glad you belong to me."
"Mom, "I've got the dishes done,"
the girl called from the door.
Her mother smiled and softly said,
"Each day I love you more."
"I've mowed the grass," the tall boy said,
"and put the mower away."
His father answered with much joy,
"You've made my happy day."

Children deserve a little praise
for tasks they're asked to do.
If they're to lead a happy life,
SO MUCH DEPENDS ON YOU.

(Author unknown)

**FIGURE 10.16.** Sample letter 5: "Which Parent Will I Be?"

From *Teaching Literacy in First Grade* by Diane Lapp, James Flood, Kelly Moore, and Maria Nichols. Copyright 2005 by The Guilford Press. Permission to photocopy this figure is granted to purchasers of this book for personal use only (see copyright page for details).

# REFERENCES

Allington, R. (2002). *Six Ts of effective elementary literacy instruction*. Bloomington, IN: Phi Delta Kappan, Bloomington.

Anderson, C. (2000). *How's it going?* Portsmouth, NH: Heinemann.

August, A., & Hakuta, K. (1997). *Improving schooling for language-minority children: A research agenda*. Washington, DC: National Academy Press.

Avery, C. (1993). *And with a light touch*. Portsmouth, NH: Heinemann.

Bader, L. A. (2002). *Reading and language inventory* (4th ed.). Upper Saddle River, NJ: Prentice-Hall.

Bear, D. R., Invernizzi, M., Templeton, S., & Johnston, F. (1996). *Words their way*. Columbus, OH: Prentice-Hall.

Beck, I. (2002). *Bringing words to life*. New York: Guilford Press.

Betts, E. (1946). *Foundations of reading instruction*. New York: American Book Company.

Botel, M. (1978). *Botel reading inventory*. Chicago: Follett.

Brassell, D., & Flood, J. (2004). *Vocabulary strategies every teacher needs to know*. San Diego, CA: Academic Professional Development.

Brown, K. J. (1999/2000). What kind of text—For whom and when? Textual scaffolding for beginning readers. *Reading Teacher, 53*, 292–307.

Brown, K., & Allen, R. (Eds.). (1976). *Developing communicative competence in children*. Skokie, IL: National Textbook.

Cairney, T. H. (1997). Acknowledging diversity in home literacy practices: Moving towards partnership with parents. *Early Childhood Development and Care, 127–128*, 61–73.

Calkins, L. (1986). *The art of teaching writing*. Portsmouth, NH: Heinemann.

Calkins, L. (2001). *The art of teaching reading*. New York: Addison-Wesley.

Chall, J. S. (1967). *Learning to read: The great debate*. New York: McGraw-Hill.

Chall, J. S. (1996). *Learning to read: The great debate* (3rd ed.). Orlando, FL: Harcourt Brace.

Chomsky, N. (1988). *Language and the problems of knowledge: The Managua lectures*. Cambridge, MA: MIT Press.

Clay, M. M. (1966). *Emergent reading behavior*. Unpublished doctoral dissertation, University of Auckland, New Zealand.

Clay, M. M. (1972). The early detection of reading difficulties: A diagnostic survey. Auckland, New Zealand: Heinemann.

Clay, M. M. (1991). *Becoming literate: The construction of inner control*. Portsmouth, NH: Heinemann.

Clay, M. M. (1998). *By different paths to common outcomes*. York, ME: Stenhouse.

Clay, M. M. (2000). *Running records for classroom teachers.* Portsmouth, NH: Heinemann.

Collier, V. (1989). How long? A synthesis of research on academic achievement in a second language. *TESOL Quarterly, 23,* 509–531.

Collier, V. (1995). Acquiring a second language for school. *Directions in Language and education, 1*(4), 6–17.

Cummins, J. (2000). *Language, power and pedagogy: Bilingual children in the crossfire.* Clevedon, UK: Multicultural Matters.

Cunningham, A. E., & Stanovich, K. E.(1997). Early reading acquisition and its relation to reading experience and ability 10 years later. *Developmental Psychology, 26,* 325–346.

Cunningham, P. (2000). *Phonics they use: Words for reading and writing* (3rd ed.). New York: HarperCollins.

Cunningham, P. M., & Cunningham, J. W. (1992). Making words: Enhancing the invented spelling–decoding connection. *Reading Teacher, 2,* 106–107.

Cunningham, P. M., & Hall, D. P. (1997). *Month by month phonics for first grade.* Greensboro, NC: Carson-Dellosa.

Daniels, H., & Bizar, M. (1998). *Methods that matter.* York, ME: Stenhouse.

Darling, S., & Westberg, L. (2004). Parent involvement in children's acquisition of reading. *Reading Teacher, 58,* 774–776.

Depree, H., & Iversen, S. (1994). *Early literacy in the classroom: A new standard for young readers.* Bothell, WA: Wright Group.

Deschenes, S., Cuban, L., & Tyack, D. (2001). Mismatch: Historical perspectives on schools and students who don't fit them. *Teachers College Record, 103*(4), 525–547.

Dolch, E. W. (1942). *Basic sight word test.* Champaign, IL: Garrard Press.

Duke, N. K. (2003). *Reading and writing informational text in the primary grades.* New York: Scholastic.

Durr, W. K. (1973). Computer study of high frequency words in popular trade juveniles. *Reading Teacher, 27,* 37–42.

Durrell, D. D., & Catterson, J. H. (1980). *Durrell analysis of reading difficulty.* New York: Psychological Corporation.

Education Department of Western Australia. (1994). *First steps reading developmental continuum.* Sydney, Australia: Addison Wesley Longman.

Ehri, L. C. (1995). Phases of development in learning to read words by sight. *Journal of Research in Reading, 2,* 116–125.

Ehri, L. C., & McCormick, S. (1998). Phases of word learning: Implications for instruction with delayed and disabled readers. *Reading and Writing Quarterly: Overcoming Learning Difficulties, 14,* 135–163.

Ekwall, E. E. (1986). *Ekwall reading inventory* (2nd ed.). Needham Heights, MA: Allyn & Bacon.

Faltis, C. J. (2001). *Joinfostering: Teaching and learning in multilingual classrooms* (3rd ed.). Columbus, OH: Merrill Prentice-Hall.

Farnan, N., & Dahl, K. (1998). *Children's writing: Perspectives from research.* Newark, DE: International Reading Association.

Ferreiro, E. (1991). Literacy acquisition. In C. Kamii, M. Manning, & G. Manning (Eds.), *Early literacy: A constructivist foundation for whole language* (pp. 31–56). Washington, DC: National Education Association.

Fisher, D, Flood, J, Lapp, D., & Frey, N. (2004). Interactive read alouds: Is there a common set of implementation practices? *Reading Teacher, 58,* 8–17.

Fletcher, R. (2001). *Writing workshop: The essential guide.* Portsmouth, NH: Heinemann.

Flood, J. (1975). *Predictor of reading achievement: An investigation of selected antecedents to reading.* Unpublished doctoral dissertation, Stanford University, Stanford, CA.

Flood, J., Lapp, D., & Fisher, D. (Eds.). (2005). *Teaching writing*. San Diego, CA: Academic Professional Development.

Fountas, I. C., & Pinnell, G. S. (1996). *Guided reading: Good first teaching for all children*. Portsmouth, NH: Heinemann.

Frey, N. (2004). *The effective teacher's guide: 50 ways for engaging students in learning*. San Diego, CA: Academic Professional Development.

Fry, E. (1980). The new instant word list. *Reading Teacher, 34,* 284–289.

Gee, J. (1996). *Social linguistics and literacies: Ideology in discourse* (2nd ed.). Bristol, PA: Taylor & Francis.

Gibson, J. T. (1999). *Developing strategies and practices for culturally diverse classrooms*. Norwood, MA: Christopher-Gordon.

Glasser, W. (1969). *Schools without failure*. New York: Harper & Row.

Glasser, W. (1990). *The quality school: Managing students without coercion*. New York: Harper & Row.

Glasser, W. (1998). *Choice theory*. New York: HarperCollins.

Goodman, Y. M. (1986). Children coming to know literacy. In W. H. Teale & E. Sulzby (Eds.), *Emergent literacy: Writing and reading* (pp. 114–131). Norwood, NJ: Ablex.

Graves, D. (1983). *Writing: Teachers and children at work*. Portsmouth, NH: Heinemann.

Graves, D. (1994). *A fresh look at writing*. Portsmouth, NH: Heinemann.

Graves, M., & Slater, W. (2004). Vocabulary instruction in content areas. In D. Lapp, J. Flood, & N. Farnan (Eds.), *Content area reading and learning: Instructional strategies* (2nd Ed., pp. 261–276). Mahwah, NJ: Erlbaum.

Harris, A. J., & Jacobson, M. D. (1982). *Basic reading vocabularies*. New York: Macmillan.

Hart, B., & Risley, T. R. (1995). *Meaningful differences in the everyday experiences of young American children*. Baltimore: Brookes.

Harwayne, S. (2001). *Writing through childhood*. Portsmouth, NH: Heinemann.

Heath, S. (1983). *Ways with words*. Cambridge, UK: Cambridge University.

Heffernan, L. (2004). *Critical literacy and writer's workshop*. Newark, DE: International Reading Association.

Herrell, A. (2000). *Fifty strategies for teaching English language learners*. Columbus, OH: Merrill-Prentice-Hall.

Hess, R. D., & Holloway, S. (1984). Family and school as educational institutions. In R. D. Parke (Ed.), *Review of child development research: Vol. 7. The family* (pp. 179–222). Chicago: University of Chicago Press.

Hillerich, R. L. (1974). Word lists: Getting it all together. *Reading Teacher, 27,* 353–360.

Hoffman, J. V., Roser, N. L., & Battle, J. (1993). Reading aloud in classrooms: From the modal to a "model." *Reading Teacher, 46,* 496–503.

Holdaway, D. (1980). *Independence in reading*. Portsmouth, NH: Heinemann.

Hoyt, L. (2003). *Exploring informational texts*. Portsmouth, NH: Heinemann.

International Reading Association. (2002, April/May). Position statement points way to stronger, better family–school partnerships. *Reading Today, 19*(5), 48.

Johns, J. L. (1994). *Basic reading inventory* (6th ed.). Dubuque, IA: Kendall Hunt.

Kamil, M. L. (Ed.). (2000). *Handbook of reading research*. Mahwah, NJ: Erlbaum.

Kamil, M. L., Mosenthal, P. B., Pearson, P. D., & Barr, R. (2000). *Handbook of reading research* (Vol. 3). Mahwah, NJ: Erlbaum.

Lapp, D., Fisher, D., & Flood, J. (2000). What we say is influenced by how we say it! Effective oral language experiences for every child. *California Reader, 33,* 25–30.

Lapp, D., Fisher, D., Flood, J., & Moore, K. (2003). "I don't want to teach it wrong:" An investigation of the role families believe they should play in the early literacy development of their children. In D. L. Schallert, C. M. Fairbanks, J. Worthy, B. Maloch, & J. V.

Hoffman (Eds.), *51st Yearbook of the National Reading Conference* (pp. 275–286). Oak Creek, WI: National Reading Conference.

Lapp, D., & Flood, J. (1974). *Teaching reading to every child.* New York: Macmillan.

Lapp, D., & Flood, J. (2004). No parent left behind. In D. Lapp, C. C. Block, E. Cooper, J. Flood, N. Roser, & J. V. Tinajero (Eds.), *Teaching all the children: Strategies for developing literacy in an urban setting* (pp. 63–72). New York: Guilford Press.

Lapp, D., & Flood, J. (2005). Exemplary reading in the urban elementary school: How reading develops/How students learn and how teachers teach. In J. Flood & P. Anders (Eds.), *The literacy development of students in urban schools* (pp. 150–179). Newark, DE: International Reading Association.

Lapp, D., Flood, J., Brock, C., & Fisher, D. (2005). *Teaching reading to every child* (4th ed.). Mahwah, NJ: Erlbaum.

Lapp, D., Flood, J., Frey, N., Moore, K., & Begley, M. (2004, May 2). *Models of writing instruction for kindergarten and first grade.* Paper presented at the International Reading Association Annual Conference, Preconvention Institute, Reno, NV.

Lapp, D., Flood, J., & Goss, K. (2000). Desks don't move—students do: In effective classroom environments. *Reading Teacher, 54,* 31–36.

LaPray, M., & Ross, R. (1969). The graded word list: Quick reading ability. *Journal of Reading, 12,* 305–307.

Laufer, B., & Nation, P. (1999). A vocabulary-size test of controlled productive ability. *Language Testing, 16*(1), 33–51.

Lipman, D. (1999). *Improving your storytelling: Beyond the basics for all who tell stories in work and play.* Little Rock, AR: August House.

Mace-Matluck, B. J. (1981). General characteristics of the children's language use in three environments. In B. J. Mace-Matluck (Ed.), *A longitudinal study of the oral language development of Texas bilingual children (Spanish-English); Findings from the second year.* Austin, TX: Southwest Educational Development Laboratory.

Marten, C. (2003). *Word crafting.* Portsmouth, NH: Heinemann.

Marzano, R. J., Marzano, J. S., & Pickering, D. J. (2003). *Classroom management that works.* Alexandria, VA: ASCD.

McCarrier, A., Pinnell G. S., & Fountas, I. (2000). *Interactive writing.* Portsmouth, NH: Heinemann.

Moore, K. (2004). *Diagnosing students' reading strengths and needs and planning their subsequent differentiated instruction: A comparative investigation of teachers' performance.* Unpublished doctoral dissertation, San Diego State University, San Diego, CA .

Morrow, L. M. (1993). *Literacy development in the early years: Helping children read and write.* Boston: Allyn & Bacon.

Morrow, L. M. (2005). *Literacy development in the early years: Helping children read and write* (5th ed.). Boston: Allyn & Bacon.

National Reading Panel. (2000). *Report of the National Reading Panel: Teaching children to read: An evidence-based assessment of the scientific research literature and its implications for reading instruction.* Washington, DC: National Institute of Child Health and Human Development and U. S. Department of Education.

Neuman, S. B., & Celano, D. (2001). Access to print in low-income and middle-income communities: An ecological study of four neighborhoods. *Reading Research Quarterly, 36,* 8–26.

New Standards Primary Literacy Committee. (1999). *New Standards.* National Council on Education and the Economy and the University of Pittsburgh.

Nia, I. (1999, August). *Units of study in the writing workshop.* Primary Voices. Urbana, IL: National Council of Teachers of English.

Otto, B. (2002). *Language development in early childhood.* Upper Saddle River, NJ: Merrill/ Prentice-Hall.

Pearson, P. D., & Gallagher, M. C. (1983). The instruction of reading comprehension. *Contemporary Educational Psychology, 8,* 317–344.

Peregoy, S. F., & Boyle, O. F. (1997). *Reading, writing, and learning in ESL: A resource book for K–12 teachers.* New York: Longman.

Piaget, J. (1973). *To understand is to invent.* New York: Viking.

Piaget, J., & Inhelder, B. (1969). *The psychology of the child.* New York: Basic Books.

Purcell-Gates, V. (1993). Issues for family literacy research: Voices from the trenches. *Language Arts, 70,* 670–677.

Purcell-Gates, V. (1995). *Other people's words: The cycle of low literacy.* Cambridge, MA: Harvard University Press.

Purcell-Gates, V. (2000). Family literacy. In M. L. Kamil, P. B. Mosenthal, P. D. Pearson, & R. Barr (Eds.), *Handbook of reading research* (Vol. 3, pp. 853–870). Newark, DE: International Reading Association.

Raban, B. (2001). Talking to think, learn, and teach. In P. G. Smith (Ed.), *Talking classrooms: Shaping children's learning through oral language instruction* (pp. 27–41). Newark, DE: International Reading Association.

Rasinski, T. (2003). *The fluent reader.* New York: Scholastic.

Ray, K. W. (1999). *Wonderous words.* Urbana, IL: National Council of Teachers of English.

Ray, K. W., & Cleveland, L. B. (2004). *About the author.* Portsmouth, NH: Heinemann

Roser, N. L., & Martinez, M. G. (1995). *Book talk and beyond: Children and teachers respond to literature.* Newark, DE: International Reading Association.

Rosow, L. (1992). The story of Irma. *Reading Teacher, 41,* 562–566.

Routman, R. (1991). *Invitations.* Portsmouth, NH: Heinemann.

Routman, R. (2003). *Reading essentials.* Portsmouth, NH: Heinemann.

Salus, P., & Flood, J. (2003). *Language: A user's guide.* San Diego: Academic Professional Development.

Serafini, F., & Giorgis, C. (2003). *Reading aloud and beyond: Fostering the intellectual life with older readers.* Portsmouth, NH: Heinemann.

Shanker, J. L., & Ekwall, E. E. (2000). *Ekwall/Shanker reading inventory* (4th ed.). Needham Heights, MA: Ally & Bacon.

Shanker, J. L., & Ekwall, E. E. (2003). *Locating and correcting reading difficulties* (8th ed.). Upper Saddle River, NJ: Prentice-Hall.

Shaver, A. V., & Walls, R. T. (1998). Effect of Title 1 parent involvement on student reading and mathematics achievement. *Journal of Research and Development in Education, 31,* 90–97.

Silvaroli, N. J., & Wheelock, W. H. (2001). *Classroom reading inventory* (9th ed.). New York: McGraw-Hill.

Smith, F. (1971). *Understanding reading.* New York: Holt, Rinehart & Winston.

Smith, F. (1988). *Joining the literacy club.* Portsmouth, NH: Heinemann.

Snow, C. E., Burns, M. S., & Griffin, P. (1998). *Preventing reading difficulties in young children.* Washington, DC: National Academy Press.

Spandell, V. (2004). *Creating young writers: Using 6 traits to enrich writing process in primary classrooms.* Boston, MA: Pearson Education.

Stead, T. (2002). *Is that a fact?* York, ME: Stenhouse.

Sulzby, E., & Teale, W. H. (1991). Emergent reading. In R. Barr, M. Kamil, P. Mosenthal, & P. D. Pearson (Eds.), *Handbook of reading research* (Vol. 2, pp. 727–758). New York: Longman.

Taylor, D. (Ed.) (1997). *Many families, many literacies: An international declaration of principles.* Portsmouth, NH: Heinemann.

Taylor, D., & Dorsey-Gaines, C. (1988). *Growing up literate: Learning from inner-city families.* Portsmouth, NH: Heinemann.

Teale, W. H. (1978). Positive environments for learning to read: What studies of early readers tell us. *Language Arts, 55,* 922–932.

U.S. Department of Education. (1986). *What works: Research about teaching and learning* (p. 7). Washington, DC: U.S. Government Printing Office.

Vygotsky, l. S. (1978). *Mind in society: The development of higher psychological processes.* Cambridge, MA: Harvard University Press.

Wang, M. C., Haertel, G. D., & Wahlberg, H. J. (1993). Toward a knowledge base for school learning. *Review of Educational Research, 63*(3), 249–294.

Yaden, D. B., & Paratore, J. R. (2003). Family literacy at the turn of the millennium: The costly future of maintaining the status quo. In J. Flood, D. Lapp, J. R. Squire, & J. M. Jensen (Eds.), *Handbook of research on teaching the English language arts* (2nd Ed., pp. 532–545). Mahwah, NJ: Erlbaum.

Yaden, D. B., Rowe, D. W., & MacGillvray, L. (2000). Emergent literacy: A matter (polyphony) of perspectives. In M. L. Kamil, P. B. Mosenthal, P. D. Pearson, & R. Barr (Eds.), *Handbook of reading research* (Vol. 3, pp. 425–454). Newark, DE: International Reading Association.

Zimmermann, S., & Keene, E. O. (1997). *Mosaic of thought.* Portsmouth, NH: Heinemann.

# INDEX

# C

# D